GENERAL AND SPECIAL EDUCATION INCLUSION IN AN AGE OF CHANGE: ROLES OF PROFESSIONALS INVOLVED

ADVANCES IN SPECIAL EDUCATION

Series Editors: Jeffrey P. Bakken and Festus E. Obiakor

Recent Volumes:

GENERAL AND SPECIAL EDUCATION INCLUSION IN AN AGE OF CHANGE: ROLES OF PROFESSIONALS INVOLVED

EDITED BY

JEFFREY P. BAKKEN
Bradley University, Peoria, IL, USA

FESTUS E. OBIAKOR
Valdosta State University, Valdosta, GA, USA

United Kingdom – North America – Japan
India – Malaysia – China

Emerald Group Publishing Limited
Howard House, Wagon Lane, Bingley BD16 1WA, UK

First edition 2016

British Library Cataloguing in Publication Data
A catalogue record for this book is available from the British Library

ISBN: 978-1-78635-544-7
ISSN: 0270-4013 (Series)

Printed and bound by CPI Group (UK) Ltd, Croydon, CR0 4YY

ISOQAR certified
Management System,
awarded to Emerald
for adherence to
Environmental
standard
ISO 14001:2004.

Certificate Number 1985
ISO 14001

INVESTOR IN PEOPLE

CONTENTS

LIST OF CONTRIBUTORS

Terese C. Aceves	School of Education, Loyola Marymount University, Los Angeles, CA, USA
Bob Algozzine	Department of Educational Leadership, University of North Carolina-Charlotte, Charlotte, NC, USA
Dimitris Anastasiou	Department of Counseling, Quantitative Methods, and Special Education, Southern Illinois University at Carbondale, Carbondale, IL, USA
Kelly Anderson	Department of Special Education and Child Development, University of North Carolina-Charlotte, Charlotte, NC, USA
Jeanmarie Badar	Innisfree Village, Crozet, VA, USA
Jeffrey P. Bakken	Graduate School, Bradley University, Peoria, IL, USA
Cynthia Baughan	Department of Special Education and Child Development, University of North Carolina-Charlotte, Charlotte, NC, USA
Bonnie Billingsley	School of Education, Virginia Tech, Blacksburg, VA, USA
Rachel J. Boit	University of North Carolina at Greensboro, Greensboro, NC, USA
Charlotte Fontenot	Department of Special Populations, Houston Baptist University, Houston, TX, USA
Bridgie A. Ford	Department of Curricular & Instructional Studies, University of Akron, Akron, OH, USA

Daryl Fridley	College of Education, Southeast Missouri State University, Cape Girardeau, MO, USA
Celia E. Johnson	Department of Teacher Education, Bradley University, Peoria, IL, USA
James M. Kauffman	Department of Curriculum, Instruction, and Special Education, University of Virginia, Charlottesville, VA, USA
James McLeskey	School of Special Education, School Psychology and Early Childhood Studies, University of Florida, Gainesville, FL, USA
Festus E. Obiakor	Department of Early Childhood and Special Education, Valdosta State University, Valdosta, GA, USA
Anthony Pellegrino	Division of Elementary, Secondary, and Literacy Education, George Mason University, Fairfax, VA, USA
Diana Rogers-Adkinson	College of Education, Southeast Missouri State University, Cape Girardeau, MO, USA
Cynthia Simpson	Department of Management, Marketing, and Business, Houston Baptist University, Houston, TX, USA
Jason C. Travers	Department of Special Education, University of Kansas, Lawrence, KS, USA
John Travis Spoede, Jr.	Department of Special Populations and Counseling, Houston Baptist University, Houston, TX, USA
Shernavaz Vakil	Department of Curricular & Instructional Studies, University of Akron, Akron, OH, USA

Nancy L. Waldron School of Special Education, School
         Psychology and Early Childhood Studies,
         University of Florida, Gainesville,
         FL, USA

Margaret P. Weiss Division of Special Education and
         Disability Research, George Mason
         University, Fairfax, VA, USA

Andrew L. Wiley School of Lifespan Development &
         Educational Sciences, Kent State
         University, Kent, OH, USA

PREFACE

General and Special Education inclusion in an Age of Change is divided into two volumes: Volume 31, Impact on Students with Disabilities and Volume 32, Roles of Professionals Involved. For many years, professionals have argued and debated about the topic of inclusion and how students with disabilities are best served. Different professionals have different beliefs on inclusion in relationship to the disability the students may have. Thoughts and attitudes vary regarding these students. The topic of full inclusion is also highly debated. Some individuals are obviously in favor of full inclusion and others are not. Even professionals with expertise in different disability groups have different viewpoints. Some say it depends on each individual child, the severity of their disability, and the school environment for which they are to receive their education. This situation has led to many different viewpoints on this very important topic that includes school professionals, parents, researchers, and communities.

Volumes 31 and 32 address the current top perspectives and issues regarding the topic of inclusion by providing chapters written by active researchers and scholarly university professors who specialize in this area. Volume 31 begins with an introduction to the topic of inclusion and then includes chapters that address inclusion and different types of disabilities and how students with these disabilities might best be served in this type of environment. Areas addressed in these chapters include: students with learning disabilities, students with emotional or behaviour disorders, students with intellectual disabilities, students that are deaf or hard of hearing, students with visual impairments, students with autism spectrum disorders, students with extensive and pervasive support needs, students with traumatic brain injuries, students with communication impairments, and students with physical disabilities and other health impairments. Volume 32 begins with a chapter that addresses preparing teachers for inclusive environments. This is followed by chapters that address the general and special educator and their roles in an inclusive environment. Next, a chapter on the principal and their leadership in an inclusive school is addressed. The volume then addresses the family, the community, meeting student needs, academics, and a chapter on thoughts moving forward. Finally, a chapter on concluding thoughts is provided.

Volumes 31 and 32 are composed of 11 and 10 chapters respectively, that are written by well-known and respected university professors who are actively involved in teaching undergraduate and graduate special education courses and engaged in research on inclusion. *General and Special Education Inclusion in an Age of Change: Roles of Professionals Involved* is an excellent supplementary text for advanced undergraduate special education majors and graduate students who are looking for detailed, comprehensive, and current information for their research papers or theses.

Jeffrey P. Bakken
Festus E. Obiakor
Series Editors

PREPARING TEACHERS FOR INCLUSIVE EDUCATION

Diana Rogers-Adkinson and Daryl Fridley

ABSTRACT

This chapter provides a brief overview of the inclusive education move-ment as related to educator preparation. External influences that have driven the push for more blended educational training for all educators, regardless of discipline, are discussed, and recommended practices for inclusive educator preparation programs are provided. In addition, systemic approaches to inclusive education and high impact practices from both the general education and special education disciplines are highlighted.

Keywords: Inclusive educator preparation

INTRODUCTION

It has been thirty years since Will (1986) called for a movement toward inclusive education. Dubbed the *Regular Education Initiative*, Will decried the negative impact of exclusionary models of special education. It was her

General and Special Education Inclusion in an Age of Change: Roles of Professionals Involved
Advances in Special Education, Volume 32, 1–19
Copyright © 2016 by Emerald Group Publishing Limited
All rights of reproduction in any form reserved
ISSN: 0270-4013/doi:10.1108/S0270-401320160000032002

belief that all children with mild to moderate disabilities should be educated in the general education classroom with their typical peers. Over time this movement has expanded to address all children with disabilities including those with severe conditions in the late 1990s. Specifically, Lipsky and Gartner advocated that fully inclusive schools are one indicator for determining the quality of a democratic society (Kernzner Lipsky & Gartner, 1999).

The inclusive school movement has continued to grow. Current proponents assert that the incorporation of practices that meet the needs of all learners will reduce the number of children requiring special education (Ashby, 2012). Some proponents go so far as to assert that implementation of inclusive practices will actually prevent the development of disabilities in many children (Fletcher & Vaughn, 2009). In addition, advocates expect greater inclusiveness to result in a majority of children with disabilities meeting "College and Career Ready" standards (Jorgensen, McSheehan, Schuh, & Sonnenmeier, 2012).

Although inclusive education originated with an emphasis on reducing segregated special education programming, the movement has extended to include children with cultural and linguistic differences as well as those impacted by poverty (Cosier & Pearson, 2016). The expansion of inclusive education to these populations has been grounded in social justice theory (McMaster, 2015; Theoharis & O'Tolle, 2011). There is a strong belief that schools must be able to embrace all students with educators suspending their traditional beliefs that children not from the cultural norm require segregated services in order to be successful.

If educators are to be effective in schools, they must receive the necessary preparation. Although attention to the rigor of preparation programs has led to the adoption of revised standards and high-stakes assessment over the past decade, these changes have primarily focused upon the knowledge and competencies of specific fields or disciplines or upon pedagogical practices developed for students identified as being within the norm. Standards for educator preparation programs related to teaching in an inclusive educational setting have not kept pace with the growth of those settings in P-12 schools. As inclusive educational models expand, educator preparation programs must provide preservice candidates with the tools needed to work within these educational environments. In order to accomplish this goal, teacher educators must understand not only the research-based imperatives driving the movement but, also, the expectations of external stakeholders. In order to meet those expectations, preparation programs must understand the dispositions, skills, and knowledge necessary for effective meeting the needs of exceptional children as well as the best practices for ensuring that teacher candidates enter the field with those in hand. This chapter provides an overview of each of those three topics.

For the purpose of this chapter inclusive teacher education is defined as a program that prepares all preservice teachers to instruct "diverse learners" including students with learning differences who, because of language, cultural background, differing ability level, disabilities, learning approaches, gender, and/or socioeconomic status, may have academic or behavioral needs that require varied instructional strategies to ensure their learning (Adapted from the Glossary included in InTASC Model Core Teaching Standards and Learning Progressions for Teachers 1.0, 2013; Council of Chief State School Officers [CCSSO], 2015, p. 3).

EXTERNAL DEMAND FOR CHANGE

To be sure, academic and social support for greater inclusion has increased consistently over the years. In fact, many have suggested that educator preparation has an obligation to provide all future teachers, regardless of discipline, the knowledge, skills, and dispositions to teach in inclusive settings (Sharma, Forlin, Lerman, & Earle, 2006). This assertion has long been the international position since the UNESCO recommendation in 1994 (UNESCO, 1994). Of late that support has translated into more concrete demands from leaders in P-12 education, institutions engaged in evaluating educator preparation programs, and the federal government.

P-12 Education

Teacher licensing standards have long held to the belief that disciplinary training in the content area is paramount to the preparation of future educators. This demarcation is represented by the trend for disciplines to be housed outside of a college of education with the content experts rather than within the education discipline with pedagogy experts. The silo model of educator preparation has resulted in a national movement of state departments of education demanding substantive changes to educator preparation programs (CCSSO Task Force, 2012). Specifically, the CCSSO task force on educator preparation and entry into the profession call for "learner-ready" graduates (CCSSO, 2012, p. iii). Learner ready is then defined as an educator that possesses not only depth in content knowledge and the curriculum to effectively teach it but also to meet the needs of students with differing needs and to differentiate curriculum on behalf of those learners (CCSSO, 2012).

The CCSSO report also criticizes the historical practice of only providing educators with an awareness approach toward disabilities. This model typically relies on a singular course about exceptionality to suffice for preparing educators for the varying needs of children with disabilities or gifts and talents (Cosier & Pearson, 2016). The intent of the course is to provide awareness of both the impact of specific disabilities as well as strategies to promote success for these learners in multiple environments. Rather, the CCSSO expects all educators to be prepared with "sensitivity to diverse populations" (CCSSO, 2012, p. 21). In addition, it calls for all states to "revise and enforce their licensure standards for teachers and principals to support the teaching of more demanding content aligned to college- and career readiness and critical thinking skills to a diverse range of students" (27).

In a follow up report, *Promises to Keep: Transforming Educator Preparation to Better Service a Diverse Range of Learners* (CCSSO Task Force, 2015), the CCSSO promotes three specific tenets for developing more inclusive educator preparation:

1. Ensure that the outcomes of all students – including students with disabilities – are an integral part of preparation program approval and educator evaluation systems.
2. Create an infrastructure that prepares candidates for enabling and promoting shared ownership, collaboration, and teamwork among all educators for all students – including students with disabilities.
3. Hold educator preparation programs accountable and provide feedback on how to improve programs to ensure candidates are prepared with the knowledge, skills, and practice opportunities necessary to teach and lead diverse learners within tiered systems of support (CCSSO, 2015, p. 2).

Evaluators of Teacher Preparation

The expectation for inclusive educator preparation is not limited to the CCSSO. The Council for the Accreditation of Educator Preparation in Standard 1 requires all programs to prepare educators to the meet the needs of "All P-12 students" defined as children or youth attending P-12 schools including, but not limited to, students with disabilities or exceptionalities, students who are gifted, and students who represent diversity based on ethnicity, race, socioeconomic status, gender, language, religion, sexual identification, and/or geographic origin (http://caepnet.org/standards/standard-1, 11). Providing a framework of inclusivity in educator preparation has also been suggested as a social justice practice for educator preparation (Conklin & Hughes, 2016).

The *National Council on Teacher Quality* (NCTQ) recommendations that all preservice educators should be prepared to support struggling readers in an inclusive framework is their belief that "the best way to reduce the portion of children in special education is to train teachers ... in the most effective strategies for preventing reading failure" (NCTQ, 2014). McLeskey and Brownell (2015) advocate that the most effective tool for improving the educational outcomes for low achieving students is to improve the effectiveness of the educator.

The Federal Government

There is also support at the federal level for a more inclusive model of educator preparation. The Collaboration for Effective Educator Development, Accountability, and Reform (CEEDAR) is a national center shared between the University of Florida, University of Kansas, the American Institute for Research, and the CCSSO with endorsements from the Council for Accreditation of Educator Preparation (CAEP), the Council for Exceptional Children (CEC), The Association for the Severely Handicapped, and the American Association of College of Teacher Education. This collaborative provides intensive support to states to facilitate transformation of teacher education to more inclusive models of educator development. Currently 15 states are involved in this inclusive educator preparation initiative. The overall goal of both universal and technical assistance by CEEDAR is to improve the learning systems for teachers and leaders on behalf of all children with disabilities.

Response to Initiatives

Despite advocacy by the stakeholders identified above, only around half of all states have licensing or certification policies that stipulate general education majors have either field experience or coursework that includes students with disabilities (http://ceedar.education.ufl.edu/portfolio/policy-snapshot-1/).

If programs that prepare educators are to meet the increasing expectations of a wide variety of stakeholders, they will need to make significant revisions to their curricula. Such a task requires, first, a clear understanding of the dispositions, skills, and knowledge necessary to teach effectively in an inclusive school.

COMPONENTS OF EFFECTIVE TEACHING IN AN INCLUSIVE SETTING

Inclusive teacher education must provide every teacher candidate with an open understanding of the needs of all learners coupled with a sense of urgency derived from the belief that teachers: (a) have the capacity to determine the needs of all learners, and (b) design effective instruction for these children. These premises assume some level of collaboration between general and special education but do not defer all designing of adapted instruction to special education. Rather, all general educators are expected to assume a primary responsibility to all children in the classroom. Inclusive educator preparation programs need to provide key critical content if candidates are to be prepared to enter into schools learner ready. There are three primary areas of practice that are integral to inclusive educator preparation curriculum: (a) collaboration skills, (b) frameworks for inclusive curriculum implementation, and (c) methods that support the learning needs of children requiring additional supports and accommodations to be successful in the inclusive school environment. Another critical component of an inclusive educator preparation program is to address the beliefs and dispositions that develop a mindset of openness toward inclusive schooling. The following have been suggested as critical to providing preservice educators the knowledge and skills needed to participate in inclusive education: (a) inclusive delivery models, (b) collaboration skills, (c) universal design for learning (UDL), (d) differentiation, behavioral support strategies, and (e) scientifically based reading instruction (Holdheide & Reschly, 2008).

Dispositions

Teachers' preconceptions about students with disabilities greatly shape their potential effectiveness in working with these students. A study by Sharma that utilized the *Attitudes Towards Inclusive Education Scale* (Wilczenski, 1992) determined educators with a more negative attitude toward students with disabilities are less likely to implement effective inclusive practices (Sharma et al., 2006). This connection between dispositions and effectiveness was also documented in a study by Moberg, Zumberg, and Reinmaa (1997) in which the authors noted the level of inclusion in a country impacted the preservices educator's attitudes toward inclusive practices.

Collaboration

Collaboration is essential in an inclusive environment. If educators are to work with a broader variety of children, they must be able to draw upon the expertise of peers. Co-teaching has become commonplace as a strategy for promoting collaborative teaching between general and special education. The goal is to provide effective shared interventions on behalf of all children demonstrating increased academic needs while simultaneously maintaining growth toward the individualized educational programs for the included students with disabilities. Initially developed by Friend and Cook (2010) the model provides a framework for instruction that relies on two educators taking joint responsibility for the inclusive classroom. The model includes six options for instruction based on the instructional and student needs in each lesson. St. Cloud State University extended this model for implementation as a practice for all educators within the student teaching experience (Bacharach, Heck, & Dahlberg, 2008, 2010). The infusion of co-teaching in the clinical experiences in educator preparation service to provide candidates with the ability to develop collaborative practices, first within their own discipline before later implementation between a content expert and special educator in professional practice. To date studies have indicated limitations in educators implementation of co-teaching specifically criticizing general education preservice students lack of knowledge in effective accommodations and preservice special educators limited content knowledge (Shin, Lee, & McKenna, 2016). To effectively infuse co-teaching into the practice of preservice educators increased evidence-based practices such as those highlighted later in this chapter must be paired with co-teaching to have positive educational results for all learners.

Understanding the Importance of Systems

The second area of key concepts for inclusive educator preparation is a depth of understanding of frameworks of practice common in inclusive schools. These frameworks include UDL and Multi-Tiered Systems of

Support (MTSS). The following paragraphs provide brief reviews of the key concepts that should be embedded in coursework in an inclusive educator preparation program.

Universal Design for Learning

UDL is a framework for development of curriculum to support better access to instruction for all learners. The general philosophy of UDL asserts that the curriculum is what is disabling rather than conditions within the student (O'Brien, Aguinaga, & Knight, 2013). The most recent reauthorization of the Elementary and Secondary Education Act, entitle the Every Student Succeeds Act (ESSA) includes UDL as a critical component of effective practice in schools (Samuels, 2016) and it has been proposed as a tool to merge general and special education (Rose & Meyer, 2006). UDL tenants are typically applied at the lesson or unit level. This allows educators to create lessons from inception that will meet the needs of all learners through elimination of barriers typically in place in traditional curriculum (CAST, 2011). The framework includes three primary principles that guide curriculum development:

- Provide Multiple Means of Representation
- Provide Multiple Means of Action and Expression
- Provide Multiple Means of Engagement (CAST, 2011, p. 5)

These principles guide lesson plan development along with three leading questions:

- What will all students do?
- What will most students do?
- What will some students do? (http://mast.ecu.edu)

UDL as a framework expects the preservice educator to know the needs of individual learners and plan for their instruction early in the process of curriculum development. Preservice educators must learn to observe for these needs in early field experiences. Providing preservice educators content specific to UDL was found to positively impact both general and special education majors' belief in their ability to design instruction with accommodation in mind (Spooner, Baker, Harris, Ahgrim-Delzell, & Browder, 2007). In addition preservice students were able to design a lesson utilizing UDL. Implementation of UDL modeled lessons that include faculty and peer impact must occur for generalization of the practice into future classrooms (Evans, Williams, King, & Metcalf, 2010).

Multi-Tiered Systems of Support

MTSS provide preservice educators a framework for considering both academic and behavioral needs of students. It is an integration of the Response to Intervention (RtI) and Positive Behavior Intervention and Support (PBIS) movements. Similar to UDL, a three-tiered intervention system is applied for assessing and determining student needs. MTSS has been included in ESSA as a critical component of effective schools (National Center for Learning Disabilities [NCLD], 2016) and is seen as one tool for ensuring all students are able to meet college and career ready standards (Hayes & Lillenstein, 2015). It is a three-tiered approach that guides progress monitoring and intervention planning on behalf of all students. Both academic and socio-emotional/behavioral needs are integrated into the framework. The three foundational components of MTSS are:

- Core universal instruction and socio-emotional/behavioral supports
- Targeted supplemental systems and supports
- Intensive individualized interventions and supports

Similar to UDL inclusive educator preparation programs must partner with school district partners implementing MTSS for field experiences to facilitate candidate understanding of school wide practices that support the needs of all learners. In addition, coursework specific to curriculum should integrate the practices of RtI with behavior management courses integrating PBIS. This combined approach facilitates the holistic view promoted by MTSS (Prasse et al., 2012). A pilot residency program that integrated MTSS in to an a nontraditional educator preparation program found that entry level interns outperformed practicing teachers when taught to implement all three tiers of instruction within initial preparation (Warren Ross & Lignugaris-Kraft, 2015).

It is critical for teacher educators to reinforce that UDL, MTSS, RtI, and PBIS are frameworks for designing and implementing curriculum on behalf of all learners (Rogers-Adkinson, 2012). Specific evidence-based methodologies that support the framework must also be components of an effective inclusive educator preparation model.

HIGH IMPACT PRACTICES FOR INCLUSIVE TEACHER EDUCATION

Integrated Field Experiences

Zeichner (2010) asserts that teacher education can no longer structure itself around preparing for future practice but rather be preparing *in* practice.

If inclusive teacher educators wish to ensure mastery and use of the practices that promote inclusive schools, opportunities must be provided to observe and implement the use of high impact inclusive practices. Educator preparation programs must adjust field practices to promote both competence in the discipline with the skills to adjust curriculum for students that are not making adequate progress.

Strong field experiences are important, not only for providing opportunities for observation and application, but also for shaping the candidate notions about students with disabilities. Attitudes toward inclusion can be significantly influenced by a teacher candidate's experiences during their own P-12 instruction. While students that have been educated with and alongside students different than themselves tend to be more accepting of students with disabilities (Rogers-Adkinson, 2007), many teacher candidates have not had those positive experiences. To address attitudinal barriers preservice educators need to experience field experiences that focus on better understanding of the needs of diverse learners. Research published in 2012 (Swain, Nordness, & Leader-Janssen, 2012) concluded that preservice educators are more likely to have positive attitudes toward inclusion and are more likely to adapt instruction if they have had a field experience which requires them to provide direct instruction to children with disabilities. That study paired the field work an introductory course in special education. Pedagogy alone does not promote the application and use of evidence-based inclusive practices in teacher candidates.

Narrative Inquiry

Kukner and Orr (2016) have suggested the narrative inquiry model to develop intellectual shifts in preservice education to a more inclusive philosophy. Four components of reflection and narrative inquiry require the candidate to reflect upon past experiences with their discipline to determine their preconceived conceptions of what it means to teach. Candidates share their narratives to develop an understanding of how their previous educators have influences how they already visualize themselves as educators. Candidates are then challenged to expand their understanding of the content and milieu of pedagogy to expand the teaching repertoire to include practices and beliefs beyond the lived experience as a student in schools or modeled in limited field experiences. Such a practice can increase the capacity of the developing educator in embrace integration curricular practices that support success for students with disabilities.

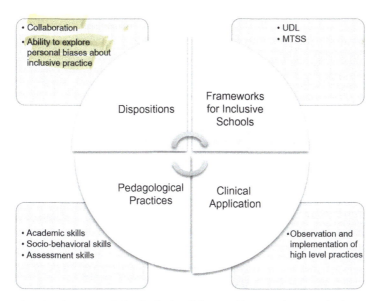

Fig. 1. Framework for Inclusive Educator Preparation Curriculum.

Evidence-Based Practices

There are several primary pedagogical practices promoted as necessary for an inclusive educator preparation program. The CCSSO, governing boards, and focused think tanks such as NTEP and CEEDAR have advocated for these practices. The new ESSA also incorporates some of these practices. Many of these practices meet the standards applied by *What Works Clearinghouse* (i.e., "gold standards") utilizing double-blind research methods to validate the practice. In some cases, however, state departments continue to advocate for practices (e.g., instruction based upon learning styles) for which little research-based evidence of impact exists (Pashler, McDaneil, Rohrer, & Bjork, 2008). As a result, some pedagogical practices described below should be included in an inclusive educator preparation program because research suggests that they are effective while other must be included because of regulatory mandate. Fig. 1 provides a model for conceptualizing the integration of these practices.

General Practices
The first sets of pedagogical practices are those that may be integrated within general or content methods course. The Institute of Education

Sciences (Pashler et al., 2007) has promoted the following as evidence-based practices that can promote increased learning for all children, including those considered at risk or "struggling." These strategies are

- Spacing learning over time
- Integrate worked examples with problem-solving exercises
- Combine graphics with verbal descriptions
- Connect abstract and concrete representations
- Effective use of quizzing
- Teach effective use of study time
- Use effective questioning techniques

Deans for Impact (2015) (deansforimpact.org/the_science_of_learning.html) have emphasized knowledge in the science of learning to improve preservice educator preparation. They suggest inclusive educator preparation can improve practice through helping preservice educators explore six critical questions.

- How do students understand new ideas?
- How do students learn and retain new information?
- How do students solve problems?
- How does learning transfer to new situations?
- What motivates students to learn?
- What are some common misconceptions about how students think and learn?

These key questions do not focus on the limitations of students but rather demand that preservice educators understand how students explore and experience new knowledge for mastery.

Literacy
State departments of education have placed increased emphasis on ensuring all educators have a better understanding of literacy instruction and supports for struggling readers. NCTQ standards also emphasize the need for all educators to have coursework specific to struggling readers (Greenberg, McKee, & Walsh, 2013). Critical to this course content is a balanced literacy approach that includes literacy experiences in phonemic awareness, phonics, fluency, comprehension, and vocabulary development (Ashby, Burns, & Royle, 2014).

Literacy instruction in an inclusive model must also include the use of strategic instructional models that support the needs of struggling students. One such model is self-regulated strategy development (SRSD). SRSD research indicates strong impact for developing student use of personal strategies for skill development (Hagaman, Casey, & Reid, 2012, 2016). For example, the RAP strategy (Schumaker, Denton, & Deshler, 1984) provides development of paraphrasing skills that improve recall of information. This model has been found to have impact at elementary (Hagaman et al., 2012), middle school (Ellis & Graves, 1990), and high school level (Lauterbach & Bender, 1995). Another similar strategy using the mnemonic TRAP to foster comprehension was found to be effective with struggling readers (Hagaman et al., 2016). Inclusive teacher education programs will need to decide what specific strategies align with their curriculum goals but should be an important component of inclusive curriculum.

Practices Specific to Special Education

The CEC in collaboration with the CEEDAR Center has also advocated for a set of practices most commonly considered special education disciplinary content. An inclusive educator preparation program, especially those that are in a dual licensure model, must incorporate these basic skills into the curriculum (McDonald, Kazemi, & Kavanaugh, 2013). These practices are listed in Table 1.

Table 1. CEC Recommended High Leverage Practices.

- Development of comprehensive learner profiles for monitoring student progress and planning of instruction
- Use of assessment data for the designing, implementation, and evaluation of instruction
- Maintaining a consistent, organized, and respectful learning environment
- Teach social behaviors
- Conduct functional behavioral assessments and implement behavior intervention plans
- Provide effective feedback to students regarding learning and behavior
- Identify long-term and short-term learning goals
- Design instruction toward a specific learning goal
- Adapt curriculum related to specific learning goals
- Use explicit teaching strategies to support learning and independence
- Scaffold instruction
- Use explicit instruction
- Use flexible grouping
- Use strategies to promote active student engagement
- Teach for generalization
- Provide for intensive instruction

Source: McLeskey and Ziegler (2015, November).

These recommendations run in tandem with the skills required under a UDL and/or MTSS framework. Instructionally teacher candidates must be able to experience the above practices through clinical applications. This requires exposure to effectively implement inclusive classrooms that demonstrate integration of both holistic and intensive instruction.

Assistive Technology
Finally, embedded across all of these competencies, inclusive educator preparation must provide candidates with the ability to implement instructional and assistive technology (AT) in the curriculum. This can provide a challenge as universities have often struggled to keep pace with emergent educational technology. Yet we must provide the adequate technology skills for educators to select and implement instructional and AT for the benefit of students (Marino, Sameshima, & Beecher, 2009). Coursework should integrate AT tools that are Type I tools which support completion of tasks efficiently and Type II that provide mechanism to use and share information (Christensen, Overall, & Knezek, 2006).

Task completion AT tools may include voice dictation software such as *Dragon Naturally Speaking* or toolbar electronic readers *Read & Write Gold* provide oral presentation of text from websites and email which may be helpful for both students with learning disabilities or ELLs. Task completion devices include apps that can facilitate oral communication via picture or word prompt, visual schedules, or social stories for behavioral support. Preservice educators must be formally taught to analyze student needs related to the curriculum and how assistive or instructional technology may enhance the learning outcomes for each student. Technology as a tool for enhancing instruction does not require a separate course but rather can and should be infused across all coursework to address applicable skills and tools across the curriculum.

Multi-Program Integration

In addition to the practices noted above, changes in the structure of programs can be effective. Counter to the traditional approach of preparing general education and special education teachers in separate silos, dual licensure or collaborative education models have been promoted as an effective framework for increasing the capacity of all educators to be prepared for practice in inclusive schools (Anderson, Smith, Olsen, & Algozzine, 2015; Jenkins, Pateman, & Black, 2002). The most prominent model is a combination of elementary and cross categorical special education, but dual early childhood programs are also prevalent. Entrenched in these licensing frameworks is a belief that educators must understand the general education system in order to support children with increased challenges (Blanton & Pugach, 2011). While an integrated curriculum communicates to teachers that they all share responsibility for students with disabilities, educator preparation programs should proceed with caution. A significant criticism of an integrated approach is that curriculum and instruction often focuses too much on developing mastery of general education practices while limiting the amount of time spent developing skills needed by special educators in more intensive interventions. In spite of this concern, combined programs for special education licensing have increased significantly in recent years despite a lack of research supporting their efficacy (Pugach & Blanton, 2011). Inclusive educator preparation programs must consider whether to dually or singularly certify preservice educators while promoting the competencies necessary to be successful in inclusive school classrooms.

CONCLUSION

That the movement to make schools more inclusive continues to grow is indisputable. In the context of that trend, it would be unconscionable for educator preparation programs to fail to prepare teachers to work effectively in inclusive educational settings. In addition, failing to address this goal would be in direct contradiction to the demands of a wide variety of social, academic, professional, and governmental stakeholders. If teacher educators are to address these expectations, they must be knowledgeable about the practices most likely to be effective in schools and the experiences that will allow novice teachers to enact those practices. Preservice educators need tools to explore their personal dispositions toward inclusive education, skills in collaborating with colleagues, frameworks for developing inclusive lessons, and practices for implementation within the discipline.

REFERENCES

Anderson, K., Smith, J. D., Olsen, J., & Algozzine, B. (2015). Systematic alignment of dual teacher preparation. *Rural Special Education Quarterly, 34*(1), 30–36.

Ashby, C. (2012). Disability studies and inclusive teacher preparation: A socially just path for teacher education. *Research and Practice for Persons with Severe Disabilities, 37*(2), 89–99.

Ashby, C., Burns, J., & Royle, J. (2014). All kids can be readers: The marriage of reading first and inclusive education. *Theory Into Practice, 53*(2), 98–105.

Bacharach, N., Heck, T., & Dahlberg, K. (2008). *Co-teaching: Enhancing the student teaching experience.* Eighth Annual IBER & TLC Conference Proceedings, Las Vegas, NV.

Bacharach, N., Heck, T., & Dahlberg, K. (2010). Changing the face of student teaching through coteaching. *Action in Teacher Education, 32*(10), 3–14.

Blanton, L. P., & Pugach, M. C. (2011). Using a classification system to probe the meaning of dual licensure in general and special education. *Teacher Education and Special Education, 34*(3), 219–234.

CAST. (2011). *Universal design for learning guidelines version 2.0.* Wakefield, MA: Author.

CCSSO Task force on Educator Preparation and Entry to the Profession. (2012). *Our responsibility, our promise: Transforming educator preparation and entry into the profession.* Washington, DC.: CCSSO. Retrieved from CCSSO.org

CCSSO Task force on Educator Preparation and Entry to the Profession. (2015). *Promises to keep: Transforming educator preparation to better serve a diverse range of learners, leveraging the policy recommendations of the CCSSO's our responsibility, our promise report.* Retrieved from http://www.ccsso.org/Documents/2015/CEEDAR%20Policy%20Framing%20-Final%20300%20dpi.pdf

Christensen, R., Overall, T., & Knezek, G. (2006). Personal education tools (PETs) for type II learning. *Computers in the Schools, 23*(1), 173–189.

Conklin, H. G., & Hughes, H. E. (2016). Practices of compassionate, critical, justice-oriented teacher education. *Journal of Teacher Education, 67*(1), 47–60.

Cosier, M., & Pearson, H. (2016). Can we talk? The underdeveloped dialogue between teacher education and disability studies. *Sage Open*, January-March, 1–10.

Deans for Impact. (2015). *The science of learning.* Austin, TX: Author. Retrieved from deansforimpact.org

Ellis, E. S., & Graves, A. W. (1990). Teaching rural students with learning disabilities: A paraphrasing strategy to increase comprehension of main ideas. *Rural Special Education Quarterly, 10*, 2–10.

Evans, C., Williams, J., King, L., & Metcalf, D. (2010). Modeling, guided instruction, and application of UDL in a rural special education teacher preparation program. *Rural Special Education Quarterly, 29*(40), 41–48.

Fletcher, J. M., & Vaughn, S. (2009). Response to intervention: Preventing and remediating academic difficulties. *Child Development Perspectives, 3*(1), 30–37. doi:10.1111/j.1750-8606.2008.00072.x

Friend, M., & Cook, L. (2010). *Interactions: Collaboration skills for school professionals* (6th ed.). Columbus, OH: Merrill.

Greenberg, J., McKee, A., & Walsh, K. (2013). *Teacher prep review: A review of the nation's teacher preparation programs.* Available at SSRN 2353894.

Hagaman, J. L., Casey, K. J., & Reid, R. (2012). The effects of the paraphrasing strategy on the reading comprehension of young students. *Remedial and Special Education, 33*(2), 110–123.

Hagaman, J. L., Casey, K. J., & Reid, R. (2016). Paraphrasing strategy instruction for struggling readers. *Preventing School Failure: Alternative Education for Children and Youth, 60*(1), 43–52.

Hayes, L., & Lillenstein, J. (2015). *A framework for coherence: College and career readiness standards, multi-tiered systems of support, and educator effectiveness.* American

Institutes for Research: Washington, DC. Retrieved from http://www.gtlcenter.org/sites/default/files/Multi-Tiered_Systems_of_Support.pdf

Holdheide, L. R., & Reschly, D. J. (2008). *Teacher preparation to deliver inclusive services to students with disabilities (TQ Connection Issue Paper)*. Washington, DC: National Comprehensive Center for Teacher Quality. Retrieved from http://www.tqsource.org/publications/%20TeacherPreparationtoDeliverInclusiveServices.pdf. Accessed on May 12, 2011.

Jenkins, A., Pateman, B., & Black, R. S. (2002). Partnerships for dual preparation in elementary, secondary, and special education. *Remedial and Special Education, 23*(6), 360–372.

Jorgensen, C. M., McSheehan, M., Schuh, M., & Sonnenmeier, R. M. (2012, July). *Essential best practices in inclusive schools*. Durham, NH: National Center on Inclusive Education Institute on Disability, University of New Hampshire.

Kernzner Lipsky, D., & Gartner, A. (1999). Inclusive education: A requirement of a democratic society. H. Daniels & P. Garner (Eds.), *Inclusive education: World yearbook of education* (pp. 12–23). New York, NY: Routledge Taylor and Francis Group.

Kukner, J. M., & Orr, A. M. (2016). Narrative inquiry in the teacher education classroom: A review of narrative inquiries into curriculum making in teacher education. *Teachers and Teaching Theory and Practice, 22*(1), 117–122.

Lauterbach, S. L., & Bender, W. M. (1995). Cognitive strategy instruction for reading comprehension: A success for high school freshmen. *High School Journal, 79*, 58–64.

Marino, M. T., Sameshima, P., & Beecher, C. C. (2009). Enhancing TPACK with assistive technology: Promoting inclusive practices in preservice teacher education. *Contemporary Issues in Technology and Teacher Education, 9*(2). Retrieved from http://www.citejournal.org/vol9/iss2/general/article1.cfm

McDonald, M., Kazemi, E., & Kavanaugh, S. (2013). Core practices of teacher education: A call for a common language and collective activity. *Journal of Teacher Education, 64*(5), 378–386.

McLeskey, J., & Brownell, M. (2015). *High-leverage practices and teacher preparation in special education*. University of Florida, Collaboration for Effective Educator, Development, Accountability, and Reform Center. (Document No. PR-1). Retrieved from http://ceedar.education.ufl.edu/tools/best-practice-review/

McLeskey, J., & Ziegler, D. (2015, Dec.) A draft of high leverage practices for special education teachers. Paper presented at the Teacher Education Division Conference, Tempe, AZ.

McMaster, C. (2015). "Where is _____?": Culture and the process of change in the development of inclusive schools. *International Journal of Whole Schooling, 11*(1), 16–34.

Moberg, S., Zumberg, M., & Reinmaa, A. (1997). Inclusive education as perceived by prospective special education teachers in Estonia, Finland, and the United States. *Research and Practice for Persons with Severe Disabilities, 22*(1), 49–55.

National Center for Learning Disabilities. (2016, Spring). *Impact update*. Retrieved from http://www.ncld.org/archives/blog/nclds-impact-update-spring-2016

National Center for Teacher Quality. (2014). Standard 4: Struggling readers. Retrieved from http://www.nctq.org/teacherPerp/review2014/ourApproach/standards/elementary.jsp?printView = T

O'Brien, C., Aguinaga, N., & Knight, V. (2013). Universal design for learning: Accessing the general curriculum with effective teaching and digital technologies. In G. Campbell-Whatley & J. Lyons (Eds.), *Leadership practices for special and general education* (pp. 146–164). Boston, MA: Pearson.

Pashler, H., Bain, P., Bottge, B., Graesser, A., Koedinger, K., McDaniel, M., & Metcalfe, J. (2007). *Organizing instruction and study to improve student learning.* Washington, DC: National Center for Education Research, Institute of Education Sciences, U.S. Department of Education. (NCER 2007–2004). Retrieved from http://ncer.ed.gov

Pashler, H., McDaneil, M., Rohrer, D., & Bjork, R. (2008). Learning styles: Concepts and evidence. *Psychological Science and the Public Interest, 9*(3), 106–119.

Prasse, D., Breunlin, R. J., Giroux, D., Hunt, J., Morrison, D., & Their, K. (2012). Embedding multi-tiered system of supports/response to intervention into teacher preparation. *Learning Disabilities: A Contemporary Journal, 10*(2), 75–93.

Pugach, M. C., & Blanton, L. P. (2011). Preservice teacher preparation across general and special education: Interrogating the meaning of collaboration and its role in teacher education reform. *Teacher Education and Special Education, 34*(30), 181–182.

Rogers-Adkinson, D. L. (2007, Fall). Finding the answers to the 'inclusion' debate. *Whitewater Magazine*, University of Whitewater Press, Whitewater, WI.

Rogers-Adkinson, D. L. (2012). Are positive behavioral interventions effective at reducing misbehavior in students with behavioral disorders? In S. Eckes & C. Russo (Eds.), *School discipline and safety* (pp. 240–247). London: Sage Publishing.

Rose, D. H., & Meyer, A. (2006). *A practical reader in universal design for learning.* Cambridge, MA: Harvard Education Press.

Samuels, S. (2016, Feb.). ESSA spotlights strategy to reach diverse learners. *Education Week*, March 6, 2016.

Schumaker, J. B., Denton, P. H., & Deshler, D. D. (1984). *The paraphrasing strategy.* Lawrence, KS: University of Kansas.

Sharma, U., Forlin, C., Lerman, T., & Earle, C. (2006). Preservice teachers' attitudes, concerns and sentiments about inclusive education: An international comparison of novice preservice teachers. *International Journal of Special Education, 21*(2), 80–93.

Shin, M., Lee, H., & McKenna, J. M. (2016). Special education and general education preservice teachers' co-teaching experiences: A comparative synthesis of qualitative research. *International Journal of Inclusive Education, 20*(1), 91–107.

Spooner, F., Baker, J. N., Harris, A. A., Ahgrim-Delzell, L., & Browder, D. M. (2007). Effects of training in universal design for learning on lesson plan development. *Remedial and Special Education, 28*(2), 108–116.

Swain, K. D., Nordness, P. D., & Leader-Janssen, E. M. (2012). Changes in preservice teacher attitudes toward inclusion. *Preventing School Failure: Alternative Education for Children and Youth, 56*(2), 75–81.

Theoharis, G., & O'Tolle, J. (2011). Leading inclusive ELL social justice leadership for English language learners. *Educational Administration Quarterly, 47*(4), 646–688.

UNESCO. (1994, June). The Salamanca statement and framework for action. Paper presented at the World Conference on Special Needs Education: Access and Quality, Salamanca, Spain.

Warren Ross, S., & Lignugaris-Kraft, B. (2015). Multi-tiered systems of support preservice residency: A pilot undergraduate teacher preparation model. *Journal of the National Association for Alternative Certification, 10*(1), 3–20.

Wilczenski, F. L. (1992). Measuring attitudes toward inclusive education. *Psychology in the Schools, 29*(4), 306–312.
Will, M. C. (1986). Educating children with learning problems: A shared responsibility. *Exceptional Children, 52*(5), 411–415.
Zeichner, K. (2010). Rethinking the connections between campus courses and field experiences in college and university based teacher education. *Journal of Teacher Education, 61*(1–2), 89–99.

THE ROLE OF THE GENERAL EDUCATOR IN THE INCLUSION CLASSROOM

Celia E. Johnson

ABSTRACT

Since the inception of Public Law 94-142, the delivery of services to children with exceptional learning needs (ELNs) has continually changed in an effort to provide optimal programming in least restrictive environments. The roles and responsibilities of teachers have also changed with the most dramatic changes likely seen in the roles of general education teachers, also known as inclusion teachers, serving children with ELNs. Federal mandates require general education teachers be actively involved in the referral and Individualized Education Program process. Once children with ELNs are serviced in inclusion classrooms, collaboration between the inclusion teacher and many professionals becomes an essential part of service delivery. This chapter focuses on elements of successful collaboration for planning, instructional delivery, and assessment, as inclusion teachers apply the principles of Universal Design for Learning and Differentiated Instruction. Academic, behavioral, and social needs of children in inclusive environments are also addressed as are essential elements addressing the collaborative roles and responsibilities of general

General and Special Education Inclusion in an Age of Change: Roles of Professionals Involved
Advances in Special Education, Volume 32, 21–38
Copyright © 2016 by Emerald Group Publishing Limited
All rights of reproduction in any form reserved
ISSN: 0270-4013/doi:10.1108/S0270-401320160000032003

education teachers as they embrace the opportunity to teach in inclusive classrooms.

Keywords: Inclusion; collaboration; collaborative teaching; universal design for learning; differentiated instruction; response to intervention

When Public Law 94-142, the Education for All Handicapped Children Act was passed in 1975, the focus was on providing an education to children with disabilities in public schools; schools receiving federal funding qualified. Later, the law was amended and re-titled the Individuals with Disabilities Education Act (IDEA) of 1990, and again amended and re-titled Individuals with Disabilities Education Improvement Act (IDEIA) of 2004. These laws ensure funding for a free appropriate public education for services to children with qualifying disabilities (Special Education News, 2016; U.S. Department of Education, 2007). Prior to 1975, few children were educated in public schools and teacher-training programs did not prepare general elementary and secondary teachers to work with children with disabilities. The passage of these laws has led to a dramatic change in teacher preparation in general and special education that continues today. Today, all teachers are likely to have children with disabilities in their classrooms as part of inclusive education.

When the public schools were charged with meeting the needs of children with disabilities, the process of changing was slow, as administrators, families, general education teachers, special education teachers, and other supportive personnel (e.g., speech therapists, physical therapists, and reading specialists) did their best to design programs for the many new children entering the doors of public schools. Efforts to offer an appropriate education progressed and the need to provide a continuum of services (Deno, 1970) to meet the many varying individual needs that ranged from mild disabilities to more severe disabilities became the challenge. A variety of models was put in place with many still being utilized today. Most public school programs have followed the concept of a continuum of services that range from least restrictive to most restrictive with the least restrictive being in the general education classroom for all content and having in place the supports necessary for the students with disabilities to succeed. In inclusive classrooms, children with and without disabilities are taught together. Students with disabilities have an Individualized Education Program (IEP) that specifies the extent of needed supports. These supports range from minimal with the special education teacher working in consultation with the general education teacher, to the student having more extensive time with the special education teacher and less time, if any, in the general education classroom or school setting. The responsibility to meet the needs of students in inclusive classrooms requires solid collaboration skills of all professionals involved in meeting the needs of individual students with disabilities as specified in their IEPs.

It is important to take a look at definition of terms when talking about inclusion. Educational terms such as "inclusion" are sometimes used loosely, resulting in misunderstandings, confusion, and even bias. Therefore, to be clear and create a common ground of communication, see Table 1 for definitions of terms relevant to this chapter.

As the educational system struggled to create public school environments where students with ELNs could experience success, both general and special education were required to examine teacher preparation programs. Many questions were asked about how to best prepare teachers to collaborate in ways they had not previously experienced. Much research has been done to identify what is necessary for successful inclusion of children with ELN in an inclusive classroom (Brownell, Adams, Sindelar, Waldron, & Vanhover, 2006; Conderman & Johnson-Rodriguez, 2009; Damore & Murray, 2009; Friend, 2000; Idol, 2006; Miller & Savage, 1995; Obiakor, Harris, Mutua, Rotatori, & Algozzine, 2012; Scruggs, Mastropieri, & McDuffie, 2007; Wallace, Anderson, & Bartolomay, 2009). The success of inclusive education for students with ELNs is dependent on both general and special education teachers assuming new roles and responsibilities. This chapter will focus on the essential roles of the general education teacher that support successful inclusion.

GENERAL EDUCATOR AS MEMBER OF THE IEP TEAM

Just as in any other endeavor, it is important to have a strong foundation. It is assumed the inclusion teacher already has the knowledge and skills necessary for successful teaching and learning in his or her general education classroom. When general education teachers open their classrooms to

Table 1.   Definition of Terms Commonly Used in the Field of General
and Special Education.

Term	Definition
Assistive Technology (AT)	AT includes any piece of equipment, product, or system that is used to "increase, maintain or improve the functional capacities of people with disabilities." AT can be low-tech, such as a magnifying glass, or high-tech, such as computer software (U.S. Department of Education, n. d.)
Collaborative Teaching	Includes a variety of teaching models such as co-teaching, cooperative teaching, team teaching, parallel teaching, and station teaching (Rainforth & England, 1997). For the purpose of this chapter, collaboration refers to the many professionals actively involved with students with exceptional learning needs (ELNs).
Continuum or Cascade of Services	A range of services from full-time placement in the general education classroom as the least restrictive to placement in a non-public residential facility as the most restrictive (Deno, 1970).
Curriculum-based Measurement	An assessment strategy for measuring student progress (in reading, math, spelling, and writing) over time using repeated probes (Gargiulo & Metcalf, 2013).
Differentiated Instruction (DI)	Teaching that includes various approaches to content, process, and product in order to meet the needs of student differences in readiness, interests, and learning needs (Tomlinson, 2001).
Exceptional Learning Needs (ELNs)	ELN is the phrase the Council for Exceptional Children has recommended when discussing children with disabilities and how to best meet their needs.
Inclusion or Full Inclusion	This term is not specifically used or defined in IDEA. For the purposes of this chapter, the term refers to students who attend a portion of their academic day in a general education setting. Full inclusion refers to students attending the general education for the full day.
Inclusion teacher	Inclusion teacher has been used to describe both the general education teacher whose classroom includes children with IEPs and special education teachers whose caseload involves children in general education classrooms. For the purpose of this chapter, inclusion teacher will refer to the general education teacher whose classroom includes children with IEPs. Associated other terms include general or regular education teacher.
Individualized Education Program (IEP)	The guidelines developed by a team that specifies appropriate services to be provided to a student who is eligible for special education. The program plan is created by the IEP Team.
IEP Team	At a minimum, the team will include the student (if appropriate) and parents/guardians, special education teacher, case manager, at least one general education teacher, school representative, school psychologist or diagnostician, and others involved or contributing to the successful learning of the student.

Table 1. (*Continued*)

Term	Definition
Probes	Frequent and repeated measures that allow for instructional planning (Gargiulo & Metcalf, 2013).
Response to Intervention (RtI)	Typically, a three-tier model to provide necessary supports for any student who is falling behind due to a variety of reasons. Ongoing assessment is used to monitor student progress and guide decisions on appropriate intervention strategies. The three tiers are designed as follows: Tier 1 – core instruction accessed by all students; Tier 2 – provides needed intervention strategies to small groups of students not making adequate progress at Tier 1 level; Tier 3 – designed for one-on-one or very small group instruction for students not making adequate progress in Tier 2 by utilizing more intense intervention strategies. Students in Tiers 2 and 3 continue to receive whole class core instruction. Students in special education may or may not need additional supports in Tiers 2 and 3. Teachers may consider a referral for special education for students not making adequate progress in Tier 3. This model is applied to academic and behavioral expectations.
Support Services for Inclusion	These services are specifically stated in the IEP and include a variety of strategies, instruction, and personnel needed for the student with an ELN to be successful in the general education classroom. For example, the general education teacher may have consultation from the special education teacher on implementation of accommodations (e.g., written directions, daily schedule, check system on homework), or, it may be specified that the student with an ELN be in the resource room when taking a test.
Universal Design for Learning (UDL)	A set of principles for curriculum development that gives all individuals equal opportunities to learn. An educational approach with three primary principles: multiple means of representation, multiple means of expression, and multiple means of engagement (National Center on Universal Design for Learning, 2013).

inclusion, it is important to be prepared with new knowledge specific to special education, as well as revisiting much of what one knows about good teaching. IDEA mandates that general education teachers be active participants in the IEP process. This process is initiated when a referral for special services has been made, typically when a child has not been performing as expected for his or her developmental age. A referral can be made initiating the process by a variety of individuals who interact with a student who is not typically progressing. General education teachers have the most contact with students and are most likely to initiate a referral after collecting data and trying different strategies to support a student's learning. Therefore, it is possible the general education teacher may have been the one making the referral initiating the process, but many times someone else has made the referral (i.e., parent, doctor, counselor, or principal). The student may have previously qualified for special education services and has received services prior to coming into the inclusion classroom. It doesn't really matter whether the process is just being initiated, or whether the process is actively in place, the mandate is that the general education teacher be included in the IEP process. Unfortunately, many teacher preparation programs leave very little space for additional hours and require only one introductory survey course in special education. As a result, most undergraduates in education today have only a basic level of knowledge about special education, inclusion, and IEPs. The inclusion teacher's role on the IEP Team is vital and it is highly recommended additional professional development (PD) focused on IEPs and inclusion be obtained. If the student with an ELN attended the general educator's classroom prior to being qualified for special education services, that teacher can provide much insight and perspective on the classroom environment, how the student learns, what his or her strengths are, and the kinds of learning challenges experienced. When the student who is eligible for special services continues or begins placement as part of inclusive education, the inclusion teacher needs to understand the responsibilities and expectations relative to implementing the IEP and needed supports. As an inclusion teacher, it is important to have an awareness of available resources for supporting the student with an ELN and resources to support the success of the inclusion teacher herself or himself. Inclusion teachers need to ask about the kinds of resources available and whether additional training or assistance is required to successfully implement the IEP. As an active and valued participant on the IEP Team, the inclusion teacher will be working with many different professionals (Teacher Vision & Council for Exceptional Children, 2016).

"... General education teachers consistently report that they do not have the skills they need to effectively instruct diverse learners, including students with disabilities" (Blanton, Pugach, & Florian, 2011). A much-needed component for successful inclusion is the availability of ongoing PD to support inclusion teachers. Having ongoing PD is a pro-active approach to helping teachers feel competent and prepared as they take on new roles and responsibilities in their inclusive classrooms. Numerous topics can be covered, but the most critical are those foundational to successful inclusion; understanding the IEP, aligning goals and standards for learning, building collaborative relationships, collaborative planning, models of collaborative teaching, applying the concepts of UDL, strategies for DI, and organizing and interpreting assessment data. PD that is ongoing rather than a minimal one-time session allows teachers to discuss and share experiences as they seek to refine their skills needed for successful inclusive teaching.

GENERAL EDUCATOR AS COLLABORATOR

Collaboration simply defined by the Merriam-Webster (2015) dictionary means, "to work with another person or group in order to achieve or do something." Applied to education, Friend and Cook (2017) address the interactions between professionals as they work toward a common goal, "how" people go about working together as they share accountability and responsibility (Wiggins & Damore, 2006). Research supports collaboration as the core foundation and best practice for successful inclusion of students with an ELN (Barnes & Turner, 2001; Brownell et al., 2006; Cross, Traub, Hutter-Pishgahi, & Shelton, 2004; Kurjan, 2000; Pena & Quinn, 2003). It would be negligent to present collaboration, between general and special education teachers, along with other professionals, and parents as the foundation to successful inclusion without also addressing its greatest obstacle, time. Ample time, along with support from administration, resources, monitoring, data collection, and evaluation are some of the primary aspects required for success. The professionals involved may be clearly committed, but without adequate common time to collaborate, success is at risk of failure. Assuming the foundational structures required for successful inclusion are in place, we can further examine how success occurs.

The inclusive classroom becomes the hub for delivery of services to students with ELNs attending the general education classroom. Service delivery may involve numerous professionals and support staff that include reading specialists, speech pathologists, occupational and physical therapists, school nurses, psychologists, counselors, behavior interventionists, and the special education teacher, in addition to the student's parents or guardians. For inclusive education to be successful, the general educator, along with other professionals involved, must continually strive to develop collaborative skills. What this collaboration looks like varies from school to school, and sometimes classroom to classroom within the same school. Looking at the inclusive classroom environment, the primary collaborators are typically the general and special education teachers who have shared responsibility to support students with ELNs in the general education classroom (Vaughn, Bos, & Schumm, 2014). This does not exclude the importance of commitment from the many others who are collaborative partners supporting the success of students with ELNs in the inclusion classroom.

Although general educators are the experts at planning, instructing, and assessing in their specific content areas, collaborating with a special education teacher and others in these areas requires a willingness to take on new perspectives and an openness to different thoughts and ideas about planning for instruction, instructional delivery, and assessment. Believing that students with ELNs can learn and be successful in the general education environment is critical and is supported by Rosenthal's extensive research during the twentieth century (Rosenthal, 1973; Rosenthal & Jacobson, 1968) and additional related research in the twenty-first century (Jussim & Harber, 2005; Kumar, Karabenick, & Burgoon, 2014). Teachers' beliefs and expectations of their students are significant factors for the success of students with ELNs in inclusive classrooms (Soodak, Podell, & Lehman, 1998). Furthermore, adopting the perspective that teachers are also learners alongside their students facilitates a reciprocity leading to rich understanding of what it really means to meet the needs of a diverse group of students in inclusive environments (Miller & Savage, 1995). Friend and Cook (2017) emphasize professional attributes important when sharing responsibilities that include cooperation, trust, and mutual respect along with other elements necessary for success such as voluntary participation, parity, shared goals, accountability, and resources as professionals collaborate in planning instruction, delivering instruction, and assessing and evaluating student progress toward learning and behavioral goals.

Collaborative Planning

Time for planning can focus on a variety of aspects critical to successful inclusion. Collaborative planning may address connections and support for different team members, especially the parents or guardians. Many aspects of the inclusion process may be focused on such things as (a) how the physical environment of the classroom supports the student with an ELN, (b) reviewing and interpreting assessment results and how to use that information for planning lessons and units, (c) designing and implementing accommodations, including AT, into the daily schedule and routines; (d) identifying where there may be problems and how to solve them; (e) integrating today's technology so that it benefits all students; and (f) incorporating all of these aspects into instruction to support students with ELNs. Common planning time is essential to successful collaboration and should be built into the daily/weekly schedule.

Starting with a review of the data presented at the IEP meeting and the specified accommodations indicated on the IEP, is the first step in planning how to best meet the needs of a student with an ELN. The focus is to be on the student's strengths and how those strengths can be used in a way for the student to have opportunity to meet learning standards specific to the classroom curriculum. The inclusion teacher, with the support of the special education teacher and others, will align IEP goals to identified learning standards while considering student strengths, prerequisite skills, and how the specified accommodations will support success. Whenever possible, accommodations that can be helpful to all students should be of priority, an approach referred to as UDL. For example, if a student needs written directions in a step-by-step format, such directions can be provided to the whole class or made available to anyone who can benefit. If a student lacks prerequisite skills and needs direct instruction prior to participating in a particular lesson, the whole class or possibly a few may benefit from direct instruction as a review, or to make up for instruction that was lost during an absence. Such accommodations can be provided by the special education teacher, para-professional, or the general education teacher. During collaborative planning is when the inclusion teacher considers what resources are available to support the success of the student with an ELN, as well as what is needed for the inclusion teacher to be successful in providing instruction to the whole class.

During collaborative planning is when decisions are made about instructional strategies, again keeping in mind the student's strengths. In order to accommodate a range of abilities, multiple intelligences, varied interests, and individual learning styles, teachers need to be deliberate in deciding how to best apply the concepts of UDL, DI, and the use of AT that must be addressed specifically on the IEP. Once again, the general education teacher will need to utilize available resources to effectively prepare for successful inclusive lessons. The inclusion teacher needs to have a clear understanding of UDL, DI, and AT in order to meet the diverse needs of the students in his or her inclusive classroom.

Universal design (UD) is a concept originating from the architectural work of Ron Mace, an individual with a disability and an advocate who defined UD as, "The design of products and environments to be usable by all people, to the greatest extent possible, without the need of specialized design" (R. L. Mace Universal Design Institute, 2016). This concept has been applied to the educational setting for learning to be more accessible to all students. The seven principles of UD can easily be applied to education, see Table 2 for the application of UD principles to UDL.

Just as UD is a concept based on seven principles, DI is a philosophy based on a set of principles (Tomlinson, 2001). This philosophy allows teachers to develop habits of thinking and learning as they plan and instruct diverse students such that inclusion teachers are able to meet the learning needs of individual students with ELNs within the inclusive classroom environment. The practice of differentiation centers on engaging students through different learning modalities, by tapping into their interests, and "by using varied rates of instruction along with varied degrees of complexity" (Tomlinson, 1999, p. 2). Gargiulo and Metcalf (2013) address how UDL supports DI by aligning the elements of both concepts as seen in Table 2. The elements of UDL involve multiple means of representation, engagement, and expression; whereas planning DI utilizes variation in content, process, and product. Content is "what" the teacher teaches and how the students access information; for example, providing background or foundational information through direct instruction or students doing

Table 2. Application of UD Principles to UDL.

Universal Design (UD)	Universal Design for Learning (UDL)
Equitable use	Website information accessible from many points; computers with speech to text software and variation in print
Flexibility in use	Materials available in a variety of formats (e.g., paper, digital, Braille); scissors for right or left hand use; compositions handwritten or on a computer
Simple and intuitive use	Labeling with words, pictures, symbols; scaffolding and prompting strategies from a variety of sources; available computer programs having ability levels
Perceptible information	Pairing of oral, written, or pictorial directions enhanced with video or closed caption features
Tolerance for error	Immediate correction and guidance provided when errors occur on computer programs or other response systems
Low physical effort	Alternative keyboards, mouse, or touch screens; speech to text software
Size and space for approach and use	Adjustable chair and table heights; space for movement; needed materials are accessible to all students

Source: Adapted from Gargiulo and Metcalf (2013).

research. Process involves "how" the teacher teaches; whether it be to the whole class, small group or pairs, or to an individual for instruction. The product deals with the assessment of the content learned; this can vary, but has pre-established criteria. Incorporating these principles when planning instruction creates a classroom environment where all students have access to the curriculum such that they have their needs met and can experience success. Once collaborative planning is accomplished, instructional options are considered. Will the inclusion teacher be teaching independently or will there be some type of collaborative instruction with another professional? If collaboration between the general and special education teachers continues into the inclusion classroom, various models of collaborative teaching have been shown to benefit students with and without ELNs in an inclusive classroom environment.

Collaborative Instruction

There are many models of collaborative teaching in inclusive classrooms with the inclusion teacher predominantly the primary leader in the general education classroom. When addressing the continuum of services to students with disabilities, one typically views the general education classroom as the least restrictive environment (LRE) at one end of the continuum, but similarly, there is a continuum of services within the general education classroom itself. For example, the supports in the inclusive classroom can range from the general education teacher having, (a) full-time support in the inclusive classroom with a para-professional serving as a one-on-one aide or a classroom aide, (b) a special education teacher as a co-teacher team teaching, (c) having a special education teacher provide in classroom instruction to small groups as needed, or (d) no other support or special education teacher in the classroom during instruction, but having support through consultation only. There are several other supportive possibilities in-between each of these models as well. In any of these models, the primary person responsible for instructional delivery to the student with an ELN is the general education inclusion teacher. Ideally, one indicator of successful collaboration supporting inclusion results in teacher parity, evident when teachers use the terms "our" and "we" when referring to students, planning, instruction, and classrooms.

Collaborative teaching, often referred to as cooperative teaching or co-teaching, has been shown to be an effective model for service delivery in inclusive classrooms. There are variety of arrangements that teachers have utilized when doing collaborative instruction or co-teaching. After numerous observations of teachers in co-teaching classrooms, Vaughn, Schumm, and Arguelles (1997) described five models of co-teaching that have been employed in inclusion classrooms; one teacher – one assist, station teaching, parallel teaching, alternative teaching, and team teaching. Research supports teachers using multiple models depending on the lesson and needs of the students, as well as having the teachers exchange roles in order to have a balanced perspective of equality between the teachers and to avoid student dependence on one teacher over the other.

One Teach – One Assist
In this model one teacher is instructing all of the students while the other teacher assists in multiple ways. Teachers should take turns being the lead teacher, if possible in this situation. For example, the assisting teacher may be moving about the room providing additional support where needed to individual students who may or may not have an ELN. Or, the assisting teacher may also be observing and collecting data on individual students.

Station Teaching
This model works very well with learning centers or work stations as it allows for two small groups to have individual attention from each of the teachers. Students will rotate around the different stations resulting in the teachers providing attention to all students within small groups while other students work independently or collaboratively at other stations.

Parallel Teaching
In this model teachers each provide the same instruction to half the class organized in two heterogeneous groups. With a lower teacher-student ratio, it is possible to give more personal attention benefitting students while avoiding attention given only to students with ELNs.

Alternative Teaching
This model allows for one teacher to instruct a small group for the purposes of pre-teaching, re-teaching, remediation, or enrichment while the other teacher instructs a heterogeneous group.

Team Teaching
The benefits of this model rely on the compatibility of the two teachers and allows for students to have equal access to each teacher at the same time.

It involves both teachers equally providing and sharing instructional activities for the whole class.

As with so many aspects of teaching, there are advantages and disadvantages for all co-teaching models. In order for co-teaching to be effective, it is critical for teachers to have adequate time to develop a teaming relationship and learn from each other; be open to new and different ideas and strategies for instruction. Additionally, the complexities at the middle and secondary levels due to curriculum structures, scheduling, and depth of content knowledge, adds dimension to the advantages and disadvantages of the co-teaching models (Weiss & Lloyd, 2002). Teachers at the middle and secondary levels also need common planning time. They should volunteer or want to co-teach in order to develop their relationship as a successful co-teaching team.

Irrespective of which arrangement or model is employed, instructional approaches that support successful inclusion of students with ELNs involve systematic procedures for appropriate learning tasks that may require scaffolding or breaking tasks down to subcomponents. Furthermore, inclusion teachers must provide clear directions and varied pacing of instruction. During active engagement, students will need frequent checks for understanding and immediate feedback on progress or needed corrections for accuracy. Students may need time extensions to complete assignments, and once completed they need positive reinforcement to promote continued success. Along with UDL, adapting instruction may require modification of materials and or activities, procedures may need to be changed, and some assignments may need to be altered or provide for an alternate choice. Hopefully, most instructional changes can be met by the creative application of UDL and DI principles.

A primary area of concern for many inclusion teachers is behavior of students with ELNs. All teachers face behavior challenges on a daily basis in their classrooms. Having clear classroom expectations, consequences, and procedures in place to provide needed structure is an absolute necessity for a strong Level One core on the three-tier RtI behavior model (see Table 1). Applying the RtI model to behavior has all students functioning with the same expectations, consequences, and procedures taught for Level One. If a student is challenged with the classroom expectation, consequences, or procedures, additional support can be provided at Level Two. For example, some students may need to be reminded of an impending transition, benefitting all students, to prepare mentally for the behavior expectation leading to the next event. An example of Level Three support might be individual instruction for a task with role playing to practice the expectation. If behavior is addressed on the IEP, the inclusion teacher can request consultation with a behavior interventionist as well as have the support of the special education teacher to implement specific behavioral interventions required beyond RtI Level One. Emphasis must focus on the use of positive strategies and require the same application of best practices identified for academic success. For example, provide clear instructions, break down tasks into subcategories, provide frequent reinforcement, and immediate correction of inappropriate behaviors. It is important to remember; behaviors are learned and will need time to change. Teach students to monitor their behavior to promote more intrinsic motivation and help students perceive their successes.

Related to behavior is social acceptance. Inclusion teachers can promote and model acceptance of students with ELNs in the classroom. Lewis and Doorlag (2011) state, "The general education teacher must participate in developing and implementing a systematic program to improve the students' social skills and to increase their social integration" (p. 133). As with all students, the inclusion teacher needs to get to know his or her students with ELNs; focus on students' interests, provide role models and mentors when needed, utilize flexible grouping arrangements, use direct instruction when necessary, praise appropriate social interaction skills, create opportunities for students to be successful and acknowledged, create classroom spaces for quiet work or collaboration, and use strategies that build classroom community. There are many strategies that support social acceptance and integration of students with ELNs that are beneficial for all students.

Another essential element related to successful inclusion is whether there is evidence that the students with ELNs are making satisfactory progress toward learning and behavioral goals established in their IEPs that are aligned with standards and goals in the general curriculum. Research outcomes strongly support inclusive education of students with disabilities. O'Rourke (2015) provides an overview of significant research worldwide that consistently establishes the benefits of inclusive education both academically and behaviorally. Additionally, Oh-Young and Filler (2015) discuss over 80 years of research indicating that students in inclusive settings outperform students in more restricted environments on both academic and social outcome measures. Over time, assessment of students with ELN in inclusive environments has emphasized ongoing or formative assessment, the process of collecting data during active engaged learning to determine what students do and don't know. Ongoing assessment allows teachers to make decisions and adjustments to instruction for the purpose of supporting student overall educational performance. Tomlinson (2008) refers to this as informative assessment and states that it is not always formal, but that it is a conscious act of paying close attention to what and how students are communicating what they know through their conversations, creations, and engaged active learning, so that teachers can make decisions supporting optimal learning.

Collaborative Assessment

Once eligibility has been determined and the LRE identified as an inclusive classroom, the inclusive teacher begins collaboration to make decisions on what types of ongoing assessment will best document the student's progress. Regular planning and progress monitoring are critical for inclusion teachers to be able to adjust instructional strategies to address problems as they arise, either academic or behavioral. Assessment information allows for long-term planning that is organized and focused for efficient use of planning time and effective selection of instructional materials and strategies. Knowing the different types of assessments and how to use assessment information will help when creating a plan for assessment that is organized, efficient, and useful. Collaborating partners determine how data will be collected and the frequency of collection. Also, it is essential for assessment to be comprehensive such that it includes all aspects related to a student's disability and how the disability affects academic performance, behavior, and social interactions. There are many methods of assessment for data collection; anecdotal notes from observations, curriculum-based measures, screening instruments, and computerized assessments that track student progress. It is recommended teachers use multiple assessments that are both formative and summative to provide more accurate and valid interpretation of results that are informative (Tomlinson, 2008).

Academically, it is necessary to review the IEP for present levels of performance in order to evaluate progress over time. Many classroom teachers use curriculum-based assessment (CBA) for ongoing documentation of student progress. CBA is defined by Deno (1987) as assessment using "direct observation and recording of a student's performance in the local curriculum as a basis for gathering information to make instructional decisions" (p. 41). It is used to measure academic progress in the basic skills of reading, math, spelling, and writing. Pemberton (2003) promotes CBA because it provides immediate information to aid in instructional decisions about what to do next, based on the results. He suggests teachers set up an area in the classroom for assessment, have material for probes organized and available, have others administer probes, involve students in scoring when appropriate, and use software programs that automatically aggregate data and graph progress. Results of CBA need to be analyzed to determine why a student is failing, as well as determine what strategies have been effective in helping the student make progress. Computer programs are also available that track CBA data and generate graphs for visual representation helpful in communicating progress to students, parents, and other professionals involved in the student's program.

In classrooms that operate by the principles of UDL and DI, performance assessment is frequently required to determine students' understanding of concepts. Performance assessment typically uses a scoring system based on specific criteria described on a rubric. Rubrics are assessment tools used to determine a student's performance on each of the specific criteria based on level of quality given a numerical value. Rubrics focus on the product or performance as opposed to the process; they are a tool that can be used for a variety of assessment situations (Gargiulo & Metcalf, 2013; Lewis & Doorlag, 2011).

CONCLUSION

Successful inclusion relies on the coordination of numerous professionals and program elements. The topics covered in this chapter are only a small part in the overall picture of what it takes for the general education teacher to successfully support students with ELNs in the inclusive classroom. Discussion of the term "success" and how it applies to all aspects of inclusive education would require numerous volumes; successful collaboration, planning, instruction, assessment, integration of students with ELN, classroom management and discipline, and PD. This chapter provided a brief overview of essential elements addressing the collaborative roles and responsibilities of general education teachers as they embrace the opportunity to teach in inclusive classrooms.

REFERENCES

Barnes, E. J., & Turner, K. D. (2001). Team collaborative practices between teachers and occupational therapists. *American Journal of Occupational Therapy*, 55(1), 83–89.
Blanton, L. P., Pugach, M. C., & Florian, L. (2011). *Preparing general education teachers to improve outcomes for students with disabilities*. Washington, DC: AACTE.

Brownell, M. T., Adams, A., Sindelar, P., Waldron, N., & Vanhover, S. (2006). Learning from collaboration: The role of teacher qualities. *Exceptional Children, 72*, 168–185.

Collaboration [Def. 1]. (2015). In *Merriam-Webster dictionary*. London: Meriam-Webster, Inc. Retrieved from http://www.merriam-webster.com/

Conderman, G., & Johnson-Rodriguez, S. (2009). Beginning teachers' views of their collaborative roles. *Preventing School Failure, 53*(4), 235–244.

Cross, A. F., Traub, E. K., Hutter-Pishgahi, L., & Shelton, G. (2004). Elements of successful inclusion for children with significant disabilities. *Topics in Early Childhood Special Education, 24*(3), 169–183.

Damore, S. J., & Murray, C. (2009). Urban elementary school teachers' perspectives regarding collaborative teaching practices. *Remedial and Special Education, 30*(4), 234–244.

Deno, E. (1970). Special education as developmental capital. *Exceptional Children, 37*, 229–237.

Deno, E. (1987). Curriculum-based measurement. *Teaching Exceptional Children, 20*, 40–42.

Friend, M. (2000). Myths and misunderstandings about professional collaboration. *Remedial and Special Education, 21*(3), 130.

Friend, M., & Cook, L. (2017). *Interactions: Collaboration skills for school professionals* (7th ed.). Upper Saddle River, NJ: Pearson Education.

Gargiulo, R. M., & Metcalf, D. (2013). *Teaching in today's inclusive classrooms: A universal design for learning approach*. Belmont, CA: Cengage/Wadsworth.

Idol, L. (2006). Toward inclusion of special education students in general education: A program evaluation of eight schools. *Remedial and Special Education, 27*(2), 77–94.

Jussim, L., & Harber, K. D. (2005). Teacher expectations and self-fulfilling prophecies: Knowns and unknowns, resolved and unresolved controversies. *Personality and Social Psychology Review, 9*, 131–155.

Kumar, R., Karabenick, S. A., & Burgoon, J. N. (2014). Teachers' implicit attitudes, explicit beliefs, and the mediating role of respect and cultural responsibility on mastery and performance-focused instructional practices. *Journal of Educational Psychology, 107*(2), 533–545.

Kurjan, R. M. (2000). The role of the school-based speech-language pathologist serving pre-school children with dysphagia: A personal perspective. *Language, Speech, and Hearing Services in Schools, 31*(1), 42–49.

Lewis, R. B., & Doorlag, D. H. (2011). *Teaching students with special needs in general education classrooms*. Boston, MA: Pearson.

Miller, K. J., & Savage, L. B. (1995). *Including general educators in inclusion*. ERIC Document Reproduction Service No. ED 381 322).

National Center on Universal Design for Learning. (2013). Retrieved from www.udlcenter.org

Obiakor, F. E., Harris, M., Mutua, K., Rotatori, A., & Algozzine, F. (2012). Making inclusion work in general education classrooms. *Education and Treatment of Children, 35*(3), 477–490.

Oh-Young, C., & Filler, J. W. (2015). A meta-analysis of the effects of placement on academic and social skill outcome measures of students with disabilities. *Research in Developmental Disabilities, 47*, 80–92.

O'Rourke, J. (2015). Inclusive schooling: If it's so good – Why is it so hard to sell? *International Journal of Inclusive Education, 19*(5), 530–546. doi:10.1080/13603116.2014.954641

Pemberton, J. B. (2003). Communicating academic progress as an integral part of assessment. *Teaching Exceptional Children, 35*(4), 16–20.

Pena, E., & Quinn, R. (2003). Developing effective collaboration teams in speech-language pathology. *Communication Disorders Quarterly*, 24(2), 53–63.

R. L. Mace Universal Design Institute. (2016). *What is universal design?* Retrieved from http://udinstitute.org/whatisud.php

Rainforth, B., & England, J. (1997). Collaboration for inclusion. *Education and Treatment of Children*, 20(1), 85.

Rosenthal, R. (1973). *On the social psychology of the self-fulfilling prophecy: Further evidence for Pygmalion effect and their mediating mechanisms*. Dover, DE: MSS Modular Publication, Inc.

Rosenthal, R., & Jacobson, L. (1968). *Pygmalion in the classroom: Teacher expectations and pupils' intellectual development*. New York, NY: Holt, Rinehart, & Winston.

Scruggs, T. E., Mastropieri, M. A., & McDuffie, K. A. (2007). Co-teaching in inclusive classrooms: A metasynthesis of qualitative research. *Exceptional Children*, 73(4), 392–416.

Soodak, L. C., Podell, D. M., & Lehman, L. R. (1998). Teacher, student, and school attributes as predictors of teachers' responses to inclusion. *The Journal of Special Education*, 33(4), 480–497.

Special Education News. (January 31, 2016). Retrieved from www.specialednews.com/the-history-or-special-education-in-the-united-states.htm

Teacher Vision & Council for Exceptional Children. (2016). *The IEP cycle: The general educator's role*. Retrieved from https://www.teachervision.com/special-education/resource/5582.html

Tomlinson, C. A. (1999). *The differentiated classroom: Responding to the needs of all learners*. Alexandria, VA: ASCD.

Tomlinson, C. A. (2001). *How to differentiate instruction in mixed-ability classrooms* (2nd ed.), Alexandria, VA: ASCD.

Tomlinson, C. A. (2008). Learning to love assessment. *Educational Leadership*, 65(4), 10–17.

U.S. Department of Education. (2007). *History: Twenty-five years of progress in educating children with disabilities through IDEA*. Retrieved from http://www2.ed.gov/print/policy/speced/leg/idea/history.html

U.S. Department of Education (n. d.). *Building the legacy: IDEA 2004*. Retrieved from http://idea.ed.gov/explore/view/p/,root,statute,I,A,602,1,

Vaughn, S. R., Bos, C. S., & Schumm, J. S. (2014). *Teaching students who are exceptional, diverse, and at risk in the general education classroom* (6th ed.). Boston, MA: Pearson.

Vaughn, S., Schumm, J. S., & Arguelles, M. E. (1997). The ABCDE's of co-teaching. *Teaching Exceptional Children*, 30, 4–10.

Wallace, T., Anderson, A. R., & Bartolomay, T. (2009). Collaboration: An element associated with the success of four inclusive high schools. *Journal of Educational and Psychological Consultation*, 13(4), 349–381.

Weiss, M. P., & Lloyd, J. W. (2002). Congruence between roles and actions of secondary special educators in co-taught and special education settings. *The Journal of Special Education*, 36(2), 58–68.

Wiggins, K., & Damore, S. (2006). "Survivors" or "friends"? A framework for assessing effective collaboration. *Teaching Exceptional Children*, 38(5), 49–56.

THE ROLE OF THE SPECIAL EDUCATOR IN THE INCLUSIVE CLASSROOM

John Travis Spoede, Jr., Charlotte Fontenot and Cynthia Simpson

ABSTRACT

In a world of ever-changing educational trends, it is essential for educators to provide a continuum of services to meet the needs of all students. Therefore, employing an inclusive structure or environment is imperative to the implementation of Special Education laws, according to Individuals with Disabilities Education Act and Every Student Succeeds Act. As stipulated in law, all students should be educated in the least restrictive environment with their typically developing peers. This chapter focuses on the role of the special education professional as it specifically relates to the mainstream or inclusion setting. Topics covered in this chapter include an overview of inclusion, the inclusion model, an in-class support model, a content mastery model, and characteristics of an effective special educator, understanding disabilities, assessing and referring to appropriate supports, collecting data for individualized education program meetings, differentiated instruction, and strategies for inclusion. The goal of the

General and Special Education Inclusion in an Age of Change: Roles of Professionals Involved
Advances in Special Education, Volume 32, 39–54
Copyright © 2016 by Emerald Group Publishing Limited
All rights of reproduction in any form reserved
ISSN: 0270-4013/doi:10.1108/S0270-401320160000032004

chapter is to provide the overall view of inclusion in today's classrooms in relation to the role of the special education teacher.

Keywords: Inclusion; special education; support; differentiated instruction; disabilities; UDL

INTRODUCTION

When asked to remember their first day as a classroom teacher, many veteran teachers recall having mixed levels of anxiety and hopefulness. They dreamt of the first day of their career with a certain level of idealism. As time passed, reality began to settle in and idealistic views of teaching in a traditional way to meet the needs of all students faded. The notion that one can just implement what they learned from textbooks began to blur. In a very short time, this new career revealed that each class is different, every student is unique, and most importantly, the design, the instruction, and the tools to teach must be individualized to meet the needs of all students. It isn't a task that presents itself with an instruction manual filled with sequential steps to teach student "A" and another process to teach student "B". All children are different and all students reach their academic success based on their own set of strengths and challenges. Teachers in an inclusive classroom can attest to this.

Over the decades, education has changed. Civil rights movements have demanded equality for all. Advocates have exposed flaws in the educational system and have begun supporting a shift in educating students with disabilities. Educators around the world have begun to embrace the challenge of creating learning environments where students identified with a variety of different disabilities and possessing a range of academic, social, and emotional abilities receive a free and appropriate education in an inclusive classroom. A new era of public education has emerged and truly inclusive classrooms have surfaced.

In the following sections, the continuum of services within an inclusion setting is discussed with a focus on the inclusion model, in-class support model, and content mastery model. Characteristics of an effective special educator, understanding disabilities, assessing and referring to appropriate supports, collecting data for individualized education program (IEP) meetings, differentiated instruction, and strategies for inclusion are highlighted and discussed in light of current trends within the education system.

WHY INCLUSION?

It is best practice and federal education laws require that a significant effort be made to create an inclusive placement for all students with exceptionalities (U.S. Department of Education, 2011). This brings about the heart of the special education professional. They tend to understand that one of the main focuses of educating students is to prepare them for transitioning into society (Association for Supervision and Curriculum Development, 2012; Banks & McGee Banks, 2009; Labaree, 1997; Spoede & Cutting, 2016). When working with students with exceptionalities, these professionals target strategies to help students regain lost ground in an attempt to re-integrate them back with their nondisabled peers because they know life does not provide them with accommodations and modification as they leave the cocoon of Pre-K-12 education (Fuchs & Fuchs, 1994; Fuchs, Fuchs, Fernstorm, & Hohn, 1999).

One goal of the professional in the field of education is preparing students for careers that are new and continually evolving (such as careers in technology, green collar jobs, and the medical industry). To this end, the field of education must be mindful of training students in transferrable skills that, once learned, can be applied across many settings. It is also important to instill the importance of being a lifelong learner.

Many of these professionals become a catalyst or agent for change for students who have been identified as individuals with exceptionalities. As effective agents of change, special education professionals need to see past the fears surrounding transformation from transitioning students from the self-contained classroom setting into the inclusive mainstreamed general education setting. The Individual with Disabilities Act (Individuals with Disabilities Education Act [IDEA], 2004) maintains that all districts must provide "a continuum of placements" for servicing students with exceptionalities.

The key to change is to let go of fear. (*Rosanne Cash*)

Federal Legislation

In December 2015, new laws were adopted related to special education. One law adopted is the Every Student Succeeds Act (ESSA), which legislates a cap of one percent of all students that can take alternate assessments. This translates to appropriately 10 percent of students with disabilities (Every

Student Succeeds Act [ESSA], 2015). The law additionally requires that a specific plan for reducing bullying and harassment, restraint and seclusion, and suspensions and expulsions be developed in the school setting. There is a body of literature supporting interventions as it relates to bullying and students in the special education setting (Spoede & Reed, 2015). Therefore, even though ESSA does not explicitly state criteria for inclusion, the law implies that inclusion is needed for the success of students with exceptionalities (ESSA, 2015; Samuels, 2015 from Education Week, December 2015). Due to ESSA, the field of special education is now preparing students with disabilities for regular accountability assessments and the preparation should occur in the least restrictive environment (LRE).

The Individuals with Disabilities Education Improvement Act of 2004 (IDEIA) refers to the LRE as a legally mandated sound model for the learning of students with exceptionalities (Heward, 2013). According to Mercer, Mercer, and Pullen (2011), it is imperative to produce an "enabling environment which will further ensure greater success for students with exceptionalities in the general education setting."

Inclusion should be driven by the students' needs as determined by the IEP team. Special educators are a required and important part of the IEP team. They bring a unique perspective of knowledge and experience related to the practical functioning of students with exceptionalities in the school setting. The team consists of the special educator, resource professionals, general educator, administrators, parents, and student when appropriate (Kauchak & Eggen, 2014). Each state has its own qualifications for becoming a professional special educator. Generally, these qualifications include education, experience, demonstration of proficiency, and assessment (Texas Education Agency, 2016).

Section 504 of the Rehabilitation Act of 1973 requires that a recipient of federal funds provide for the education of each of its qualified handicapped persons with persons who are not handicapped to the maximum extent appropriate to the needs of the handicapped person. This portion of the Rehabilitation Act of 1973 is in place to provide support to students needing additional assistance, but do not qualify for special education services under federal law (Evers & Spencer, 2011).

Inclusion Model

What is inclusion? Inclusion means including students with exceptionalities in a general education classroom; it also means including the student with exceptionalities in the day-to-day real-world applications as their abilities will allow. According to Obiakor, Harris, Mutua, Rotatori, and Algozzine (2012), one of the goals of inclusion is to provide increased normalcy in the lives of students with disabilities, such as environments provided through the general education setting. Inclusion is being a part of what others are actively engaged with, which includes being welcomed and embraced as a member of society. Inclusion is not a trade-off of support and services for placement in the mainstream class and is not a trade-off of achievement of individual goals. Inclusion must be created with proper planning, preparation, and support. The following are instructional options often provided by special educators: inclusion support, in-class support, co-teach support, and content mastery.

Inclusion Support/Consultation Model
This is a setting in which students are placed into the mainstream or general education setting to receive instruction; however, the general education teacher receives ongoing support from the special education professional (Heward, 2013). This support may be focused on the implementation and modification of teaching strategies to increase student success (Vaughn & Bos, 2012). Support from the special education professional can occur at predetermined intervals, or on an as-needed basis. However, it is important for a spirit of collaboration to occur between the two professionals in order to provide the highest level of instruction for students – especially students with exceptionalities. Many times this collaboration has a positive effect on student learning outcomes such as testing and classroom performance (Hick, Kershner, & Farrell, 2008). This model is designed to support students that are experiencing difficulties with organization, motivation, attention, and basic study skills (Heward, 2013).

In-Class Support Model
Generally, in-class support consists of a trained special education professional who has a presence in the classroom to assist with accommodations for students receiving special education services. The professional acts as a support for the general education teacher to assist with the day-to-day functions of the classroom (Heward, 2013). The special education professional provides direct services and assists with basic functions such as providing academic intervention while collecting data for future IEP meetings, accommodations from the IEP meeting, repeating directions as needed, monitoring and attending to students staying on-task, and intervening and monitoring behavior challenges identified by the students IEP team.

Accommodation in the special education arena is utilized to assist students with disabilities with meeting academic skills successfully. According to publications from the Florida State Department of Education (1999), "... accommodations involve a wide range of technics and support systems that helps students with a disability work around any limitations that result from their disability" (p. 1).

Co-Teach Support Model
Co-teach support consists of collaboration between general education and special education teachers in a general education setting. Both professionals provide instructional services and modification. There are several formats in the co-teach model. One format is team teaching where both professionals share time in teaching. This includes both professionals spending time planning and preparing to teach an entire lesson collaboratively. Another style is complementary instruction. In this format one educator is primarily responsible for teaching a specific subject matter, while the other educator is primarily responsible for teaching skills and learning strategies and re-teaching utilizing differentiated instructional approaches (Gurgur & Uzuner, 2010). The third type of co-teach model is commonly referred to as supportive learning activities. This form of co-teaching involves one educator providing instruction, where the other educator develops and implements supplementary and supportive learning activities (Gurgur & Uzuner, 2010).

Content Mastery Model
Content mastery is designed to support students assigned to general education classes in all academic and nonacademic areas (Vannest et al., 2009). In the content mastery setting, one-on-one assistance can be given to students. One-on-one assistance can be given in the following areas: test adaptations, specialized activities, formulized instruction in test taking strategies and study skills, and instructional modifications and accommodations as indicated by the students IEP. Test adaptions can include modifications, such as deleting a test answer choice, reading the test aloud to students, and chunking the test. Specialized materials may include physical models for math and science, assistive technology, and manipulatives for hands-on reinforcement for instruction in the general education classroom. Instruction on test taking and study skills can include such things as the use of − and monitoring the use − of the planner, teaching and monitoring the development of time management skills, and reviewing general test taking aids/strategies. Instructional modifications and accommodations are specifically discussed and determined within the IEP meeting and may

include such interventions as simplifying instruction, monitoring student progress, checking for student understanding, and/or any other agreed-upon intervention that assists students with mastering the curriculum. There are researchers who suggest that content mastery has some benefits for students with disabilities as an intermittent step to accessing general education curriculum in the classroom. In this model, students are able to attend the general education classroom and access the special education classroom as needed to bolster their learning and success (Turnbull, Turnbull, & Wehmeyer, 2010).

CHARACTERISTICS OF AN EFFECTIVE SPECIAL EDUCATOR

Special education professionals often find themselves thinking outside of the box and going the distance to ensure that all students can be successful in the general education and special education settings that are deemed necessary to maximize student mastery of content. Some characteristics that can be noted with these professionals consist of the following: a correct mindset, good classroom management skills, providing a safe learning environment, having students' best interest at heart while establishing positive relationships with students, improving teaching based on assessment data, and possessing a realistic mindset about working with students with disabilities (Thompson & Shamberger, 2012).

According to Codell (2009) general educators believe that students can excel in their studies. They also place high expectations on their students and are willing to go over and above to provide support for student learning. The work in their classrooms tend to be interesting, relevant, and comprehensible. Finally, Codell (2009) indicated that these professionals utilize diverse instructional strategies to enhance and engage student learning at all levels. Kafele (2009) indicated that these professionals have a core belief that it is their responsibility to provide high-quality instruction to students in any educational environment.

Good classroom management skills such as clearly communicating expectations from the start of school are best practice for all students and educational settings. Instead of having a punitive mindset, these professionals are equitable to all students and exhibit an understanding of working with students that demonstrate minor behavior infractions. Above all, they value the learning of all students and will prevent classroom distractions that inhibit a productive instructional environment while incorporating the emphasis of a safe learning environment in the professionals' classroom (Thompson, 2010).

Additionally, characteristics noted by researchers found that special educators ensure that students believe in the power and benefits of being well educated, as education prepares them for practical everyday skills for real world applications (Gruell, 1999; McCourt, 2006). Professionals take a consistent active role in the overall welfare of their students (Codell, 2009). Codell furthermore indicated that effective special educators also collect data on students that helps to inform their practice and goals for ensuring student mastery of content as demonstrated by improved standardized test scores (2009). Effective educators do not expect perfect or ideal classroom conditions, but instead expend their energy, effort, and focus on what they can control in doing their best work for their students (Thompson, 2010). Resilience, regardless of the school climate and culture in which the teacher finds himself or herself, allows the teacher to provide an outstanding education to all students entrusted in their care (Benard, 2004).

Understanding Disabilities

The base of knowledge related to understanding disabilities is an ever-growing and evolving field. One recent example of the changes in the field was the release and use of the Diagnostic and Statistical Manual of Mental Disorders DSM 5 (American Psychiatric Association, 2013) and changes in defining and treating disabilities such as autism spectrum disorder. The fully trained special education professional has completed thorough specialized training related to various disabilities. This training generally occurred through specialized classes and experiential learning during the educator's education preparation program. The educator further demonstrates proficiency, understanding, and comprehension of various disabilities on teacher certification exams and through classroom observations conducted by seasoned educators and administrators. According to the U.S. Department of Education (2011), there are 13 categories in which individuals may receive special education services:

1. Autism Spectrum Disorder
2. Learning Disability
3. Emotional and Behavior Disorders
4. Intellectual Disabilities
5. Speech and Language Impairment
6. Hearing Impairment

7. Visual Impairment
8. Orthopedic Impairment
9. Other Health Impairment (such as AD/HD, fetal alcohol syndrome)
10. Multiple Disabilities
11. Developmental Delay
12. Traumatic Brain Injury
13. Deaf-Blindness

It is simple enough to list the 13 categories of disabilities. However, simply knowing the names of the categories is only the first step in developing a more complete understanding of the disabilities, the characteristics of the disabilities, and how to most effectively create and monitor educational interventions for students with the specific disabilities within the inclusive classroom environment. To this end, even within the field of special education professionals, there are clusters of professionals who have exerted effort and are invested in developing explicit specialties. Within these specialties, educators learn about best practices and evidence-based practices when working with students within a certain disability category. Within the 13 categories of disabilities within the IDEIA, there is potential for special education teachers to develop specific and tailored professional identity. See Table 1 for examples of this.

Accessing and Referring to Appropriate Supports

In general, the goal of the special education professional is to provide services in the LRE. To this end, educational systems across the United States have developed a continuum of services to ensure that every effort is made to instruct the students in the general education setting as much as possible. The role of the special educator is to provide insights to other educators on the campus when traditional interventions are not effective. According to Heward (2013), there are multiple tiers of interventions. These tiers consist of:

1. Classroom interventions which are created, implemented, and monitored by the teacher of record.
2. English as a Second Language Services.
3. Referral to the Response to Intervention process
   a. Tier 1 – Includes interventions for the entire class, based on students' needs.

Table 1.   Approaches to Cultivating Specialties for Working with Students
in Specific Disability Categories.

Category	Examples

Learning	1. Academic pursuits such as
	  a. initial certification programs
	  b. advanced graduate degrees
	  c. specialized trainings
	  d. specialized certification (i.e., applied behavior analysis)
	2. Lifelong learning opportunities, such as:
	  a. professional development
	  b. continuing educational
	  c. conferences
	  d. workshops
	3. Serves as the conduit for translational research application in sundried real-life educational settings.

Consultation and Collaboration	1. Joining professional organizations, such as:
	  a. Council for Exceptional Children
	  b. National Education Association
	  c. Council for Learning Disabilities
	  d. Other state-level organizations
	2. Advocacy work at the local, state, and federal levels with an emphasis on influencing:
	  a. public policy
	  b. social justice
	  c. law
	  d. funding for research
	  e. funding for educating all disability categories
	3. Provide professional development to general education teachers in the areas of
	  a. understanding criteria for disabilities
	  b. understanding causes and underlying factors related to the development of specific disabilities
	  c. understanding most effective treatment for specific disabilities
	  d. best practices for working with students with disabilities on an individual, classroom, and schoolwide levels
	4. Through providing consultation about students with disabilities to various educational professionals such as:
	  a. administrators
	  b. counselors
	  c. curriculum and instructional specialist
	  d. general education teachers
	  e. paraprofessionals
	5. Through providing consultation to parents and community members
	6. Develop a network of professionals who can serve as consultants for working with students with disabilities throughout the school district, state, and national levels.

Table 1. (*Continued*)

Category	Examples
Experiential learning	1. Professional experience, such as years of teaching a population of students with specific categories disabilities. 2. Targeted volunteering, which allows the teacher an opportunity to connect and empathize with advocates, families, and students within various disability categories.
Research	1. Serves as the conduit for translational research application in sundry real-life educational settings. 2. Develops expertise in data-driven assessments which informs teaching practices and student IEP meeting. 3. Peer-reviewed activities such as: a. presenting sessions at professional conferences b. facilitating poster sessions at professional conferences c. leading round table discussion at professional conferences d. publishing books and articles 4. Develop written research summaries to inform and impact educational practices for campus and districts.

This table was compiled from resources such as Council for Exceptional Children (2016), Council for Learning Disabilities (2016), Family to Family Network (2016), Halverson, Grigg, Prichett, and Thomas (2007), and Heward (2013).

    b. Tier 2 – Within this tier, teachers instruct students within small group settings.
    c. Tier 3 – Individualized instruction, which may lead to special education referral for services.
4. Referral to specialized programing, such as 504 or special education services.

It is important to remember that the special education professional is a part of a team that works to prevent over identification of students into the special education program. More specifically, the special education professional acts as an advocate to ensure students are educated in the mainstream to the maximum extent allowed by the disability (Boyle & Scanlon, 2010).

Collecting Data for IEP Meetings

Many special education professionals also serve as the case manager for students with disabilities. In their role as case manager, the professional will distribute pertinent information from the IEP meeting to the general education teachers, provide clarity and consultation on an as-needed basis, monitor student progress through data collection, and report student progress to the IEP team. Several types of data that can be collected within the general education setting, according to Taylor, Smiley, and Richards (2009), consist of:

1. Observational data such as behaviors related to learning performance and emotional states.
2. Academic data such as grades on class assignments, homework, and both formative and summative assessments.
3. Social interaction data especially for those that are experiencing social skill deficits.
4. Functional behavior checklist and data.
5. Data describing communication skills, such as verbal, written, and nonverbal.

Differentiated Instruction

As an effective professional special education inclusion specialist, it is important to know how each student in the class learns best. This includes knowing students learning style and strengths and weaknesses. Providing differentiated instruction ensures that the needs of all students are being met. According to Willis (2009), differentiated instruction is in place when students are offered choices in how they will engage in learning to master the content being taught. One tool utilized by differentiating instruction is the Universal Design for Learning (UDL).

This design is inclusive of all students, regardless of their learning level. With UDL, it is essential that methods, materials, and assessments are included to establish a connecting point for all students. Some other benefits for utilizing UDL consist of the curriculum transitioning into an innately flexible design so that all students' needs are met. Adaptability is yet another advantage of the UDL process. Simply integrating the use of UDL as another tool in the professional toolkit is not optimal. UDL design is best implemented through a consistent systematic approach in the classroom, so that students are able to function effectively in the learning environment that is created with the design (Boyle & Scanlon, 2010). This requires the professional to consistently learn, implement, and maintain the UDL design for all students in the classroom. Further positive anticipated outcomes from the use of UDL, according to Willis (2009), includes the minimization of barriers and maximizing of access to

Table 2. Differentiated Instructional Strategies across Content Areas.

Differentiated Activities	Definition	Content Areas it Can Be Used In
Leveled Learning Centers	Group students together according to their ability levels for the benefit of targeted instruction	Language Arts Mathematics Science Social Studies Physical Education Electives
Menus	Providing a list of options of activities to increase student motivation, engagement, and learning	Language Arts Mathematics Science Social Studies Electives
Think, Pair, Share	A collaborative effort between 2 and 4 students, where students process and engage in educational dialog, and report back to the class about a given topic	Language Arts Mathematics Science Social Studies Physical Education Electives
K-W-L Charts	Implementing the use of a three-column organizer where students brainstorm: K – what they know W – What they want to know L – What they learned	Language Arts Mathematics Science Social Studies Physical Education Electives
Graphic Organizers	A symbolic representation or way to consolidate information through a collection of information and thoughts regarding the content	Language Arts Mathematics Science Social Studies Electives
Sticky Note Discussions	The use of sticky notes, to allow students to mark specific sections they intend to bring up during classroom discussion to get more information	Language Arts Science Social Studies

Sources: Conklin (2012), Gregory and Chapman (2007), McCarney and Wunderlich (2014), Mercer et al. (2011), Nunley (2002), Santa et al. (1988), and Tomlinson and Eidson (2003).

both information and learning. It is also essential within the UDL design that appropriate assistive technology is utilized to further enhance assessment, placement, and learning for all students (Fontenot, Marvil, & Houser, 2013). Therefore, a special education professional providing services in an inclusive environment should be well versed in the literature and practicalities of implementing UDL across all educational setting, subjects, and curriculum.

STRATEGIES FOR INCLUSION

In addition to the seamless integration of special education teachers into the inclusion setting, it is helpful to also have strategies to engage students with disabilities. Many times these strategies can be learned via training such as Project CRISS — Creating Independence through Student-owned Strategies (Santa, Havens, & Maycumber, 1988). However, learning strategies is only the first step. It then becomes important for educators to implement the strategies through practical application in the classroom setting. In an effort to assist with the practical implementation of various inclusion strategies, Table 2 acts as a summary for a sampling of differentiation activities, definitions, and suggested content areas where the strategy could be executed. However, it should be noted that this is by no means an exhaustive or comprehensive list, rather a limited selection of example strategies that can be pragmatically introduced into the classroom setting.

CONCLUSION

Over the course of this chapter, specific terms, concepts, and special education laws were reviewed in light of the impact on special education professionals implementing an inclusive educational system in their schools. Though a wide variety of topics were discussed in this chapter, it is imperative to process and integrate the knowledge gained in such a way that special education professionals are able to create and maintain an inclusive environment for students with disabilities. Although the field of special education has advanced in efforts to include students into the LRE with their nondisabled peers, there is much work and research left to be done in order for the field to become fully developed and truly inclusive for ALL students.

REFERENCES

American Psychiatric Association. (2013). *Diagnostic and statistical manual of mental disorders: DSM-5.* Washington, DC: American Psychiatric Association.

Association for Supervision and Curriculum Development. (2012). *What is the purpose of education?* Retrieved from http://www.ascd.org/ASCD/pdf/journals/ed_update/eu201207_ infographic.pdf

Banks, J. A., & McGee Banks, C. A. (2009). *Multicultural education: Issues and perspectives* (7th ed.). Hoboken, NJ: John Wiley & Sons, Inc.

Benard, B. (2004). *Resiliency: What we have learned.* San Francisco, CA: WestEd.

Boyle, J., & Scanlon, D. (2010). *Methods and strategies for teaching students with mild disabilities: A case-based approach.* Boston, MA: Wadsworth Cengage Learning.

Codell, E. R. (2009). *Educating Esme: Diary of a teacher's first year* (expanded ed.). New York, NY: Algonquin.

Conklin, W. (2012). *Activities for a differentiated classroom: Standards and research based.* Huntington Beach, CA: Shell Education.

Council for Exceptional Children. (2016). Retrieved from https://www.cec.sped.org/

Council for Learning Disabilities. (2016). Retrieved from http://www.council-for-learning-disabilities.org/

Evers, R. B., & Spencer, S. S. (2011). *Planning effective instruction: For students with learning and behavioral problems.* New York, NY: Pearson.

Every Student Succeeds Act. (2015). House of Representatives: Washington, DC.

Family to Family Network. (2016). Retrieved from http://www.familytofamilynetwork.org/

Florida Department of Education. (1999). *Assisting students with disabilities: A guide for educators.* Retrieved from http://files.eric.ed.gov/fulltext/ED444288.pdf

Fontenot, C., Marvil, M. A., & Houser, M. (2013). Assessment: Utilizing the IPad as assistive technology. *The Journal of the Texas Educational Diagnosticians' Association: The Dialog, 42*(1), 15–18.

Fuchs, D., & Fuchs, L. S. (1994). *What's "special" about special education? A field under siege. Viewpoints.* Retrieved from http://files.eric.ed.gov/fulltext/ED379817.pdf

Fuchs, D., Fuchs, L. S., Fernstorm, P., & Hohn, M. (1999). *Achieving responsible reintegration of behaviorally disordered students.* Retrieved from http://files.eric.ed.gov/fulltext/ ED313857.pdf

Gregory, G. H., & Chapman, C. (2007). *Differentiated instructional strategies: One size doesn't fit all.* Thousand Oaks, CA: Corwin Press.

Gruell, E. (1999). *The freedom writer's diary: How a teacher and 150 teens used writing to change themselves and the world around them.* New York, NY: Broadway.

Gurgur, H., & Uzuner, Y. (2010). A phenomenological analysis of the views on co-teaching applications in the inclusion classroom. *Education Sciences: Theory and Practice, 10*(1), 311–331.

Halverson, R., Grigg, J., Prichett, R., & Thomas, C. (2007). The new instructional leadership: Creating data-driven instructional systems in school. *Journal of School Leadership, 17*(2), 159–194.

Heward, W. L. (2013). *Exceptional children: An introduction to special education* (10th ed.). Boston, MA: Pearson.

Hick, P., Kershner, R., & Farrell, P. (2008). *Psychology for inclusive education: New directions in theory and practice.* New York, NY: Routledge.

Individuals with Disabilities Education Act. 20 U.S.C. § 1400 (2004).

Kafele, B. (2009). *Motivating black males to achieve in school and in life.* Alexandria, VA: ASCD.

Kauchak, D., & Eggen, P. (2014). *Introduction to teaching: Becoming a professional* (5th ed.). Boston, MA: Pearson.

Labaree, D. F. (1997). Public goods, private goods: The American struggle over educational goals. *American Educational Research Journal, 34*(1), 39–81.

McCarney, S. B., & Wunderlich, K. C. (2014). *Pre-referral intervention manual: The most common learning and behavior problems encountered in the education environment* (4th ed.). Columbia, MO: Hawthorne Educational Services, Inc.

McCourt, F. (2006). *Teacher man: A memoir*. New York, NY: Scribner.

Mercer, C. D., Mercer, A. R., & Pullen, P. C. (2011). *Teaching students with learning problems* (8th ed.). Upper Saddle River, NJ: Pearson.

Nunley, K. F. (2002). *Layered curriculum: The practical solution for teachers with more than one student in their classroom*. Kearney, NE: Morris Publishing.

Obiakor, F. E., Harris, M., Mutua, K., Rotatori, A., & Algozzine, B. (2012). Making inclusion work in general education classrooms. *Education and Treatment of Children, 35*(3), 477–490.

Samuels, C. (2015). What does ESSA mean for special education? *Education Week*. Retrieved from http://mobile.edweek.org/c.jsp?cid = 25920011&item = http%3A%2F%2Fapi.edweek.org%2Fv1%2Fblogs%2F58%2F%3Fuuid%3D55844

Santa, C. M., Havens, L. T., & Maycumber, E. M. (1988). *Project CRISS* (2nd ed.). Dubuque, IA: Kendall/Hunt Publishing.

Spoede, J., & Cutting, R. (2016). Successfully transitioning students with disabilities DiaLog-Journal of the Texas Educational Diagnosticians' Association. *The Journal of Texas Educational Diagnosticians' Association: The Dialog, 45*(1), 24–27.

Spoede, J., & Reed, D. (2015). Issues update: Special education and bullying. *The Journal of Texas Educational Diagnosticians' Association: The Dialog, 44*(2), 17–20.

Taylor, R. L., Smiley, L. R., & Richards, S. B. (2009). *Exceptional students: Preparing teachers for the 21st century*. New York, NY: McGraw-Hill.

Texas Education Agency. (2016). *Becoming a classroom teacher in Texas*. Retrieved from http://tea.texas.gov/interiorpage.aspx?id = 25769812519

Thompson, G. (2010). *The power of one: How you can help or harm African American students*. Thousand Oaks, CA: Corwin Press.

Thompson, G. L., & Shamberger, C. T. (2012). What really matters: Six characteristics about outstanding teachers in challenging schools. *ASCD Express, 8*(2). Retrieved from http://www.ascd.org/ascd-express/vol8/802-thompson.aspx

Tomlinson, C. A., & Eidson, C. C. (2003). *Differentiation in practice: A resource guide for differentiating curriculum*. Alexandria, VA: Association of Supervision and Curriculum Development.

Turnbull, A., Turnbull, R., & Wehmeyer, M. L. (2010). *Exceptional lives: Special education in today's schools* (6th ed.). Columbus, OH: Merrill.

U.S. Department of Education. (2011). *Individuals with Disabilities Education Act (IDEA) data*. Washington, DC: Author.

Vannest, K. J., Mason, B. A., Brown, L., Dyer, N., Mainey, S., & Adiguzul, T. (2009). Instructional settings in science for students with disabilities: Implications for teacher education. *Journal of Science Teacher Education, 20*(4), 353–363.

Vaughn, S., & Bos, C. S. (2012). *Strategies for teaching students with learning and behavior problems* (8th ed.). Boston, MA: Pearson.

Willis, C. (2009). *Creating inclusive learning environments for young children: What to do on Monday morning*. Thousand Oaks, CA: Corwin Press.

PRINCIPAL LEADERSHIP FOR EFFECTIVE INCLUSIVE SCHOOLS

James McLeskey, Bonnie Billingsley
and Nancy L. Waldron

ABSTRACT

Research in general education has demonstrated that school principals have a substantial impact on the effectiveness of schools and related student achievement. This is not a direct impact, but rather relates to how principals indirectly impact student learning by improving the learning environment of a school and the practice of teachers. More specifically, the dimensions of principal practice that are most influential in improving schools and student achievement relate to establishing a shared vision, facilitating a high-quality learning environment for students, building the professional capacity of teachers, creating a supportive organization for learning, and connecting with external partners. Only in recent years has research begun to emerge related to the role of the principal in supporting improved achievement for students with disabilities in schools that are effective and inclusive. In this chapter, we review research related to what principals can do to facilitate the development of inclusive schools that are also effective in improving achievement for students with disabilities and other students who struggle to learn. After reviewing these dimensions of principal practice, we then provide a brief case study that

General and Special Education Inclusion in an Age of Change: Roles of Professionals Involved
Advances in Special Education, Volume 32, 55−74
Copyright © 2016 by Emerald Group Publishing Limited
All rights of reproduction in any form reserved
ISSN: 0270-4013/doi:10.1108/S0270-401320160000032005

illustrates how a principal in an effective inclusive school applied several of these practices, including staff collaboration, progress monitoring, and professional development to improve teacher practice and student outcomes.

Keywords: Inclusion; principal; professional development; progress monitoring; collaboration

INTRODUCTION

The impact of principal leadership on student achievement has been documented by researchers for over four decades (Hitt & Tucker, 2015), and syntheses of this research have identified specific dimensions of leadership behavior that are associated with student achievement (e.g., see Hitt & Tucker, 2015; Leithwood, Louis, Anderson, & Wahlstrom, 2004; Robinson, Lloyd, & Rowe, 2008). In a recent synthesis, Hitt and Tucker identified five key leadership domains linked to student learning, which include "(a) establishing and conveying the vision, (b) facilitating a high-quality learning experience for students, (c) building professional capacity, (d) creating a supportive organization for learning, and (e) connecting with external partners" (p. 12). As these domains suggest, effective principals influence instructional leadership through those "leadership practices that affect the context within which teachers and students work" (Bellamy, Crockett, & Nordengren, 2014, p. 8).

Many of the dimensions of leadership practice that make a difference in student achievement are incorporated into leadership standards. Most recently, the new Professional Standards for Educational Leaders (PSEL) (formerly the Interstate School Leaders Licensure Consortium [ISLLC] Standards, Council of Chief State School Officers [CCSSO], 2008) have been "recast with a stronger, clearer emphasis on students and student learning ... so that each child is well-educated and prepared for the 21st century" (National Policy Board for Educational Administration, 2015, p. 2). All of these 10 professional leadership standards ends with an emphasis on "each student," emphasizing the importance of leaders' work in helping all learners, including those with disabilities, meet high achievement standards.

Principals today are also expected to play a major role in creating inclusive schools for students with disabilities, with the vast majority of these students receiving instruction in general education settings for at least part of the school day (U.S. Department of Education, 2015). It is clear that principals have a challenging charge – to lead inclusive schools that support each student with a disability in becoming well educated and pre-pared for success in the 21st century. Although the new PSEL leadership standards provide general recommendations for principals, they do not provide sufficient guidance for describing the leadership activities of princi-pals as they lead effective and inclusive schools for students with disabil-ities. Unfortunately, evidence also suggests that preparation programs do little to help prepare principals to address the needs of these learners (Angelle & Bilton, 2009; Burdette, 2010; Lynch, 2012; Pazey & Cole, 2013; Steinbrecher, Fix, Mahal, Serna, & McKeown, 2016).

A major question that needs to be addressed is, what can principals do to facilitate the development of inclusive schools that are also effective in improv-ing achievement for students with disabilities and other students who struggle to learn? This chapter describes selected leadership dimensions and behaviors that principals should consider as they work with others school professionals to increase student achievement in inclusive schools (see Billingsley, McLeskey, & Crockett, 2014, for a more extensive description of these and other dimen-sions). After this review, we provide a brief case study that illustrates the work of one principal and how she fostered a school environment that supported inclusive and effective instruction for students with disabilities through staff collaboration, progress monitoring, and professional development.

INSTRUCTIONAL LEADERSHIP FOR STUDENTS WITH DISABILITIES

Principals are in a key position to systematically plan for instructional effectiveness by attending to a wide range of variables, such as protecting instructional time, minimizing disruptions, promoting powerful instruc-tional practices, fostering teacher learning, monitoring student progress, and giving teachers specific feedback about their instruction (Deshler & Cornett, 2012). In this chapter we focus on several dimensions of principal leadership that are particularly important to helping students with disabil-ities and those who struggle. We address the need for principals to support: (1) high achievement expectations, (2) effective instruction and progress moni-toring, including teaching prosocial behavior, (3) working conditions that sup-port effective instruction, with a focus on collaboration, and (4) professional learning opportunities. It is important to note that while each of these are rele-vant to school leadership for all students, special considerations are necessary to foster better outcomes for students with disabilities.

High Achievement Expectations

High achievement expectations, academic focus, achievement orientation, and academic press are terms used in leadership research to describe the practice of setting "high but achievable school goals and classroom academic standards" (Leithwood, Patten, & Jantzi, 2010, p. 699). Leadership behaviors promoting academic press have been linked to student achievement across research studies and syntheses (e.g., Hitt & Tucker, 2015; Leithwood et al., 2004, 2010; Robinson et al., 2008). Principals clearly have an important role in facilitating a school-wide commitment to high achievement expectations and setting the conditions for special and general educators to work together so that students with disabilities have opportunities to learn the curriculum standards set for all students (Billingsley et al., 2014). Improving expectations for achievement for students with disabilities will often require that leaders challenge preconceived notions about what these students are able to achieve. Unfortunately, low expectations for students with disabilities have been a long-standing problem (Hehir, 2005) and continue to persist even though the performance of these students has improved on state tests over time (Thurlow, Quenemoem, & Lazarus, 2012). It is essential that principals work with school staff to assure that they are both prepared for and committed to teaching students with disabilities, and have high expectations for their achievement.

Effective Instruction and Progress Monitoring

Assuring that all learners receive high-quality instruction is critically important, and districts and schools have incorporated frameworks such as Universal Design for Learning (cast.org) and differentiated instruction (Tomlinson, 2008) as a way of responding to the diversity of students' instructional needs. However, students with disabilities also require individual consideration (Crockett, 2002) and benefit from evidence-based instructional practices (EBPs) that have been shown to be effective in improving their learning (Cook & Smith, 2012). Because principals may have limited awareness of these EBPs (Steinbrecher et al., 2016), they need to work with those who are knowledgeable (e.g., special education teachers, district leaders, university faculty) in identifying and promoting effective instruction for students with disabilities.

A particularly compelling framework for planning and monitoring instructional effectiveness is the use of Multi-Tiered Systems of Support

(MTSS) frameworks, which are used to systematically design, deliver, and monitor instruction that results in improved student outcomes (Algozzine et al., 2012). A key aspect of MTSS is defining and assuring quality instruction at each tier (Crockett & Gillespie, 2007). MTSS supports flexibility in instruction (e.g., goals, group size, and frequency of progress monitoring), allowing instruction to be tailored to the individual needs of students (Batsche, 2014). For example, students who struggle in Tier 1 may need focused interventions such as class-wide peer tutoring (Bowman-Perrott et al., 2013) at Tier 2. Others who are substantially below grade level may need highly intensive interventions at Tier 3 to progress, such as the use of small group, intensive instruction focusing on basic reading skills (McLeskey & Waldron, 2011). Across all tiers, progress is monitored to assess student achievement and inform instructional decisions.

Another example of MTSS is the use of School-Wide Positive Behavioral Supports (SWPBS) to promote a positive school culture and productive learning environment by teaching desired behavior and preventing undesirable behavior (Sugai, O'Keeffe, Horner, & Lewis, 2012). In Tier 1, all students in the school are taught the same agreed upon behavioral expectations, and these are supervised and reinforced by everyone in the school. For students who do not respond and have behavioral challenges, additional supports are provided in Tier 2, such as increasing structure, supervision, and using additional contingencies (Horner, Sugai, & Anderson, 2010). Tier 3 is then designed for a relatively small proportion of students who continue to exhibit ongoing challenging or high-risk behavior. Support plans in Tier 3 are more extensive and specific to meet individual student needs (e.g., modify the social context, teach new skills) (Horner et al., 2010). The research on SWPBS demonstrates the effectiveness of this approach in improving academic outcomes, school safety, and staff satisfaction (Horner et al., 2010), as well as reduced disciplinary referrals (Horner et al., 2009). Another advantage is that SWPBS provides differentiated supports to all students in the school, irrespective of their disability status.

Working Conditions that Support Effective Instruction and Collaboration

Organizing for instruction requires attending to those conditions that allow special and general education teachers to collaborate productively to address the needs of students with disabilities (Friend & Cook, 2013). Leaders have the responsibility to work with all professionals in the school to facilitate the development of a collaborative culture and to assure that staff have opportunities to collectively address the needs of students with disabilities through planning and collaborative service-delivery (Causton-Theoharis, Theoharis, Bull, Cosier, & Dempf-Aldrich, 2011; Friend & Cook, 2013). Setting the stage for collaboration requires helping all involved align expectations about collaboration, its purpose, and activities. For example, collaboration requires that leaders support the development of schedules and routines that allow teachers and other service-providers to collaboratively plan instruction, monitor student progress, coordinate transition and related services, and facilitate the work of paraprofessionals.

Teacher effectiveness depends on teachers' opportunities to engage in "well-structured, deliberate, and thoughtful work" (Billingsley, 2011, p. 401). The literature suggests that special educators' jobs may be poorly designed (Gersten, Keating, Yovanoff, & Harniss, 2001; Otis-Wilborn, Winn, Griffin, & Kilgore, 2005), that their time is fragmented by a wide range of noninstructional responsibilities, including paperwork, meetings, and compliance activities (Vannest & Hagan-Burke, 2010), and that special educators often see their jobs as unmanageable (Billingsley, Carlson, & Klein, 2004). Supporting effective instruction requires that principals work with teachers to consider how structures can be put in place that support instruction and collaboration so these educators can work toward productive, student-oriented goals.

Professional Learning Opportunities

School leaders play a critical role in fostering teacher learning. Robinson et al. (2008) reported that after controlling for student background factors, the more teachers reported that their principals were actively involved in teacher professional development, the better students did on learning outcomes. Hitt and Tucker (2015) discuss that this "side by side learning" serves to improve the leader's knowledge about "curriculum, instruction and assessment" and also serves to "strengthen teacher perceptions of the leader's credibility and legitimacy as an instructional leader, and it better equips the principal to be a source of knowledge and assistance" (p. 18).

One of the most challenging tasks for principals in supporting an effective, inclusive school is ensuring that teachers have the knowledge and skills to meet the needs of a diverse range of students (McLeskey & Waldron, 2011). While the success of these programs largely depends on the ability of teachers to collaborate with others and deliver content to all students, many teachers do not feel that they are well prepared to meet the needs of students with disabilities who are included in their classrooms (Jenkins & Yoshimura, 2010). Extensive research over several decades has revealed that the majority of general education teachers (about 70%) feel that they lack the expertise to address the needs of students with disabilities in general education classrooms (Scruggs & Mastropieri, 1996; Waldron, 2007). Given this lack of preparation, it is critical for general education teachers to have intensive and well-planned professional development to effectively teach in these settings (Scruggs & Mastropieri, 1996). School-wide professional development is needed if all teachers are to be prepared to address the needs of the diverse range of students in their classrooms, and should focus on those skills that are strongly related to improved student outcomes (Englert & Rozendal, 2004; Fuchs & Fuchs, 2001).

Two forms of professional development that are used to improve teacher practice (among other things) are defined in Table 1. A substantial research base exists to support the perspective that when Expert Centered Professional Development (ECPD) or the "sage on the stage" approach is

Table 1. Descriptions of ECPD and LCPD.

ECPD	LCPD
ECPD focuses on disseminating knowledge to teachers. This is typically done by an outsider who is an expert related to the topic or innovation being addressed, through lecture, written material, demonstrations, and/or practice over a short period of time. Little or no follow up is provided as newly learned information is applied in the classroom. Follow up is not viewed as necessary, as teachers are viewed as passive recipients of the information, and are expected to implement innovations in their classroom exactly as they were presented with few adaptations (Duffy & Kear, 2007). This fidelity of implementation ensures that the practice is effective, and if teachers don't implement the innovation with fidelity, they are viewed as resistant and maybe even recalcitrant (Richardson & Placier, 2001).	LCPD is typically directed toward topics or innovations that are selected by teachers, and should fit the teacher's knowledge and beliefs about teaching. Teachers should collectively participate in these activities with other professionals who share similar interests. Professional development should initially provide teachers with a deep understanding of the innovation, including a rationale for the use of the innovation and how it may be adapted to the needs of the teacher's classroom and students. Professional development should include modeling and demonstration in a setting that simulates the classroom, and teachers should practice the innovation under similar simulated conditions (e.g., peer teaching). Professional development should be of sufficient length and depth to provide teachers with deep knowledge of the practice. Teachers should receive ongoing support from peers (e.g., reflection on the innovation, coaching in the classroom) as they implement the innovation in their classrooms.

Source: Adapted from McLeskey (2011).

used, teachers' classroom practices seldom change (Desimone, 2009; Leko & Brownell, 2009; McLeskey, 2011). In contrast, research has revealed that significantly more teachers in general and special education improve their classroom practices when Learner Centered Professional Development (LCPD) is employed (Desimone, 2009; Leko & Brownell, 2009; McLeskey, 2011).

LCPD includes learning communities, defined as "professionals in a school, typically groups of teachers, who work collaboratively to improve practice and enhance student learning" (Blanton & Perez, 2011, p. 6). Characteristics of Professional Learning Communities (PLCs) include a shared vision for student-centered school improvement, a supportive environment, ongoing examination of data, and open dialogue regarding areas in need of improvement (Blanton & Perez, 2011; Waldron & McLeskey, 2010).

THE IMPORTANCE OF PRINCIPAL SUPPORT FOR EFFECTIVE INCLUSIVE EDUCATION

Principals play a range of critical roles in developing and supporting effective inclusive classrooms and schools (Billingsley & McLeskey, 2014; Sindelar, Shearer, Yendol-Hoppey, & Liebert, 2006; Waldron, McLeskey, & Redd, 2011). This includes leadership for inclusive education related to building a shared vision and school-wide commitment to support inclusive education (Burstein, Sears, Wilcoxen, Cabello & Spagna, 2004; Guzman, 1997; McLeskey & Waldron, 2015; Ryndak, Reardon, Benner, & Ward, 2007), redesigning the school to support inclusive education (Billingsley, 2012), and engaging others in shared leadership (Burstein et al., 2004; Hoppey & McLeskey, 2013). A recent review of research concluded that "more than anything else, a commitment to a set of core values by teachers and administrators is part of what makes inclusive schools successful" (McLeskey & Waldron, 2015, p. 69).

This commitment then provides teachers and other professionals with the motivation to work collaboratively to redesign the organization to support inclusive education. This includes changes in varied practices, including curriculum, instructional practices, teacher and administrator beliefs, and teacher roles (Fullan, 2015; Hoppey & McLeskey, 2013; McLeskey & Waldron, 2006; Sindelar et al., 2006). Finally, any major school improvement effort requires that a range of stakeholders take on leadership roles, and this is the case when inclusive schools are developed

(Burstein et al., 2004; Ryndak et al., 2007). Shared leadership in inclusive schools is often done strategically by principals, as they maintain responsibility in certain areas (e.g., developing vision and a share commitment to inclusive education), while sharing leadership with teachers and other professionals in key areas such as designing and implementing changes as inclusive programs are developed (Sindelar et al., 2006).

In addition to these areas of leadership, principals support effective inclusive schools through instructional leadership, which includes high achievement expectations, a positive disciplinary climate, effective instruction and progress monitoring, working conditions that promote instructional effectiveness, and support for ongoing professional learning (Billingsley et al., 2014). In the following section, we include a brief case study that describes how a principal in an effective inclusive elementary school supported her teachers in developing the skills that they needed to work effectively with all students, including those with disabilities.

SUPPORTING IMPROVED TEACHER INSTRUCTION: A BRIEF CASE STUDY

Previous research provides very little descriptive information regarding how schools that are engaged in developing inclusive programs address the need for high-quality professional development that improves teacher practice (Leko & Brownell, 2009; McLeskey, 2011). Research that has been conducted suggests that it has been "… much more difficult than anticipated to provide teachers with professional development that influences classroom practice" (McLeskey, 2011, p. 42). In the following section, we provide a description of how a principal in one effective inclusive elementary school provided high-quality professional development to support her teachers in gaining the skills they needed to be successful. This description comes from a larger case study that addressed the qualities of an effective inclusive school (see McLeskey, Waldron, & Redd, 2014; Waldron et al., 2011, for further information regarding this case study).

High-Quality Professional Development at Creekside Elementary School

This description of professional development comes from an elementary school that included students with disabilities in general education classrooms at a level that was well above the district and state averages, and obtained achievement levels in reading and math for students with disabilities and students from high poverty backgrounds that were well above the district and state averages. Creekside Elementary School (CES) is a K-4 school that enrolls approximately 480 students. (Note that the name of this school and names used for professional staff at CES are pseudonyms.) About one-third of the students are from African American, Hispanic, and multiracial or other ethnic groups, while 52% are from high poverty backgrounds. A total of approximately 17% of the students at CES are identified with a full range of disabilities.

A summary of the themes that emerged related to the successful use of professional development to support teacher practice at CES is included in Table 2. The overall themes that emerged suggest that teachers at CES were immersed in opportunities for participating in high quality, LCPD; data were systematically used to provide direction for professional development as well as teacher incentive for participating in these activities; and a PLC emerged to support professional learning and growth at CES. Each of these themes is subsequently described.

Teachers are Immersed in LCPD

At CES teachers and administrators developed a school-wide system of support for LCPD to ensure that all teachers developed the skills they needed to make CES a highly effective, inclusive school. Teachers at CES were immersed in LCPD, and the principal at Creekside, Ms. Richards, was the primary person who ensured that this occurred. How far was Ms. Richards willing to go to do this? Consider her comment regarding faculty meetings:

> Why sit through an hour and a half faculty meeting when you can write a memo? When I have the whole faculty sitting there I'd much rather it be things they can use in their classrooms. There is some really successful professional development coming out of our faculty meetings. Not just them sitting there thinking about what they should be doing or somebody standing there talking.

Using highly valued faculty meeting time for professional development clearly showed teachers how much Ms. Richards valued their professional learning and improved classroom practice. As a kindergarten teacher said: "At every faculty meeting we're taught something new that helps instruction. We collaborate a lot across grade levels, and learn from one another."

Table 2.   Themes Related to the Successful Use of LCPD at CES.

Teachers are Immersed in LCPD
  Use every opportunity for LCPD
    Faculty meetings
    Grade level and team meetings
    Ad hoc groups to address issues (inclusion, co-teaching)
    Book studies
  Support with
    Common planning time to meet and visit classrooms
    Development of experts in the school
Data are Used to Provide Direction and Motivation
  Develop an authentic data system to monitor student progress
    Reflects what is taught in classrooms
    Accepted by teachers as authentic and useful data
  Use data to
    Have productive conversations with teachers
    Make decisions about professional development needs
    Monitor progress of groups of students
    Determine additional classroom support
    Ensure high expectations for all students
  Use data in positive and supportive ways whenever possible
    Focus on the needs of all students
    Celebrate successes
    Share responsibility among all teachers for successes and shortcomings
A PLC Supports Teacher Learning
  Characteristics of PLC guide meetings
    Shared vision for student-centered school improvement
    Supportive environment
    Ongoing examination of data
    Open dialogue regarding areas in need of improvement
  Ensure a trusting and supportive atmosphere in the school
  Principal does not micromanage classroom practice or PD
  Principal shares major decisions with teachers
  Principal ensures that problems are addressed

A second grade teacher similarly commented "I take a lot of ideas from faculty meetings. In faculty meetings we have teachers sharing ideas they're using in their classrooms." This time was thus used for several aspects of LCPD, as teachers learned about innovations, reflected on and practiced these activities, and received feedback on how other teachers were using effective practices.

Any possible opportunity for professional learning was used at CES, including meetings of teachers and administrators in grade level teams or inclusion planning teams. Teachers also met for specific purposes to address professional learning when something was not working well. For example, when problems arose with co-teaching partnerships, teachers began meeting for co-teach chats, which provided time to reflect on and discuss issues as they emerged, and figure out how to address these problems.

Ms. Richards and the teachers at CES ensured that common planning time was built into the school schedule so that teachers would have the opportunity to work together to address issues, as well as to observe practices in other teachers' classes. This common planning time also provided the teachers with the opportunity to engage in book studies and other types of collaborative professional development, which many teachers found very useful.

A final approach used by Ms. Richards to ensure that her teachers were immersed in LCPD was to place an emphasis on developing experts in her school who provided support to other teachers. These experts were readily available, provided others with in-depth information regarding innovations, and provided coaching in classrooms as teachers learned to apply the innovations. Ms. Richards addressed this topic by saying:

> I don't like to send teachers off to something and then only those two teachers that go know anything about it. I've always believed in trying to create experts in our building and encourage them to coach others. We've tried to do that with a lot of things–with technology, with inclusion. With so many things that we've tried to do over the years, we've had people who learn it and learn it well. They're good communicators, so they can share it with others, they're willing to go into other classrooms or willing to have people come into their classroom.

Data are Used to Provide Direction and Motivation

While Ms. Richards placed an emphasis on improving instruction to meet the needs of all students at Creekside, she realized that she needed to know which students were struggling and needed additional assistance, and where professional development should be focused to address these needs. As she stated "How can I have conversations with teachers without individual data about students? We had to come up with ways to monitor student data to have good conversations about how kids are doing. How can we get them moving, what resources do we need?"

While statewide accountability data were monitored at Creekside, Ms. Richards and the school staff did not perceive these data to be useful in ongoing monitoring of student progress. Ms. Richards described the comprehensive, electronic data system that was developed at Creekside as "all self-created. We include (state accountability test data), but real data (addresses) what they're doing in the classroom. How many letters do they know? How many sounds do they know? That's the data we collect and track here. Real data is what they're seeing in the classroom and how (the students are) progressing."

Ms. Richards used these data in monthly meetings with teachers to examine the progress of students and have conversations with teachers based on data that all agreed were accurate and useful. These meetings helped focus teachers on individual student needs, as well as the need to improve their practice in certain areas. Ms. Richards further noted:

> We look at data on ALL children 'These children are doing ok, these aren't gaining.' Just by showing a teacher that, and talking about every child, they get the message that I'm looking at every child's gains. When we go through their professional development plans–any effective teacher is going to say I'd better start paying attention to individual child needs (and how I need to improve my practice). Just by looking at data for every child and holding them accountable, they get the message that 'I better pay attention to every child'.

The data were also used to monitor groups of students (e.g., third graders, students with disabilities) to determine how well they were progressing. Ms. Richards said "When we started looking at student data and who was successful, it was glaringly obvious when I showed them several years of (state accountability) data and classroom data, a lot of students with disabilities were not being successful." This led to changes in how services were delivered, an emphasis on inclusion, and a shared responsibility by both general and special educators for improving teacher practices and outcomes for these students.

Ms. Richards believes "if you're going to do school-wide improvement, our school-wide data has to be out there and on the table." However, she also recognized that this public availability of data at Creekside could produce a negative reaction from teachers unless it was handled carefully and respectfully. She addressed this issue in several ways. "When we started looking at (the data), it was like accountability, but with accomplishment, and with praise, and with resources. I'm sure they felt pressure, but they also got pats on the back and praise." In short, to ensure that the accountability system was accepted and supported by teachers, Ms. Richards emphasized that all teachers share responsibility for student outcomes, focused on the positives, and provided support to teachers (i.e., professional development) to overcome any negative connotations.

For example, one approach that was used was to ensure that student progress was emphasized and celebrated school-wide. As Ms. Richards noted "If I could capture something from data that we did well on, we celebrated, we made a big deal about it, we showed it to everybody. We celebrated every little step, because I knew every teacher loves to celebrate and get that pat on the back." She went on to state that the data system soon became part of the school culture, as teachers would point out "look at how far we've come, look at how we've grown." She went on to note that whenever student progress was celebrated, or areas of weakness were pointed out, the focus of discussion was not on a certain group of teachers, but was shared by everyone.

The positive, supportive approach that was used at Creekside when considering student accountability data ensured that teachers had a positive view of the school-wide accountability system and viewed this information as useful in monitoring student progress and improving teacher practice. Furthermore, the emphasis on sharing positive outcomes and sharing responsibility for these outcomes helped to support the development of a PLC at Creekside. In the next section, we describe how PLCs provided a foundation for the teacher learning that occurred at Creekside to support the effectiveness of the inclusive program.

A PLC is Used to Support Teacher Learning

The characteristics of a PLC were frequently found when teachers worked together at Creekside, whether in grade level teams, inclusion support team, as part of co-teaching arrangements, or during faculty meetings. For example, as we illustrated previously, these characteristics were an integral part of how professional development works at CES, as faculty worked collaboratively to support one another in learning new skills and improving student outcomes. Similarly, the availability of a school-wide data system and how the data were used to make decisions were supportive of the development of a PLC at CES.

While the approach used to provide professional development illustrates how the PLC worked and the data system was integral to the work of the PLC, it would not be possible to maintain the PLC without the trusting and supportive atmosphere that Ms. Richards and her teachers created at CES. This was illustrated in the previous section, which detailed how

Ms. Richards used the school-wide accountability system in ways that were very respectful and supportive of her teachers.

This respect and support was further reflected in the level of trust Ms. Richards had for her teachers. For example, she never micromanaged what they did, but rather she set high expectations for students and let teachers do their jobs. Ms. Wood, a special education teacher, addressed this by saying "she doesn't make you fit into a mold, she allows you to be the teacher that you are. As long as you are doing what's right for children, you're teaching to the standards, and you're making progress with children." Ms. Richards echoed this perspective when she said that teachers "do what they want to do as long as kids are being successful. What makes a school great is that you have all these different personalities and all these different teaching styles."

Ms. Richards also manifested respect and trust for her teachers by sharing responsibility for decision-making whenever possible. One way she did this was by discussing data to identify areas that needed improvement. She also shared decision-making regarding the focus of professional development. As Ms. Richards described "we sit down, talk about what our problems are, what articles and books we can read, where we can go to see (effective practice). At times we'll take a whole team to a conference and (after going to relevant sessions) we'll stay up at night and sketch out what we're going to do to address the problem." She also noted the importance of her involvement in these activities, as she learned about problems and shared decision-making with teachers. "If it's going to be important, I need to be right in the middle of it. I need to learn with them. I need to know that this is not working or this is difficult, because I need to be thinking the whole time, what can I do to help, what resources can I provide, what professional development do we need?"

If PLCs are to be successful, teachers and administrators must engage in dialogue regarding areas in need of improvement. Identifying and addressing areas in need of improvement was part of the culture at CES. As we noted previously, the data system was used to help identify weaknesses, and the administration and staff were willing to engage in open dialogue as they developed strategies to improve student performance. Ms. Richards addressed this issue when she said, "It's much less stressful not to deal with issues. Much easier. But once you begin to face issues and solve problems, teachers will start to react as well. '(Those problems) are not good for our school and climate!' We create a collective belief in what we are, it's just a fact now that we address issues and problems. That snowballs on everything and keeps us going." A special education teacher, Ms. Wood addressed this topic when she said, "One of the reasons we've been so successful is that when we have bumps, instead of ignoring them, we address them. Ms. Richards will get a team together, and we will meet and talk about what will work better."

CONCLUSION

Previous research has revealed that principals play a key role in improving schools and student outcomes (Fullan, 2015; Leithwood et al., 2004). This certainly is the case related to the development schools that are inclusive and effective – that is, schools that welcome and value students with disabilities as actively participating members of the school community, and provide supports needed to ensure the academic and behavioral success of these students (Billingsley & McLeskey, 2014; McLeskey & Waldron, 2015). In this chapter, we reviewed professional literature which revealed that in developing and supporting schools that are effective and inclusive, principals engage in activities that enhance high achievement expectations for all students, including those with disabilities, ensure that effective instruction guided by student progress monitoring data is provided, support working conditions that enhance effective instruction and collaborative work among professionals, and ensure that professional learning opportunities that improve teacher practice are provided. While these practices have been shown to improve achievement outcomes for all students, we describe special conditions regarding each that are necessary to support improved outcomes for students with disabilities.

After reviewing this research, we provided a brief case study that demonstrates how a principal in an effective inclusive school employed several dimensions of effective principal practice to support teachers in gaining the skills they needed to successfully support all students, including those with disabilities. The success of Ms. Richards in CES suggests that when used in combination, the identified dimensions of effective principal practice can have a powerful effect on student learning for those who struggle in school, including students with disabilities and those form high poverty backgrounds.

In spite of research evidence that strongly suggests that principals are a key lever for ensuring that students with disabilities receive a high-quality education, evidence suggests that principal preparation programs provide very limited preparation related to these issues in general, and do not prepare principals with the skills needed to proactively address the needs of students with disabilities in their schools (Angelle & Bilton, 2009; Burdette, 2010; Lynch, 2012; Pazey & Cole, 2013; Steinbrecher et al., 2016). Furthermore, standards for the preparation and ongoing professional development of principals and other leaders (i.e., CCSSO, 2008; National Policy Board for Educational Administration, 2015) include scant information related to knowledge and skills that might be developed by principals to address these pressing concerns.

In conclusion, this research points to the need to substantially improve the preparation of principals related to addressing the needs of students with disabilities and others who struggle academically and behaviorally in schools. Principals who are well prepared to support high achievement expectations and effective instruction for all students, including those with disabilities, can have a substantial impact on the achievement gap that currently exists for students with disabilities. This preparation can lead to substantially improved schooling for these students in effective inclusive settings, and ensure that students with disabilities and others who struggle to learn have improved opportunities for success in school, and as importantly, they will leave school better prepared for college and their careers. These improvements are long overdue in our schools.

REFERENCES

Algozzine, B., Wang, C., White, R., Cooke, N., Marr, M. B., Algozzine, K., ... Duran, G. Z. (2012). Effects of multi-tier academic and behavior instruction on difficult to teach students. *Exceptional Children, 79*(1), 45–64.

Angelle, P., & Bilton, L. (2009). Confronting the unknown: Principal preparation training in issues related to special education. *AASA Journal of Scholarship & Practice, 5*(4), 5–9.

Batsche, G. (2014). Multi-tiered system of supports for inclusive schools. In J. McLeskey, N. L. Waldron, F. Spooner, & B. Algozzine (Eds.), *Handbook of effective inclusive schools: Research and practice* (pp. 183–196). New York, NY: Routledge.

Bellamy, G. T., Crockett, J. B., & Nordengren, C. (2014). *Preparing school leaders for every student's learning (Document No. LS-2)*. Retrieved from University of Florida, Collaboration for Effective Educator, Development, Accountability, and Reform Center website http://ceedar.education.ufl.edu/tools/literature-syntheses/

Billingsley, B. (2011). Factors influencing special education teacher quality and effectiveness. In J. M. Kauffman & D. P. Hallahan (Eds.), *Handbook of special education* (pp. 91–405). New York, NY: Taylor & Francis.

Billingsley, B., Carlson, E., & Klein, S. (2004). The working conditions and induction support of early career special educators. *Exceptional Children, 70*(3), 333–347.

Billingsley, B., & McLeskey, J. (2014). What are the roles of principals in inclusive schools? In J. McLeskey, N. Waldron, F. Spooner, & B. Algozzine (Eds.), *Handbook of effective inclusive schools: Research and practice* (pp. 67–79). New York, NY: Routledge.

Billingsley, B., McLeskey, J., & Crockett, J. B. (2014). *Principal leadership: Moving toward inclusive and high-achieving schools for students with disabilities (Document No. IC-8)*. Retrieved from University of Florida, Collaboration for Effective Educator, Development, Accountability, and Reform Center website http://ceedar.education.ufl.edu/tools/innovation-configurations/

Billingsley, B. S. (2012). Inclusive school reform: Distributed leadership through the phases of change. In J. B. Crockett, B. S. Billingsley, & M. L. Boscardin (Eds.), *Handbook of leadership and administration for special education* (pp. 170–190). New York, NY: Taylor & Francis.

Blanton, L., & Perez. (2011). Exploring the relationship between special education teachers and professional learning communities. Implications of research for administrators. *Journal of Special Education Leadership, 24*(1), 6–16.

Bowman-Perrott, L., Davis, H., Vannest, K., Williams, L., Greenwood, C., & Parker, R. (2013). Academic benefits of peer tutoring: A meta-analytic review of single-case research. *School Psychology Review, 41*(1), 39–55.

Burdette, P. (2010). *Principal preparedness to support students with disabilities and other diverse learners*. Alexandria, VA: National Association of State Directors of Special Education.

Burstein, N., Sears, S., Wilcoxen, A., Cabello, B., & Spagna, M. (2004). Moving toward inclusive practices. *Remedial & Special Education, 25*(2), 104–116.

Causton-Theoharis, J., Theoharis, G., Bull, T., Cosier, M., & Dempf-Aldrich, K. (2011). Schools of promise: A school district-university partnership centered on inclusive school reform. *Remedial and Special Education, 32*(3), 190–205.

Cook, B. G., & Smith, G. J. (2012). Leadership and instruction: Evidence-based practices in Special Education. In J. B. Crockett, B. S. Billingsley, & M. L. Boscardin (Eds.), *Handbook of leadership and administration for special education* (pp. 281–296). New York, NY: Taylor & Francis.

Council of Chief State School Officers. (2008). *Educational leadership policy standards: Interstate school leadership licensure consortium (ISLLC 2008)*. Retrieved from http://www.npbea.org/projects.php

Crockett, J. B. (2002). Special education's role in preparing responsive leaders for inclusive schools. *Remedial and Special Education, 23*(3), 157–168.

Crockett, J. B., & Gillespie, D. N. (2007). Getting ready for RTI: A principal's guide to response to intervention. *ERS Spectrum, 25*(4), 1–9.

Deshler, D. D., & Cornett, J. (2012). Leading to improve teacher effectiveness: implications for practice, reform, research, and policy. In J. B. Crockett, B. S. Billingsley, & M. L. Boscardin (Eds.), *Handbook of leadership and administration for special education* (pp. 239–259). New York, NY: Taylor & Francis.

Desimone, L. (2009). Improving impact studies of teachers' professional development: Toward better conceptualizations and measures. *Educational Researcher, 38*, 181–199.

Duffy, G., & Kear, K. (2007). Compliance or adaptation: What is the real message about research-based practices. *Phi Delta Kappan, 88*, 579–581.

Englert, C. S., & Rozendal, M. (2004). A model of professional development in special education. *Teacher Education and Special Education, 27*, 24–46.

Friend, M., & Cook, L. (2013). *Interactions: Collaboration skills for school professionals*. Boston, MA: Pearson.

Fuchs, L., & Fuchs, D. (2001). Principles for the prevention and intervention of mathematics difficulties. *Learning Disabilities Research & Practice, 16*, 85–95.

Fullan, M. (2015). *The new meaning of educational change* (5th ed.). New York, NY: Teachers College Press.

Gersten, R., Keating, T., Yovanoff, P., & Harniss, M. K. (2001). Working in special education: Factors that enhance special educators' intent to stay. *Exceptional Children, 67*(4), 549–567.

Guzman, N. (1997). Leadership for successful inclusive schools. *Journal of Educational Administration, 35*(5), 439–450.

Hehir, T. (2005). *New directions in special education: Eliminating ableism in policy and practice.* Cambridge, MA: Harvard Education Press.

Hitt, D. H., & Tucker, P. D. (2015). Systematic review of key leader practices found to influence students' achievement: A unified framework. *Review of Educational Research, 86*(2), 531–569. doi:10.3102/0034654315614911

Hoppey, D., & McLeskey, J. (2013). A case study of principal leadership in an effective inclusive school. *The Journal of Special Education, 46*(4), 245–256.

Horner, R. H., Sugai, G., & Anderson, C. M. (2010). Examining the evidence base for school-wide positive behavior support. *Focus on Exceptional Children, 42*(8), 1–14.

Horner, R., Sugai, G., Smolkowski, K., Todd, A., Nakasato, J., & Esperanza, J. (2009). A randomized control trial of school-wide positive behavior support in elementary schools. *Journal of Positive Behavior Interventions, 11*(3), 133–144.

Jenkins, A., & Yoshimura, J. (2010). Not another inservice! Meeting the special education professional development needs of elementary general educators. *Teaching Exceptional Children, 42*(5), 36–43.

Leithwood, K., Louis, K. S., Anderson, S., & Wahlstrom, K. (2004). *Review of research: How leadership influences student learning.* Minneapolis, MN: University of Minnesota, Center for Applied Research and Educational Improvement.

Leithwood, K., Patten, S., & Jantzi, D. (2010). Testing a conception of how school leadership influences student learning. *Educational Administration Quarterly, 46*(5), 671–706.

Leko, M., & Brownell, M. (2009). Crafting quality professional development for special educators. *Teaching Exceptional Children, 42*(1), 64–70.

Lynch, J. M. (2012). Responsibilities of today's principal: Implications for principal preparation programs and principal certification policies. *Rural Special Education Quarterly, 31*, 40–47.

McLeskey, J. (2011). Supporting improved practice for special education teachers: The importance of learner centered professional development. *Journal of Special Education Leadership, 24*(1), 26–35.

McLeskey, J., & Waldron, N. (2006). Comprehensive school reform and inclusive schools. Improving schools for all students. *Theory into Practice, 45*(3), 269–278.

McLeskey, J., & Waldron, N. (2011). Educational programs for students with learning disabilities: Can they be both effective and inclusive? *Learning Disabilities Research & Practice, 26*(1), 48–57.

McLeskey, J., & Waldron, N. (2015). Effective leadership makes schools truly inclusive. *Phi Delta Kappan, 96*(5), 68–73.

McLeskey, J., Waldron, N., & Redd, L. (2014). A case study of a highly effective inclusive elementary school. *Journal of Special Education, 48*(1), 59–70. doi:10.1177/0022466912440455

National Policy Board for Educational Administration. (2015). *Professional standards for educational leaders 2015*. Reston, VA: Author.

Otis-Wilborn, A., Winn, J., Griffin, C., & Kilgore, K. (2005). Beginning special educators' forays into general education. *Teacher Education and Special Education*, 28(3−4), 143−152.

Pazey, B. L., & Cole, H. (2013). The role of special education training in the development of socially just leaders: Building an equity consciousness in educational leadership programs. *Educational Administration Quarterly*, 49, 243−271. doi:10.1177/0013161X12463934

Richardson, V., & Placier (2001). Teacher change. In V. Richardson (Ed.), *Handbook of research on teaching* (4th ed., pp. 905−947). Washington, DC: American Educational Research Association.

Robinson, V., Lloyd, C., & Rowe, K. (2008). The impact of leadership on student outcomes: An analysis of differential effects of leadership types. *Educational Administration Quarterly*, 44, 635−674 .doi:10.1177/0013161X08321509

Ryndak, D., Reardon, R., Benner, S. R., & Ward, T. (2007). Transitioning to and sustaining district-wide inclusive services: A 7-year study of a district's ongoing journey and its accompanying complexities. *Research & Practice for Persons with Severe Disabilities*, 32(4), 228−246.

Scruggs, T., & Mastropieri, M. (1996). Teacher perceptions of mainstreaming/inclusion, 1958−1995. *Exceptional Children*, 63, 59−74.

Sindelar, P., Shearer, D., Yendol-Hoppey, D., & Liebert, T. (2006). The sustainability of inclusive school reform. *Exceptional Children*, 72(3), 317−331.

Steinbrecher, T. D., Fix, R., Mahal, M. A., Serna, L. A., & McKeown, D. (2016). All you need is patience and flexibility: Administrators' perspectives on special educator knowledge and skills. *Journal of Special Education Leadership*, 28(2), 89−102.

Sugai, G., O'Keeffe, B., Horner, R. H., & Lewis, T. J. (2012). School leadership and schoolwide positive behavior support. In J. B. Crockett, B. S. Billingsley, & M. L. Boscardin (Eds.), *Handbook of leadership and administration for special education* (pp. 37−51). New York, NY: Routledge.

Thurlow, M. L., Quenemoem, R. F., & Lazarus, S. S. (2012). Leadership for student performance in an era of accountability. In J. B. Crockett, B. S. Billingsley, & M. L. Boscardin (Eds.), *Handbook of leadership and administration for special education* (pp. 3−16). New York, NY: Taylor & Francis.

Tomlinson, C. A. (2008). The goals of differentiation. *Educational Leadership*, 66(3), 26−30.

U.S. Department of Education. (2015). *Thirty-seventh annual report to congress on the implementation of the individuals with disabilities education act*. Washington, DC: Office of Special Education and Rehabilitative Services, Office of Special Education Programs.

Vannest, K. J., & Hagan-Burke, S. (2010). Teacher time use in special education. *Remedial and Special Education*, 31(2), 126−142.

Waldron, N. (2007). Teacher attitudes toward inclusion. In J. McLeskey (Ed.), *Reflections on inclusion: Classic articles that shaped out thinking* (pp. 163−187). Arlington, VA: CEC.

Waldron, N., & McLeskey, J. (2010). Establishing a collaborative school culture through comprehensive school reform. *Journal of Educational and Psychological Consultation*, 20(1), 58−74.

Waldron, N., McLeskey, J., & Redd, L. (2011). Setting the direction: The role of the principal in developing an effective, inclusive school. *Journal of Special Education Leadership*, 24, 51−60.

FAMILY ENGAGEMENT WITHIN INCLUSIVE SETTINGS

Bridgie A. Ford, Shernavaz Vakil and Rachel J. Boit

ABSTRACT

The essentiality of family involvement in the schooling process is evident from the vast directives embedded within federal mandates, professional standards for teachers and administrators, parent organizations, and advocacy groups. Yet, as explicit as legislative mandates and professional standards are regarding parental rights and involvement, they do not require definitive roles of the family. Several factors influence the lack of a decisive definition regarding the role of the family in the schooling process. Those include the different perspectives on what constitutes a family structurally and functionally, the socio-cultural and political diversity within and among populations, the move to an inclusive education framework, the various terms used to describe parental involvement, the realization that no one family model fits the demographic diversity existing in today's school districts, and the rights of family members to select their level of involvement. Given the importance of family engagement and student outcomes, three fundamental questions addressed in this chapter are, "How can inclusive schools enhance productive collaborative family engagement networks?" "How can the family be empowered to voluntarily participate within those networks?" and "How can

General and Special Education Inclusion in an Age of Change: Roles of Professionals Involved
Advances in Special Education, Volume 32, 75–98
ISSN: 0270-4013/doi:10.1108/S0270-401320160000032006

inclusive schools connect with teacher preparation programs to promote the competency of educators for those collaborative family/school engagement networks?" In this chapter we delineate an interactive triad conceptual model with the school as the "connecting agent" to build relationships with families and teacher preparation, setting the stage for productive family engagement as partners in inclusive settings.

Keywords: Cultural and linguistic diversity; family engagement; collaborative family and school models; inclusive settings; special education; teacher preparation

---

Vignette

The following vignette illustrates the power of parent (family) engagement to inform change:

Over the last 10 years a large mid-west urban school district's student population had become increasingly ethnically and racially diverse with African American students comprising the largest group and an increase of English Language Learners. Concerned parents sought to improve the district's parental engagement practices. Working with a district level administrator, the parents created and distributed flyers through the district's web-site and "word-of-mouth" inviting other parents to join a core team, "Parent Engagement Project" (PEP). A University faculty member (Ford) with expertise in school/family/community collaboration was asked to help structure and facilitate the investigative process. At the conclusion PEP Team members were invited to present their recommendations to local Board members and select members of the business community. To assist in funding PEP, the University facilitator wrote and secured a grant from a local foundation. The core PEP team consisted of 15 members representing parents of children from elementary, middle school and high school as well as diverse ethnic racial groups and SES. Pre-assessment activities and discussion revealed the level of current parental involvement among the PEP Team ranged from deeply involved (e.g., building level decision-making team members, PTA, consistent volunteer) to moderate levels (e.g., parent–teacher conferences, open house). Childcare and transportation were provided to assist PEP Team members.

Eight sessions were held during the evening (6:00–8:00 p.m.) at the neutral location of the University Library. Written notes of sessions were taken by the facilitator's graduate student. The facilitator used a focus group method and interactive activities to guide and listen to the discussion of parental concerns/challenges surrounding parental engagement and possible solutions/recommendations. PEP Team members participated in pre-assessment inventory activities to obtain information regarding their perceptions/opinions about the strengths and challenges of district' current parental engagement processes. Collectively, the responses revealed parents believed specific factors influencing schools in positively engaging with parents were: those parents who were more assertive and vocal about their needs, those parents who were members of the PTA, those parents who were knowledgeable about their rights, those parents who had personal relationship with school personnel, and those parents from similar ethnic/racial groups. Focus group dialogue and interactive activities highlighted that although individual school buildings had many strengths, inconsistency in and across school buildings was a major problem; four themes emerged regarding the district's inconsistency: (a) lack of a culture of trust and reliability, (b) ineffective communication systems and engagement skills by school personnel, (c) restrictive systems for disseminating information and resources to parents and (d) lack of parent training. The PEP Team provided numerous and explicit examples aligned with these themes. The facilitator summarized PEP Team members' concerns and recommendations and assisted them in preparing for the formal presentation to the board. As a result of the PEP Team's formal recommendations to the district's board, new parent responsive initiatives are being instituted.

INTRODUCTION

The essentiality of family involvement in the schooling process is evident from the vast directives embedded with federal legislation (Individuals with Disabilities Education Act [IDEA], U.S. Department for Education, 2004, and Title I, 2015); professional standards for teachers and administrators such as the Council for the Accreditation of Educator Preparation (CAEP), Council For Exceptional Children (CEC), National Education

Association (NEA); and parent organizations, and advocacy groups. In addition, research-based models of parental involvement highlight key strategies and processes to inform parent participation in the school. Those include Epstein's Framework of Six Types of Parent Involvement (Epstein, 2009), Comer's School Development Program (Anson, 1991), and Turnbull and Turnbull's Family Systems Theory (Turnbull, Turnbull, Erwin, Soodak, & Shogren, 2015). The Individuals with Disabilities Education Act (IDEA) details specific ways families of children and youth with disabilities must be involved in the processes resulting in Free Appropriate Public Education. These are intertwined throughout the law as they refer to the mandates regarding nondiscriminatory evaluations, Individualized Education Programs (IEPs), and the Least Restrictive Environment (LRE) which requires parent permission and involvement (Cartledge, Gardner & Ford, 2009; Harry, 2008; U.S. Department for Education, 2004). As explicit as IDEA is regarding parental rights and involvement, this mandate does not require definitive roles of the family. This also applies to Title I and parent involvement models. Several factors influence the lack of a decisive definition regarding the role of the family in the schooling process. Those include the different perspectives on what constitutes a family structurally and functionally, the socio-cultural and political diversity within and among populations, the move to an inclusive education framework, the various terms used to describe parental involvement, the realization that no one family model fits the demographic diversity existing in today's school districts, and the rights of family members to select their level of involvement (Abrams & Gibbs, 2002; Huang & Mason, 2008; Turnbull et al., 2015).

Recognizing (Abrams & Gibbs, 2002; Banks, 1997; Comer, 1980; Díaz-Rico, 2013; Henderson, Mapp, & Averett, 2002; Huang & Mason, 2008; Sanders, 2001) that measurable differences have been attributed to family involvement in the areas of students' grades, attendance, school persistence, and behavior for all students, including students with a disability, English Language Learners (ELLs), and other traditionally marginalized groups of learners (e.g., students from racial/ethnic minority populations, learners from low socioeconomic backgrounds, etc.). It is essential that we have a better understanding of the dynamics that promote as well as those that inhibit the nature and degree of family engagement in the schooling process is a necessity. With the shift to inclusive and diverse schools this understanding is paramount if family engagement is to positively impact outcomes for all learners, including those with disabilities. As we move toward more inclusive educational settings for children and seek parent engagement to inform students' outcomes, Abrams and Gibbs (2002) investigation of school practices and policies that influence patterns of "meaningful" inclusion and exclusion surrounding parent involvement is particularly relevant. Furthermore Abrams and Gibbs point out that parents and schools relationships mirror the context and inequitable power struggle existing in society; consequently, strengthening ties between the two is a complex task.

Among the most fundamental changes in the U.S. education system is inclusion, the requirement to provide educational services to students with disabilities in the regular education setting to the maximum extent possible. It is the optimum form of service which addresses the needs of the whole child (Allen & Cowdery, 2015). Implementing inclusion effectively requires many skills, including knowledge of the needs of all students within the context of their families, which then allows for optimum collaboration with school professionals and families (Friend, 2008). With the trend toward more inclusiveness and providing increased authentic access to the general education services, the need to systemically address the role of the family becomes more critical. Due to historic and present barriers, some families are deeply cautious about interacting with school officials. This is especially true for some families from culturally and/or linguistically diverse (CLD) populations.

Additionally, a critical phenomenon impacting schools today is the changing demographics within the student populations which are becoming increasingly CLD. Schools in the United States are often the first point of contact for children from immigrant families as they acculturate into American society (Stuff & Brogadir, 2011) and engaging with families strengthens the cultural competency of teachers with a positive impact on ELLs (Díaz-Rico, 2013). Crucial then are culturally responsive practices between administrators, teachers, and CLD families. Team interactions which acknowledge values and beliefs, systems of communication and cultural group identity are more likely to enhance the success for individuals from CLD backgrounds (Ford & Vakil, 2009). Also, meaningful participation of CLD families of students in the learning process necessitates schools redefining parent−teacher engagement. There is a need to critically reexamine our existing structures and practices to ascertain overt and subtle patterns of exclusion of family engagement. To promote a higher probability of educators' sensitivity to the development of culturally responsive family−teacher engagement, teachers must refine their perspectives regarding strengths of CLD families (Ford, 2002; Geenen, Powers, & Lopez-Vasquez, 2001; Kim & Morningstar, 2005).

Redefining the structure of teacher−parent communication and engagement begins with the need for teachers to reflect on their own biases and assumptions. Many families from CLD backgrounds place more value on nonverbal communication regarded as high context communication rather than verbal communication, low context which is often emphasized by the mainstream culture (Díaz-Rico, 2013). Rather than regarding communication and engagement from their own perspective, school personnel need to be willing to attend carefully to both verbal and nonverbal messages.

Given the importance of family engagement and student outcomes, three fundamental questions are, "How can inclusive schools enhance productive collaborative family engagement networks?" "How can the family be empowered to voluntarily participate within those networks?" and "How can inclusive schools connect with teacher preparation programs to promote the competency of educators for those collaborative family/school engagement networks?" This chapter responds to the above questions by addressing: (1) Family defined, (2) Factors influencing family engagement, and (3) Restructuring for reciprocal relationships. Within this perspective, we propose an interactive triad conceptual model with the school as the "connecting agent" to build relationships with families and teacher preparation, setting the stage for productive family engagement as partners in inclusive settings.

FAMILY DEFINED

Definition — Family

In his book, Empowering Parent—Teacher Partnerships, Coleman (2013) notes that, in contemporary American society, scholars in the field of family studies have replaced the traditional phrase "the American Family" with "American Families." This signifies the diversity of family and of family life experiences found in contemporary society. This shift in terminology extends beyond the traditional structural definition to a sociological contextual one. Coleman (2013) provides definitions of family from three perspectives, namely; personal, professional, and legal.

From one's *personal* perspective, family can be defined according to one's personal beliefs as to how families should be structured and how they should behave. Therefore, one will define family depending on their experiences (negative or positive). A personal definition will also be dependent on the influences and events that shape our views of the world in general and our interpersonal relationships.

Secondly, *professional* definitions are provided by organizations that set professional standards for their members. Examples of such definitions are:

(a) The family is a group of individuals with a continuing legal, genetic, and/or emotional relationship. The family group provides for the economic and protective needs of the individual especially children and the elderly.
(b) A family consists of two or more people who share resources, responsibilities for daily decisions, share goals and values, and show a commitment to one another over time.

A *legal* definition defines family as a group of two or more people (one of whom is a householder) related by birth, marriage or adoption and residing together. Embracing the ever-changing nature of the family today, in this chapter, we define family as *a group of people who care and support one another. These individuals may be living together or residing in different residences. They may be related by blood, adoption or grouped under fictive or affiliated kin (individuals who have no biological or legal relationship to family members but are nevertheless viewed as part of the family and given family responsibilities).* It is imperative that schools permit families to define the "significant" individuals who constitute their family unit and ultimately permit them to participate in family/school engagement process.

FACTORS INFLUENCING FAMILY ENGAGEMENT

Legal Perspectives

Family engagement is federally mandated under Title I of the Elementary and Secondary Education Act of 1965, now The Every Student Succeeds Act 2015 (White House Report, 2016) and calls for the establishment of parent partnerships with schools for the betterment of student achievement (Grant & Ray, 2010). As reported in Howard and Reynolds' (2008) examination of parental involvement of African American parents of students in middle class schools, a criticism of Title I No Child Left Behind (NCLB) focused on enforcement mechanisms to ensure compliance about parental engagement at state and local levels. They point out that school systems cannot be sure that schools are actually complying with the federal mandate of parental engagement. IDEA goes beyond necessitating parent— teacher partnerships to requiring specific responsibilities from schools when interacting with families of children with disabilities. Under IDEA, parents have a say in the educational decisions the school makes about their child and at every point of the process, the law gives parents specific rights and protections. They have the right to participate in the development of the IEP or the Individualized Family Service Plan (IFSP) and they can request a due process hearing if needed. IDEA also gives parents the right to consent to evaluating their child for eligibility, participate in both the assessment and IEP/IFSP development and placement for their child in the LRE. This entails that families be kept informed and involved in the special education process, especially related to assessment and services provided as outlined in the IEP/IFSP. Assessment and identification of a disability must emphasize more than results on standardized tests which are often viewed as culturally biased against CLD families. Multiple forms of assessment including authentic, informal assessment and the funds of knowledge families can bring a more accurate and holistic understanding of their child (Amaro-Jiménez, & Semingson, 2010; González, Moll, & Amanti, 2005).

At the core of these relationships are interactions based on trust and respect which begins with confidentiality of communications, an important mandate under IDEA. It is vital that families trust teachers to share information with them with the confidence that the knowledge will not be shared with others in passing conversations (Allen & Cowdery, 2015). This distrust is further exacerbated by fewer communications between school personnel and families who are given fewer opportunities to be equal partners in their child's education (Cartledge et al., 2009). Collectively, IDEA focuses on the family supporting the child's educational services. In their examination of motivations of African American parental involvement of their young children's learning, Huang and Mason (2008) identified three themes: parents need to develop relationships (with school personnel), parents need to influence their children's learning (have a voice in decision-making), and the belief that education is the key for their children to achieve.

In order to authentically respond to the federal mandates and utilize family engagement to improve achievement and close achievement gaps among all students, schools must believe in the benefits and put forth a policy and plan that will lead to effective parent engagement in schools. A 2003 analysis of national survey questionnaires by Public Agenda, a nonpartisan public opinion research organization, revealed that 65 percent of the teachers say students would do better in school if their parents were more involved, 72 percent of the parents feel that children whose parents are not involved sometimes "fall through the cracks" and end up with the less-than desirable teachers (Johnson & Duffett, 2003). The report further stated that few parents reported that they have participated in any school management decisions such as interviewing prospective teachers. This aligned with the results that both parents and teachers felt the best way for parents to be involved is to pay attention to what's going on in the home (e.g., checking homework) and this was more important than getting involved with curriculum or personnel issues. In Abrams and Gibbs' (2002) study African American parents are found to be more alienated from public school institutions than White American parents. However, they further elaborate that "moments of inclusion" occurred when African American parents are encouraged to participate in school activities such as parent–teacher conferences and athletic events, but they found that interaction with African American parents often did not occur outside of these traditional invitations. According to Salinas, director for the Center on School, Family, and Community Partnerships at Johns Hopkins University, "A lot of it is perception. Teachers perceive that families don't want to be involved when, in fact, families don't know how to be involved" (The Center, 2005, p. 1).

Although IDEA outlines parental rights and provides for varying levels of parental involvement, it does not designate a specific role for parents/ families. Attempting to describe parental engagement from a "role" of the family assumes a checklist approach and when families do not participate on one of the areas/items, they are perceived from deficit perspective and not caring at an appropriate level (Turnbull et al., 2015). It is a restrictive disempowering framework. Describing parental engagement based on a continuum and as part of a collaborative team network views families from an empowering status (Friend, 2008).

Impact of Changes in Terminology

Increased pressure from parents and professionals, parental involvement requirements aligned with federal mandates, consistent documentation supporting the vital benefits of family engagement in students' educational advancement, and the fiscal benefits of family engagement have led to districts refining their operational practices to institute collaborative family (and community) school networks (Shartrand, Weiss, Kreider, & Lopez, 1997). Today, terms such as engagement, partnerships, and collaborative networks reflect school districts' framework of viewing the family as partners and valuable resources to affect educational outcomes (Lareau & Horvat, 1999). The realization that schools alone cannot adequately address the multitude of complex problems and needs confronted by today's youth and that "family engagement matters," districts' are beginning to move away from perceiving the family as external entities toward a united "combining of resources" paradigm (Ford, 2002; Hardre et al., 2013). This parental engagement reform movement is not without its challenges. For us, successful family engagement is defined as: *The active, ongoing participation of the family in the education of their child. Participation is defined as access to the schools' range of parental involvement and the rights of families to select their level of involvement whether at home (e.g., assisting with homework, discussing their child's experiences at school, creating supporting environments or expressing their expectations of school performance) or school (e.g., volunteering in the classroom, serving on decision-making teams, working with the PTA).*

Many schools continue to struggle with defining and measuring meaningful parental involvement, and many don't feel that their efforts are successful. A survey of American teachers revealed that 20 percent of new teachers and nearly one-fourth of principals identify their relationships with parents as a cause of significant stress in their jobs (MetLife, 2005). Schools are more likely to extend and participate in critical cooperative and interdependent networks with social groups who are not poor and/or from multicultural backgrounds (Ford, 2004). Teacher preparation and district professional programs have failed to systematically equip teachers with the knowledge, skills, and attitudes required to develop culturally responsive family (and community) partnerships. The majority of teachers and administrators do not reside in the communities of the multicultural students they serve. This creates a professional disconnect between schools and families while simultaneously supporting a decline in ethnical and racially diverse teachers. The establishment of genuine relationships between teachers and families continues to challenge practitioners. A majority of the 25 largest school systems in the country are heavily composed of students from multicultural groups (MetLife, 2005). This demographic shift must be taken into consideration when instituting districts attempt to promote increased parental engagement and family-school partnerships. Also, disproportionate representation of minority students in special education is a national problem impacting educational equity (Artiles, Trent, & Palmer, 2004). This issue has the potential to affect the perception of culturally diverse families and ultimately their engagement in the schooling process. If school districts are to effectively establish and maintain family—school partnerships as a strategy to positively inform educational outcomes for all students in inclusive settings, including those from multi-cultural backgrounds, special training must be provided.

Professional Perspective

Rigorous standards for teacher preparation programs, licensure/certification, and professional practice ensure that teachers at all levels recognize that effective teaching depends upon partnerships with children's families. The National Association for the Education of Young Children (NAEYC), the CEC, the National Board for Professional Teaching Standards (NBPTS), Interstate Teacher Assessment and Support Consortium (InTASC), and CAEP have all identified knowledge, skills, and dispositions related to parent, family (and community) connections in their standards for professional practice. Helping teachers to embrace a professional framework that emphasizes the concept of fairness, the understanding that all students can become successful learners, that family members care about their children's future, and as such are valuable advocates, and that family members have the right to determine school engagement in those areas not legally "mandated."

Professional competence should be guided by principles which reflect ethical practices. Special educators are often challenged by the demand to balance the needs and wants of many different educational stakeholders from teachers and administrators to parents and, most importantly, students (Brilliant, 2001; Christenson, & Hirsch, 1998; Harrisa & Goodall, 2008). Ethical choices must be made in regards to many different topics. These include but are not limited to making sure assessments and interventions do not harm students physically or emotionally, confidentiality, developing relationships with families and the student, advocate for the student and conduct one self and the team with integrity and professional judgment in inclusive settings (Kampwirth & Powers, 2016).

It is important to note that as the mandate for inclusive education becomes stronger schools are faced with the challenge of meeting the needs of an increasing population of diverse students with varied academic and behavioral needs. IDEA (U.S. Department for Education, 2004) has consistently leaned towards inclusion being among the first options within the continuum of placement options among the LREs. Also, families are more aware of their rights and are more ready to exercise them which have resulted in an increase in children accessing the general education curriculum (Bauer & Shea, 2003). While access to the regular education curriculum has received a lot of attention, communication and team process often deteriorate when discussing the needs of students with disabilities in inclusive settings (Grant & Ray, 2010). During the teaming process, collaboration and communication with families on behalf of the child is key to the academic success of children with special needs (Grant & Ray, 2010; Wright, Stegelin, & Hartle, 2007). Epstein (1995) stated that both schools and families care about the students, want them to succeed and want to work together as partners. However, collaborative teams often struggle to build positive relationships and adversarial relationships often arise. This she identifies as a "rhetoric rut" in which educators talk about collaboration and partnerships but are unable to actually put these statements into action.

The belief that "all children can learn" appears to be very fundamental and almost simplistic; however, this concept is far more complex when applied to children with disabilities. Too often this deficit framework also applies to children from CLD backgrounds. The lack of this belief by school personnel has implications for family engagement in the school. Schools must recognize that all students irrespective of their diversity are capable of learning in inclusive settings when given opportunities and taught in responsive settings that facilitate the most optimum levels of learning (Allen & Cowdery, 2015; Vakil & Welton, 2010). In order to implement inclusion, educators must focus on the strengths diverse families bring to the classroom, and refrain from predicting what they believe the student may be incapable of doing because of the identified label.

Fairness for children with disabilities goes beyond the dimension of equality where it is interpreted as sameness. Rather, it should demonstrate the concept of fairness as equity pedagogy, where fairness is providing children with disabilities educational opportunities which match instruction to their learning style and needs (Welton & Vakil, 2010). This need-based definition focuses on the rights of individuals with disabilities and their families to be provided with educational opportunities that seek to empower them with the same fundamental rights as everyone else: a quality education (Cartledge et al., 2009).

Inclusion stresses the value of recognizing the individuals and their families as more than the disability, and the importance of people-first terminology when referring to them. The power of words cannot be ignored and language used to describe individuals with disabilities has a tremendous impact on not only on our perceptions of disabilities but also our willingness to include them in the inclusive setting and their families in collaborative decision-making networks (Ford, 2004; Welton & Vakil, 2010). The reauthorization of the IDEA (1990) further mandates respect for children with disabilities and their families by introducing "people first" language. This awareness and respect of students with special needs as learners with feelings and not a disability has brought about a willingness from educators to include them in their classrooms (Welton & Vakil, 2010) and engage in productive interactions with families.

RESTRUCTURING FOR RECIPROCAL RELATIONSHIPS

Parent—teacher interactions are often based on the premise that teachers are the experts and parents are passive recipients of the interactions (Hardre et al., 2013; Turnbull et al., 2015). This power-based, one-directional mode of communication creates an unwelcoming environment for families to participate. An effective engagement is one that is reciprocal in nature, and encourages equitable participation by both parties. Productive engagement includes trust and respect between all parties involved and should be earned by both sides. Trust and respect which are often dictated by the dominant culture, determines the context in which these values are viewed (Harry, 2008) and should be restructured to include CLD perspectives.

Barriers of Reciprocal Relationships

Research indicates that, many parents, especially those for whom English is a second language, parents of students with disabilities, minority parents, and parents from low income households, routinely have difficulty communicating with the teachers of their children (Ladson-Billings & Tate, 1995). Where the parent—teacher relationships should be strong and meaningful, they are instead often detached and distant or even strained and distrustful (Brilliant, 2001). This distrust is further exacerbated by fewer communications between school personnel and families who are given fewer opportunities to be equal partners in their child's education (Cartledge et al., 2009). This goes a long way in shaping an understanding of the reality of these relationships in our schools today. Research (Harrisa & Goodall, 2008; Moles, 1993) suggests that many families, including those from CLD and/

or economically disadvantaged backgrounds, want to interact more with teachers and be more involved in their children's schooling, but are prevented from doing so because of work, child care responsibilities, transportation, and other psychological and cultural barriers families may face when communicating with teachers and school officials. Multifaceted racial, cultural, socioeconomic, and political reasons further exacerbate problems of CLD families who are at a higher risk for encountering difficulties and are less likely to be appropriately engaged in the education process therefore ultimately resulting in fewer positive outcomes (Ford & Vakil, 2009; Geenen et al., 2001; Kim & Morningstar, 2005).

This is especially true for parents of children with CLD backgrounds who have special needs. The lack of cultural competence, the ability to recognize the background, and traditions and values often create a cross cultural dissonance which impacts mutual trust, respect, and communication, and results in a blame game which does not support learning (Cartledge et al., 2009). Rather than acknowledging the significance of community-based informal systems of supports to CLD families, many teachers prefer to ignore those (Ford & Vakil, 2009). As noted by Lea (2006) in her ethnographic study of five African American mothers and one White mother, the deficits viewed by service providers in the mothering abilities of these families blinded them to the strengths these mothers and families brought to the schools (Harry, 2008).

To address effective family participation of families in inclusive settings, the structure of meetings and reciprocal relationships between teachers, professionals, and families should be framed to maximize parent input. Rather than recognizing the need to consult with the family members, plan instruction and interact on an ongoing basis with family members (Utley & Obiakor, 2001), families often report negative interactions and one-way communications from the teacher, which further intensify negative perceptions, such as, not being listened to, not understanding the information, withholding of information, and feeling intimidated (Minke & Anderson, 2003). Educators must be willing to shed their preconceived notions and be willing to exchange information and listen to families (Ladson-Billings & Tate, 1995). The expertise families may bring increases the opportunities for optimal inclusion (Turnbull et al., 2015). While all team members are concerned with the student, the educator's connection is to specific services, tasks and staff, rather than the parent — or student which likely leads to parental detachment or, at best, passive participation (Gessler Werts, Mamlin, & Mayfield Pogoloff, 2002). Families are often the only constant in students with disabilities lives and rather than forcing families into defensive or angry behaviors when advocating for their children school personnel, should recognize families as a valuable source of information and integral members of the intervention team (McLoughlin, McLoughlin, & Stewart, 1979).

Pathways toward Reciprocal Relationships

Fundamental to engagement between teachers and parents/families is effective communication founded on respect, clarity, integrity, and most important a value for cultural and linguistic differences. Among the steps to successful inclusion is communication between all team members. Essential then to communication is the trust between educators, professionals providing related services and family members to an ethical belief in the process of inclusion (Friend & Cook, 2016). Communication is the exchange of a message, not only what is said but how it is said, and what is not said. It can be verbal or nonverbal (Cartledge et al., 2009). Language used at team meetings should always be professional and exclude a lot of the jargon, especially when families are present (Friend & Cook, 2016).

Culturally responsive communication and engagement should include a transparent plan where family priorities are considered and valued. School teams must collaborate with families as well as the informal systems of support in the community. This then becomes the framework on which to rely so that instruction and experiences can be authentic and community based. The shift in the power structure from schools alone being actively involved at several levels, to include families as equal rather than passive participants and gives a voice to the culture and values of the person (Vakil, Welton, & Ford, 2010). In his classical work, Cummins (1986) concluded that the major reason as to previous attempts at educational reform have been unsuccessful is that the relationships between teachers and students and between schools and communities have remained essentially unchanged. He emphasized that the required changes needed to involve personal redefinitions of the way classroom teachers interact with children and the communities they serve. Many multicultural families have a history of negative experiences with and mistrust of the school. Differences in income, language, dialects, value, and belief systems or insensitivity to religious beliefs impact involvement of multicultural parents and communities with the school. Consequentially, families are reluctant and/or intimidated to take advantage of their legal rights (Banks, 1997; Cummins, 1986; Harry, 2008). For those parents, a "neutral" mechanism is needed to empower them with information and skills to advocate for their children. Significant Multicultural Community Resources (SMCRs) may be used as a strategy to promote increased parental involvement (Ford, 2002). SMCRs include multicultural not-for-profit services or social organizations, sororities, fraternities, clubs or agencies, religious groups/churches, and individuals that local community residents perceive as providing valuable *significant* services. As detailed by Ford (2004), within many segments of the Black community, the Black church and sororities and fraternities often extend a host of outreach programs to support educational programs. Given today's increasing diverse communities and families, connecting with SMCRs operating within the local multicultural community becomes even more essential.

The need for effective communication between schools and parents/families for children in special education cannot be overstated as they progress through the assessment, IEP, and instructional process. Together they should plan a consistent process to share information. When parents and teachers engage and collaborate they learn from each other and enhance student performance. As previously stated, IDEA explicitly includes families in the education of their children with special needs. Despite these legal mandates to enhance the effectiveness of parent−teacher engagement, the system is often fraught with challenges and stresses for all families in particular those from culturally linguistically diverse backgrounds and/or families with access to resources. This often leaves these individuals and families ill prepared to deal with activities which would either enhance development or lead to more productive lives (Ford & Vakil, 2009). Additionally, evidence-based practices suggest that decisions for students should be made in collaboration with parents/families and based on data which includes a focus on the strengths (Turnbull et al., 2015). Families from diverse backgrounds may focus on different priorities and goals for their children and this often creates uneasiness and tension. Teachers need to acknowledge the cultural or linguistic differences and involve them actively through their strengths as families (Cartledge et al., 2009).

Through school−family−community partnerships, teachers are challenged to establish authentic bonds with significant community resources that empower families and enable them to better advocate for the children educationally as well as provide them with valuable services (Epstein, 2005; Ford, 2004). Delpit (2006) discusses the phenomenon of "other people children" where educators view children from poor and/or culturally diverse backgrounds as different from them, in essence, as other people children rather than "our children." The "Other People Children" paradigm inhibits educator' interaction with family members as equitable partners. Interaction with SMCRs that advocate on behalf of those children may help educators shift their paradigms to "our children" and promote family–school engagement.

As noted by Garcia (1991) public schools are a community affair; made up of children from the community surrounding the school and, with minor exceptions reflect their human communities. The school's community consists of varied social groups who interact with each other, developing cooperative and interdependent networks of relationships. However, schools are more likely to extend and participate in the critical cooperative and interdependent networks with social groups who are not poor and/or from multicultural backgrounds. When schools engage in school–community partnerships, Sanders (2001) revealed that they *underutilize* community partners such as faith-based organizations (e.g., churches), volunteer organizations, community-based organizations (e.g., sororities, fraternities, and neighborhood associations), and individuals in the school community volunteering their time, energy, and talents. These are essential elements of many multicultural communities. Broadened usage, rather than underutilization is needed.

Both general and special educators often possess certain knowledge of and/or first-hand experiences with public service providers (e.g., medical and mental agencies, social services, and juvenile service). In establishing school–community networks, educators must increase their awareness of those informal resources. These include religious groups/churches, homeless support centers, women rescue centers, civic clubs/agencies, social clubs, sport clubs, charities, etc.; family/parent advocacy organizations (e.g., specific disability organizations, National Council of Jewish Women, Urban League, and crisis-related centers/clinics).

AN INTERACTIVE TRIAD CONCEPTUAL FAMILY ENGAGEMENT MODEL

Teacher preparation and district in-service programs have failed to fully equip teacher candidates and practicing teachers respectively with the knowledge, skills, and dispositions required to develop school–community partnerships. Too often the relationship between teacher preparation programs, schools, and families has been in one direction with teacher preparation programs expecting from schools (e.g., field placements) and schools having expectations from families (e.g., supervision of homework). In the section below we propose an interactive triad conceptual model with the school as the "connecting agent" to build relationships with families and teacher preparation, setting the stage for productive family engagement as partners in inclusive settings. See Fig. 1 for a depiction of the model.

The United States has been undergoing progressive reform as a result of legislation, accreditation expectations, and general philosophical changes towards the inclusion of all children including those with disabilities. Inclusion is now more common place in public schools and it is incumbent on teacher preparation programs to prepare teacher candidates who demonstrate skills with academic content, pedagogy, and dispositions. Institutions preparing teachers and schools professional development programs must keep pace with the rapid changes both legislative and social with their education curricula and to maintain accountability. Being able to work effectively with families is an integral component of teacher accreditation

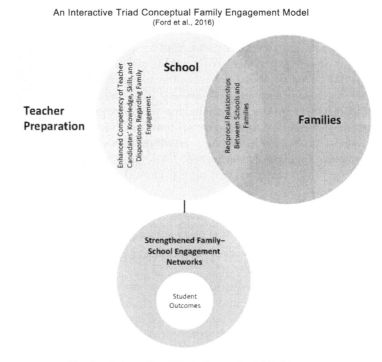

An Interactive Triad Conceptual Family Engagement Model
(Ford et al., 2016)

Fig. 1. Interactive Triad Conceptual Model.

organizations (CAEP) and federal education mandates. Yet, as documented, this remains a challenge for schools and a critical area to be systemically embedded in teacher preparation programs. Therefore, teacher preparation curricula should focus on paradigms for working with all families including those of children with disabilities, ELLs, and other traditionally margina-lized groups of learners (e.g., students from racial/ethnic minority popula-tions, learners from low socioeconomic backgrounds, etc.) in public schools. This is crucial especially in middle or high school instruction where the focus tends to be on content rather than pedagogy.

The next step then goes to recognizing the need to identify the path that teacher preparation programs take to prepare teacher candidates to engage families reflective of the needs of the area schools and the diverse popula-tions they serve. That path demands interactive relationships between schools and teacher preparation programs targeting the area of family engagement. Too often teacher candidates have limited opportunities to observe or demonstrate utilization of best practices of family engagement in diverse, inclusive settings during their field/clinical and student teaching experiences. Working interactively with teacher preparation programs schools can create authentic, guided field experiences targeted towards tea-cher candidates to learn and demonstrate effective engagement with diverse families in inclusive settings. These experiences should emphasize in their curricula, communications which build mutual trust and respect when interacting with families. They may include participating in IEP/IFSP meet-ings or communicating with diverse families during their field experiences.

Within their relationship with teacher preparation programs schools can use this valuable resource to identify and access significant community assets to share with schools thereby strengthening their curriculum and impacting student outcomes in inclusive settings. Under guidance and instruction from university faculty, teacher candidates can collaborate with schools and families to plan and host events which are culturally responsive and respond to family needs and interests along with events to promote academic needs. Teachers today rarely live in the community in which they teach or make home visits. To further enhance family engagements, teacher candidates can make home visits, talk to families, participate in community activities, and share their experiences with schools to help schools acquire better insight into the community in which their students belong. Additionally, often community resources identified by schools are more formal and often not sought out by families with diverse needs. Unique informal resources available in the community are often unknown, under-utilized, or ignored by schools. Teacher candidates can play a valuable role in identifying specific informal supports in a community to enhance family engagement in inclusive settings. Ford's (2004) Three Phase Model for Preparing Educators for School Partnerships with SMCR can be used as a guide to help teachers connect with significant community resources.

Parent–school relations are socially constructed (Abrams & Gibbs, 2002); deliberate equitable culturally responsive communications with families can influence or change the traditional framework of these relations. Practices of access and family inclusion are evident when school paradigms, policies, and practices result in patterns of interaction with family members as equitable partners. Teachers must have a commitment to the principles of fairness, respect, and the belief in all children's ability to learn. Osguthorpe (2008) states that "… good teaching requires that the teacher be knowledgeable in content, skilled in methods and virtuous in disposition and character" (p. 288). It is important for educators to internalize these dispositions and so that it impacts all schools do in their daily practice and interactions. The family, rather than being recipients of advice and services, is equal partners of the team. It is the engagement with families and their funds of knowledge that should guide teachers in integrating in their curriculum cultural and social values of the family, and the needs of diverse children in inclusive settings.

Parents are the first teachers for their children, and school's need to access their wealth of knowledge and community resources (Ford, 2004; Moll, 2005). Crucial to the success of our interactive triad conceptual model is participation by families in their children's education. Family engagement should be mutually respectful with shared communication and trust. While it is imperative that schools collaborate with families in a culturally responsive manner, in our opinion, parents are also obligated to be involved at school or home to the maximum extent possible and to advocate for their child. This includes participating in school-sponsored parent training programs, accessing the schools' systems of communication to obtain information, and in special education using resources offered by the school to participate fully in their child's education. Additionally, they can utilize community resources to support and advocate for their children.

CONCLUSION

In this chapter we operate under the premise that family engagement is crucial to student outcomes. Changes in demographics, the fluidity of families, the increasingly diverse populations within inclusive schools all influence practices of family engagement. Too often those practices of engagement are inhibitive rather than affirming and consequently must be refined. We posited three crucial questions that must be addressed to advance family school engagement. The chapter presented the legal and professional perspectives supporting family engagement. We further outlined the barriers to effective family engagement in inclusive settings for all, as well as those from CLD backgrounds. We then delineated pathways to reciprocal relations to enhance family and school engagement. We proposed our Interactive Triad Conceptual model that combines the resources of teacher preparation programs, the schools, and families (and their communities) as a forum to enhance family–school engagement. The ultimate purpose of the model is to highlight the essential interactive processes resulting in positive outcomes for students in inclusive settings.

REFERENCES

Abrams, L. S., & Gibbs, J. T. (2002). Disrupting the logic of home-school relations: Parent involvement strategies and practices of inclusion and exclusion. *Urban Education, 37*(3), 384–407.

Allen, K. E., & Cowdery, G. E. (2015). *The exceptional child: Inclusion in early childhood education.* Albany, NY: Delmar.

Amaro-Jiménez, C., & Semingson, P. (2010). Sometimes I don't know how to help you, but I'll try: Latina mothers' participation in their children's biliteracy learning in the home. *National Journal of Urban Education and Practice, 4*(2), 33–48.

Anson, A. R. (1991). The comer school development program: A theoretical analysis. *Urban Education, 26*(1), 56–82.

Artiles, A. J., Trent, S. C., & Palmer, J. (2004). Culturally diverse students in special education: Legacies and prospects. In J. A. Banks & C. M. Banks (Eds.), *Handbook of research on multicultural education* (2nd ed., pp. 716–735). San Francisco, CA: Jossey-Bass.

Banks, J. A. (1997). *Educating citizens in a multicultural society. Multicultural education series.* New York, NY: Teachers College Press.

Bauer, A. M., & Shea, T. M. (2003). *Parents and schools: Creating a successful partnership for students with special needs.* Upper Saddle River, NJ: Merrill/Prentice Hall.

Brilliant, C. D. G. (2001). Parental involvement in education: Attitudes and activities of Spanish-speakers as affected by training. *Bilingual Research Journal, 25*(3), 251–274.

Cartledge, G., Gardner, R., & Ford, D. Y. (2009). *Diverse learners with exceptionalities: Culturally responsive teaching in the inclusive classroom.* Upper Saddle River, NJ: Pearson.

Christenson, S. L., & Hirsch, J. (1998). Facilitating partnerships and conflict resolution between families and schools. In K. C. Stoiber & T. Kratochwill (Eds.), *Handbook of group interventions for children and families* (pp. 307–344). Boston, MA: Allyn & Bacon.

Coleman, M. (2013). *Empowering family-teacher partnerships: Building connections within diverse communities.* Los Angeles, CA: Sage.

Comer, J. P. (1980). *School power: Implications of an intervention project: With a new preface and epilogue.* New York, NY: The Free Press.

Cummins, J. (1986). Empowering minority students: A framework for intervention. *Harvard Educational Review, 56*(1), 18–37.

Delpit, L. D. (2006). *Other people's children: Cultural conflict in the classroom.* New York, NY: The New Press.

Díaz-Rico, L. T. (2013). *The cross-cultural language and academic development handbook: A complete K-12 reference guide* (5th ed.). New York, NY: Pearson.

Epstein, J. L. (1995). School/family/community partnerships. *Phi Delta Kappa, 76*(9), 701.

Epstein, J. L. (2005). *Epstein's framework of six types of involvement (Including: Sample practices, challenges, redefinitions, and expected results).* Center for the Social Organization of Schools, Baltimore, MD. Retrieved from http://www.schoolengagement.org/TruancypreventionRegistry/Admin/Resources/Resources/32.pdf

Ford, B. A. (2002). African American community resources: Essential education enhancers for African American children and youth. In F. E. Obiakor & B. A. Ford (Eds.), *Creating successful learning environments for African American learners with exceptionalities* (pp. 159–173). Thousand Oaks, CA: Corwin Press.

Ford, B. A. (2004). Preparing special educators for culturally responsive school-community partnerships. *Teacher Education and Special Education, 27*(3), 224–230.

Ford, B. A., & Vakil, S. (2009). Maximizing the transition process culturally/linguistically diverse youth: Essential practices. *Proceedings of International Association of Special Education, 11*, 256–259.

Friend, M. (Ed.) (2008). *Special education: Contemporary perspective for school professionals.* Boston, MA: Pearson.

Friend, M. P., & Cook, L. (2016). *Interactions: Collaboration skills for school professionals.* Boston, MA: Pearson.

Garcia, R. L. (1991). *Teaching in a pluralistic society: Concepts, models, strategies.* New York, NY: Harper Collins.

Geenen, S., Powers, L. E., & Lopez-Vasquez, A. (2001). Multicultural aspects of parent involvement in transition planning. *Exceptional Children, 67*(2), 265–282.

Gessler Werts, M., Mamlin, N., & Mayfield Pogoloff, S. (2002). Knowing what to expect: Introducing preservice teachers to IEP meetings. *Teacher Education and Special Education, 25*(4), 413–418.

González, N., Moll, L., & Amanti, C. (2005). *Funds of knowledge: Theorizing practices in households, communities, and classrooms.* New Jersey.

Grant, K. B., & Ray, J. A. (2010). *Home, school, and community collaboration: Culturally responsive family involvement.* Thousand Oaks, CA: Sage.

Hardre, P., Ling, C., Shehab, R., Nanny, M., Nollert, M., Refai, H., … Wollega, E. (2013). Teachers in an interdisciplinary learning community: Engaging, integrating, and strengthening K-12 education. *Journal of Teacher Education, 64*(5), 409–425.

Harrisa, A., & Goodall, J. (2008). Do parents know they matter? Engaging all parents in learning. *Educational Research, 50*(3), 277–289.

Harry, B. (2008). Collaboration with culturally and linguistically diverse families: Ideal verses reality. *Exceptional Children, 74*(3), 372–388.

Henderson, A. T., Mapp, K. L., & Averett, A. (2002). *A new wave of evidence: The impact of school, family, and community connections on student achievement.* Austin, TX: National Center for Family & Community Connections with Schools. Retrieved from http://www.sedl.org/connections/resources/evidence.pdf

Howard, T. C., & Reynolds, R. (2008). Examining parent involvement in reversing the underachievement of African American students in middle-class schools. *The Journal of Educational Foundations, 22*(1/2), 79.

Huang, G. H. C., & Mason, K. L. (2008). Motivations of parental involvement in children's learning: Voices from urban African American families of preschoolers. *Multicultural Education, 15*(3), 20.

Johnson, J., & Duffett, A. (2003). *Where we are now: 12 Things you need to know about public opinion and public schools. A digest of a decade of survey research.* New York, NY: Public Agenda.

Kampwirth, T. J., & Powers, K. M. (2016). *Collaborative consultation in the schools: Effective practices for students with learning and behavior problems.* Boston, MA: Pearson.

Kim, K. H., & Morningstar, M. E. (2005). Transition planning involving culturally and linguistically diverse families. *Career Development for Exceptional Individuals, 28*(2), 92–103.

Ladson-Billings, G., & Tate, W. F. (1995). Toward a critical theory of education. *Teachers College Record, 97*(1), 47–68.

Lareau, A., & Horvat, E. M. (1999). Moments of social inclusion and exclusion race, class, and cultural capital in family-school relationships. *Sociology of Education, 72*(1), 37–53.

Lea, D. (2006). "You don't know me like that": Patterns of disconnect between adolescent mothers of children with disabilities and their early interventions. *Journal of Early Intervention, 28*(4), 264–282.

McLoughlin, J., McLoughlin, R., & Stewart, W. (1979). Advocacy for parents of the handicapped: A professional responsibility and challenge. *Learning Disability Quarterly, 2*(3), 51–57.

MetLife (2005). *The MetLife survey of the American teacher: Transitions and the role of supportive relationships; A survey of teachers, principals and students.* New York, NY: Author. Retrieved from http://www.metlife.com/WPSAssets/34996838801118758796VlFATS_2004.pdf. Accessed on August 4, 2005.

Minke, K., & Anderson, K. (2003). Restructuring routine parent-teacher conferences: The family-school conference model. *The Elementary School Journal, 104*(1), 49–69.

Moles, O. C. (1993). Collaboration between schools and disadvantaged parents: Obstacles and openings. *Families and Schools in a Pluralistic Society, 168*, 21–49.

Osguthorpe, R. D. (2008). On the reasons we want teachers of good disposition and moral character. *Journal of Teacher Education, 59*(4), 288–299.

Sanders, M. (2001). *New paradigm or old wine? The status of technology education practice in the United States.* Retrieved from http://scholar.lib.vt.edu/ejournals/JTE/v12n2/sanders.html

Shartrand, A. M., Weiss, H. B., Kreider, H. M., & Lopez, M. E. (1997). *New skills for new schools: Preparing teachers in family involvement.* Cambridge, MA: Harvard Family Research Project.

Stuff, D., & Brogadir, R. (2011). Urban principals' facilitation of English language learning in public schools. *Education and Urban Society, 43*(5), 560–575. (pp. 583–607). New York, NY: Wiley.

The Center for Comprehensive School Reform and Improvement. (August, 2005). *Meeting the challenge: Getting parents involved in schools.* Washington, DC: Author.

Turnbull, A. P., Turnbull, H. R., Erwin, E. J., Soodak, L. C., & Shogren, K. A. (2015). *Families, professionals, and exceptionality: Positive outcomes through partnerships and trust.* Upper Saddle River, NJ: Pearson.

U.S. Department for Education. (2004). *Individuals with Disabilities Education Act of 2004.* Retrieved from http://idea.ed.gov

Utley, C. A. R., & Obiakor, F. E. (2001). *Special education, multicultural education, and school reform: Components of quality education for learners with mild disabilities.* Springfield, IL: Charles C. Thomas.

Vakil, S., Welton, E. N., & Ford, B. A. (2010). Citizenship and self-determination for individuals with cognitive disabilities: The interdependence of social studies and special education. *Action in Teacher Education, 32*(2), 4–11.

Welton, E., & Vakil, S. (2010). Enhancing the development of dispositions in pre-service teacher preparation programs. *Journal of Psychology of the Romanian Academy, 56*(3–4), 261–268.

White House Report. (2016, April 9). *White House Report: The every student succeeds act.* Retrieved from https://www.whitehouse.gov/the-press-office/2015/12/10/white-house-report-every-student-succeeds-act

Wright, K., Stegelin, D. A., & Hartle, L. (2007). *Building family, school, and community partnerships.* Upper Saddle River, NJ: Prentice Hall.

THE ROLE OF THE COMMUNITY IN INCLUSIVE EDUCATION

Terese C. Aceves

ABSTRACT

The United Nation's Convention of the Rights of Persons with Disabilities *in 2006 declared the need for countries to facilitate the right of individuals with disabilities to their full inclusion and participation within communities across the globe. The community clearly plays a necessary role in the overall preparation and quality of life of students with disabilities and their families. The present chapter will specifically address the role of the community within instructional programming and parent advocacy. First, the chapter discusses the importance of integrating community experiences within inclusive K-12 preparation for students with disabilities for the purpose of enhancing students' postsecondary outcomes. Second, the chapter reviews the role of community organizations in supporting parental advocacy for effective inclusive programming while highlighting the work of two specific community agencies. These sections are followed by concluding comments emphasizing the role of schools and community-based organizations in supporting inclusive education, community-based instruction, and family advocacy for students with disabilities.*

Keywords: Community; family advocacy; community agencies; inclusion; students with disabilities

General and Special Education Inclusion in an Age of Change: Roles of Professionals Involved
Advances in Special Education, Volume 32, 99–118
Copyright © 2016 by Emerald Group Publishing Limited
All rights of reproduction in any form reserved
ISSN: 0270-4013/doi:10.1108/S0270-401320160000032007

The United Nation's *Convention of the Rights of Persons with Disabilities* in 2006 recognized the need for individuals with disabilities to live and actively participate within their own communities. The Convention was the first international agreement addressing disability rights globally and articulated the importance of being included within the community as a critical goal for consideration and action (Thoma, Cain, & Walther-Thomas, 2015). Specifically, article 19 states "… Parties to this Convention recognize the equal right of all persons with disabilities to live in the community, with choices equal to others, and shall take effective and appropriate measures to facilitate full enjoyment by persons with disabilities of this right and their full inclusion and participation in the community" (The United Nations, 2006, p. 15).

More recently in the United States, a similar call for supporting community participation for individuals with disabilities was underscored during the 2015 *National Goals in Research, Practice and Policy Conference* in Washington DC. The intent of the working meeting was to establish a set of national goals for the next 10 years in specific focus areas all related to pushing forward research, practice, and policy for and with individuals with intellectual and developmental disabilities. Attendees including experts, researchers, and advocates recommended the identification, implementation, and evaluation of best practices that promote opportunities specifically for self-determination across different community environments (Shogren, Wehmeyer, Palmer, Rifenbark, & Little, 2015).

In order to support meaningful community integration of individuals with disabilities, school professionals in K-12 settings can facilitate this process by designing specialized services for students within more inclusive, community-based settings. Inclusive educational programming can better prepare students with disabilities for future integrated experiences within educational, employment, and recreation/leisure activities (Cosier, Causton-Theoharis, & Theoharis, 2013; Rojewski, Lee, & Gregg, 2013). However, accessing inclusive and community-based programming for students with disabilities often depends on a parent's ability to advocate for these options for their child as well as the supports necessary for their child to experience success within these settings (Turnbull, Turnbull, & Kyzar, 2009; Turnbull, Turnbull, Erwin, Soodak, & Shogren, 2015). Parents often seek assistance outside of their child's school from experts within their communities, to acquire the information and skills to advocate for their child's right to appropriate programming.

Therefore, it becomes clear that communities hold incredible value and purpose in supporting students with disabilities and their families when these students are educated within inclusive settings. The purpose of this chapter is to review how special educators and families access the community to support students with disabilities and optimize students' access to and success within inclusive K-12 settings. Initially, the chapter reviews evidence from the literature documenting how schools include educational programming for students with disabilities within the community, referred to in this chapter as community-based instructional programs. Subsequently, the chapter highlights how parents obtain assistance from community agencies to support their work in advocating for their children who are placed within inclusive general education settings.

COMMUNITY-BASED PROGRAMMING

Community-based programs allow children and youth to apply academic, social, and behavioral skill learning essential to their formation and growth outside of school and within real-world settings (Ysseldyke & Algozzine, 2006). Providing community-based experiences for students with disabilities who are also placed within inclusive general education settings has the potential to produce better postschool outcomes for these students (Gaumer, Morningstar, & Clark, 2004). The reauthorization of the Individuals with Disabilities Education Act in 1990 specifically required transition planning and services to better prepare students for postsecondary life experiences within their communities. Interagency collaboration, curriculum, and instruction focused on enhancing specific postschool outcomes are essential components of such programs (Morningstar et al., 2010). Morningstar et al. (2010) found that students who reported higher levels of self-advocacy after graduating from high school also reported having greater opportunities and instruction in postsecondary skill development during secondary preparation. Self-advocacy is a necessary skill for enhanced quality of life and successful community engagement. Community-based experiences for students with disabilities during K-12 programming can enhance the instruction they receive and the associated postsecondary benefits these experiences can provide.

Research investigating K-12 community-based instruction that prepares students for community living across multiple domains (e.g., vocational, daily living, recreation) has reported positive results demonstrating increases in targeted skills (Walker, Uphold, Richter, & Test, 2010). Walker et al. (2010) conducted a review of 23 transition intervention studies from 1990 to 2006 documenting the ability of students with disabilities to learn necessary daily living skills including banking, safety, grocery shopping, and general social skills within natural community environments. The research reviewed was conducted with students across varying ages and grade levels with much of this work based on students placed in secondary settings and conducted exclusively at specific sites within the community. Although the research supports the benefits of community-based instruction for students with disabilities, it is important to better understand successful programming within integrated settings involving both students with and without disabilities.

Andrews, Falkmer, and Girdler (2015) conducted an extensive review of community-based interventions involving both students with and without disabilities. Their review included studies involving children and youth, 5–18 years of age and having a neurodevelopmental disorder (e.g., Rett's syndrome, Down syndrome, cerebral palsy, or autism). The intervention focus of these studies targeted community participation, self-esteem, and/or quality of life. The team identified 13 out of 396 studies meeting inclusion and quality criteria. Of the 13 studies, 7 studies specifically involved students engaging in inclusive programming within the community and involving both students with and without disabilities (see Table 1).

These studies targeted a variety of outcomes including making improvements in students' friendships (Carter et al., 2004; Fennick & Royle, 2003; Haring & Breen, 1992; Kasari et al., 2012; Schleien et al., 1987; Siperstein et al., 2009), quality of life (Becker & Dusing, 2010), social interaction (Haring & Breen, 1992), and recreational/activity participation (Carter et al., 2004; Fennick & Royle, 2003). These studies employed a number of different outcome measures (e.g., observations, verbal and written feedback by parents and children, parental surveys, teacher reports) to evaluate effectiveness. Studies included a variety of research designs including pretest/posttest (Carter et al., 2004; Fennick & Royle, 2003; Schleien et al., 1987), randomized control trial (Kasari et al., 2012), multiple-baseline (Haring & Breen, 1992), repeated measures (Siperstein et al., 2009), case study (Becker & Dusing, 2010), and qualitative observations (Becker & Dusing, 2010; Haring & Breen, 1992). The authors from each study found significant improvements in the general quality and/or quantity of students' friendships (Becker & Dusing, 2010; Carter et al., 2004; Fennick & Royle, 2003; Haring & Breen, 1992; Kasari et al., 2012; Schleien et al., 1987; Siperstein et al., 2009), improvements in facilitating recreational participation (Becker & Dusing, 2010; Carter et al., 2004; Fennick & Royle, 2003; Schleien et al.,

Table 1. Community Participation for Children/Adolescents with Intellectual Disability.

Findings of Studies

Author, Year, Country	Design Number of Participants	Participants	Intervention Group	Control Group	Outcome Measures	Results
Kasari, Rotheram-Fuller, and Locke (2012) USA	RCT (*n* = 75)	Children with high functioning ASD (*n* = 30)	Peer-mediated group (*n* = 60)	No Intervention; Children with high functioning ASD (*n* = 15)	*Friendships* Social network Survey (child); Playground; Observation; (assessor); Self, peer, and teacher reports	*Friendships* Increase in social network, number of friendship nominations and teacher report of social skills in classroom. Decrease in isolation on playground.
		Children without ASD (*n* = 45) 6–11 years	Aim: develop friendships 2 sessions/week for 6 week; Recess and lunch at school		*Social skills* Teachers report	*Social skills* Increased social skills;
Becker and Dusing (2010) USA	Case report (*n* = 1)	Girl with Down Syndrome (11 years, mild cognitive impairment)	Performing arts group		*Quality of Life (QOL)* PedsQL (parent)	Increased QOL and self-confidence
		Children without Down syndrome (8–14 years)	Aim: participation in dance, voice, acting 14 weekly sessions Community performing arts center		*Friendships, Self-confidence, Engagement* Observations Parent Report	Increased interaction and engagement with peers Increased motivation for other community programs
Haring and Breen (1992) USA	Multiple-baseline (*n* = 11)	Adolescents with autism (*n* = 1) and intellectual disability (*n* = 1)	Social network group. Aim: facilitate social interaction and inclusion		*Social interactions/friendships*	*Friendships*

Table 1. *(Continued)*

Findings of Studies

Author, Year, Country	Design Number of Participants	Participants	Intervention Group	Control Group	Outcome Measures	Results
		Adolescents without autism and intellectual disability (n = 9)	Weekly sessions 2 Groups: 1 (n = 5). 2 (n = 6) Recess, lunch, and classroom (after-hours)		Observations – (assessor) Qualitative – satisfaction, peer interaction/relationship (child and peers)	Increased friendships (quality, quantity, interactions) Increased peer interaction outside of school and continued peer network *Social skills* Increased knowledge of social skills
Siperstein, Glick, and Parker (2009) USA	One-way repeated measures (n = 67)	Children with mild intellectual disability (n = 29)	Summer recreational program		*Friendships* Peer hang-out with friendship inventory (child)	*Friendships* Children with ID made new friends and more accepted by peers
		Children without intellectual disability (n = 38) 8–13 years old	Aim: participation in swimming, basketball, soccer, free play, arts, and crafts 5 sessions/week for 4 weeks 12 per group. Leisure center		*Recreational participation* Adapted sports skills assessment (investigators)	*Recreational participation* Significant increase in swimming and soccer skills for children with ID (p < 0.001) Strong relationship between sport skills and building relationships (p < 0.01)

Study	Design	Participants	Program/Aim	Outcomes measured	Results
Fennick and Royle (2003) USA	Two group pretest/posttest (n = not specified)	Children with mild to severe autism (n = 5); Children without autism 6–13 years old	Recreation group. Aim: participation in swimming, gymnastics, develop friendships 2 groups: 1 swimming (n = 3); 2 gymnastics (n = 2). Leisure center	Recreational participation/ Friendships: Observations – participation, attendance, and enjoyment; Parent survey	Recreational participation: Positive feedback on programs; Friendships: No improvement in friendships; Increased participation in group community programs
Schleien, Krotee, Mustonen Kelterborn, and Schermer (1987) USA	One group pretest/posttest (n = 69)	Children with severe autism (n = 2); Children without autism (n = 67) 7–12 years old	Summer recreation program. Aim: participation in badminton, basketball, volleyball, gymnastics, swimming, tennis, squash, free time 5 sessions/week for 3 weeks; 3 age groups: 7–8 years old; 9–10 years old; 11–12 years old. University campus (community)	Friendships: Attitude acceptance scale (peers); Play/Participation: Behavioral observations – in play and with peers (children and peers)	Friendships: Increase in appropriate interaction; Play/Participation: Appropriate play significantly increased in recreational activities; Increase depending of participants preferred activities
Carter et al. (2004) USA	Two groups pretest/posttest (n = 10)	Children with Asperger's syndrome 8–15 years old	Friendship club. Aim: develop friendship skills. 6 weekly sessions. 2 age groups: 8–10 years (n = 6); 11–15 years old (n = 4). Classroom (after hours) and community	Friendships, enjoyment, activity participation: Observations Verbal and written feedback from children and parents	Friendships: Most children had increased friendships; Activity participation: Increase in activity participation and enjoyment

Source: Andrews et al. (2015) and reproduced with their permission.

1987; Siperstein et al., 2009), and improvements in parental reported quality of life (Becker & Dusing, 2010).

An example of this work includes Siperstein colleague's (2009) study involving 67 children enrolled in a summer day camp (29 with intellectual disabilities and 38 without disabilities) and included students from racially diverse backgrounds (58% African American, 27% Caucasian, 12% Latino, 3% Asian American). The primary purpose of the study was to improve students' socialization skills. Participants ranged from 8 to 13 years of age and were enrolled in 3rd through 6th grade. The program followed a traditional Monday through Friday schedule from 8:30 a.m. to 2:30 p.m. Administrative and program staff provided a 3 to 1 child to adult staff ratio. Children were grouped according to teams with equal distribution of children with and without disabilities on each team. Teams remained intact for 4-week cycles and engaged in recreational activities including swimming, basketball, and soccer. Facilitators provided opportunities for team building within teams and encouraged socialization across teams through nonsport activities such as snack, arts and crafts time, and field trips. The research team collected measures on children's social relationships and friendship groups and their skill ability in different sports areas. The social relationship measures were administered during the last 2 days of camp while the skill ability in different sports activities were collected at the beginning and end of the study. Overall, the authors found that children with disabilities were nominated as being significant peers or friends by nondisabled children just as much as children without disabilities. All participants with and without disabilities were able to form positive relationships with peers as a result of the program.

Although the methodology and outcomes of this research base varies considerably, this work provides useful evidence regarding the benefits of community-based programming involving students with and without disabilities across different age groups, and having a variety of disabilities. Moreover, these studies demonstrate an impact on multiple student outcomes including students' friendships, self-confidence, recreational participation, and social skills. Inclusive programming within the community can offer students with disabilities greater interaction with nondisabled peers, more challenging curricula, higher expectations, and more meaningful experiences overall in comparison to programming within more restrictive settings (Cosier et al., 2013). However, in order to gain access to such programming and experiences, parents must actively collaborate with educational professionals to ensure these options are considered and implemented successfully.

COMMUNITY ADVOCACY TO SUPPORT INCLUSIVE PROGRAMMING

The reauthorization of the Individuals with Disabilities Education Improvement Act (2004) requires collaboration with families as an essential component of the individualized education program (IEP) process to support all students with disabilities. Home—school collaboration is particularly essential when planning for successful inclusive programming and working towards fulfilling postschool experiences. For students with disabilities to benefit from inclusive placements they must have programming that supports active and meaningful engagement in these settings (Cosier et al., 2013; Rojewski et al., 2013). However, in order to experience success within more inclusive general education programs, parents must often take a lead role in advocating for their child to receive necessary supports (Turnbull et al., 2009, 2015). Obtaining services and supports is often difficult for low-income diverse families who may not have the educational, financial, cultural, and/or linguistic knowledge to understand how best to advocate for their child's service delivery (Aceves, 2014; Harry & Klingner, 2014; Kalyanpur, Harry, & Skrtic, 2000). These families may reach out to community agencies and organizations for additional resources and support when necessary to effectively understand and navigate the system of special education service delivery (Aceves & Higareda, 2014; Aceves, 2014).

Educating families and equipping them with knowledge and skills in special education advocacy is essential to achieving the desired quality of life for themselves and their child or family member with a disability. During the 2015 *National Goals in Research, Practice and Policy Conference* experts called for the field to extend research to understand the experiences of families within communities recognizing their need to obtain formal and informal support from different community systems. Specifically, "... increased access to information, relationships, and tangible supports from within their own community offers families additional opportunities beyond only traditional eligibility based services" (Reynolds et al., 2015, p. 262). Parents seek community assistance for problem solving, accessing informal supports, networking and connecting with other families having similar experiences and needs ultimately with the purpose of building necessary social capital (Aceves & Higareda, 2014; Reynolds et al., 2015). Additional research is necessary to investigate the unique needs of families from diverse racial and ethnic communities in their ability to access various supports given the difficulties these families often face in obtaining accessible services (Harry & Klingner, 2014; Magaña, Lopez, Aguinaga, & Morton, 2013).

The current section of this chapter describes the work of two community agencies and their collaboration with schools and families to support students with disabilities within inclusive settings. After a brief description of each organization, the section describes how each organization supports families through parent training and how they work directly to support schools and districts towards successful inclusive programming.

Community Agency Descriptions

Fiesta Educativa
Based in California, Fiesta Educativa, Inc. is a community organization founded in 1978 for the purpose of supporting primarily Latino families who have a child with a disability. Fiesta's work has been replicated in New Mexico. The organization's goals include:

- Assisting families to gain knowledge, access key resources, and understand their fundamental rights;
- Influencing the advancement and rehabilitative potential of Latinos with special developmental needs;
- Increasing the consciousness of professionals about the unique cultural characteristics and needs of Latino children and their families; and
- Expanding and developing culturally sensitive programs and services. (About us, 2016)

This community organization's work includes organizing annual parent conferences, parent-lead trainings, home-based and school-site support, and an autism education program for parents in English and Spanish. In addition, Fiesta Educativa actively engages in research with multiple institutions and is committed to collaborating with researchers to increase diverse families' participation in research involving children and youth with disabilities.

Learning Rights Law Center
The Learning Rights Law Center (LRLC) is a nonprofit legal organization in Los Angeles, California, providing legal services, training, advocacy, and policy work to support the educational rights of children and youth with and without disabilities. Learning Rights "... seeks to ensure that all students are provided with equitable access to the public education system,

with a focus on low-income children that have disabilities, face discrimination or are involved in the dependency or juvenile justice systems" (Mission statement, 2016). The organization provides brief legal service clinics, advocacy, direct representation, and an extensive parent-training program known as TIGER (Training Individuals for Grassroots Education Reform).

Supporting Inclusion through Direct Family Support

Both community organizations engage in targeted individualized parent support and organized parent training to assist families to understand their child's disability, special education systems and services, the IEP process, the law, and their rights and responsibilities. Schools often do not have the resources or time to share this and related information with families in a meaningful or consistent manner. When necessary, families seek this information and support from outside resources within the community. This is particularly critical in the case of families choosing to place their children within more inclusive settings within the schools. In segregated settings, some families may perceive the programming to be repetitive and lacking in meaning and relevance for their child (Harry & Klingner, 2014). As an alternative, families may consider general education placements in lieu of more restrictive settings due to perceived higher expectations, a more rigorous curriculum and greater interaction with same age nondisabled peers. However, placement in these settings does not necessarily equal appropriate inclusion within these settings (Burke, 2015). Parents must learn to advocate for the necessary resources and supports required to make these placements appropriate (Turnbull et al., 2009). Specifically, advocating for instructional methods, professional training for service providers, and more individualized one-on-one support (if required and appropriate) becomes a necessary part of the process once families choose inclusive programming (Burke, 2015).

Some organizations provide more formal training in special education advocacy however, much of this training is often not accessible to low-income diverse families (Burke, 2015). Two trainings including the nationally available Special Education Advocacy Training (SEAT) and the Volunteer Advocacy Project (VAP) in Tennessee involve numerous hours of instruction and practicum requirements. Although incredibly valuable, this type of training may not consider the specific needs of full-time working parents, or families from culturally and linguistically diverse low-income backgrounds (Burke, 2015). Engaging with professionals within the community and external to the school, like Fiesta Educativa and LRLC, allows parents to learn how to advocate for inclusive programming while benefitting from direct advocacy assistance when needed. The goal of these organizations fortunately is not only to empower parents in this process but also to maintain positive relationships between schools and families.

LRLC's TIGER program provides hands-on monthly training sessions for parents across southern California. Since 2005 they have trained over 2,500 families from low-income communities. Through their training, parents learn about special education services, procedures, the law, and the IEP process. Parents often learn for the first time the meaning behind least restrictive environment and their child's right to receive services within inclusive settings. Trainings involve 3 hour monthly sessions within the community and lead by a special education advocate, attorney, university faculty, or special education teacher trainer. Parents receive instruction and material in their preferred language with classes currently being conducted in English, Spanish, and Korean. As part of a regular evaluation of the program's effectiveness, the program administers a pre- and posttest assessment of basic knowledge related to special education advocacy. During the 2015 calendar year, parents participating in the Beginner TIGER training program demonstrated significant gains in their special education knowledge and advocacy skills upon completing a 12-month cycle (Aceves & Chavez-Valdivia, 2016).

Learning Rights' TIGER trainings equip parents with the support and skills necessary to advocate for inclusion. Often families may not understand or consider inclusive programming for their child given a lack of information or consideration by their child's school team for this option. Community organizations are often the first ones to present to families the possibility of inclusive programming for their child (I. Kuperschmit, personal communication, February 11, 2016).

> It takes a more empowered parent in order to consider the idea of inclusion because it takes a lot more work. Other less educated or financially secure families want to take their child to school without the drama. A family who is wrestling with poverty issues may opt for an easier path. By requesting inclusive programming, you are asking to work with schools and teachers who may resist this decision and be hostile. Successful inclusion has to address students' learning issues, not only allow them to be physically included in general education classrooms. Inclusion takes more hands-on work. You have to support inclusive placements one student at a time. (J. Steel and I. Kuperschmit, personal communication, February 11, 2016)

Families seek this level of support within the community in order to gain the skills necessary to advocate for their child's special needs and ensure an appropriate education and quality of life for their child.

Accessible, no to low-cost parent training within the community is key to providing access to the knowledge and skills necessary for parents to feel empowered to support their child's inclusive education throughout their lifetime.

Supporting Inclusion through Community Agency-School Partnerships

Community organizations have the ability to use their external resources, connections, expertise, and funding to establish and improve successful inclusive programming for students with disabilities by building direct partnerships with schools (Ysseldyke & Algozzine, 2006). Schools often have limited funding and personnel with necessary training and experience to support students with disabilities regardless of the student's educational placement. Community agencies can provide greater access to a variety of specialists and information in particular areas of need such as transition, assistive technology, behavior, and mental health for parents and school staff alike.

The literature clearly identifies interagency collaboration as facilitating postschool employment and educational outcomes for all students with disabilities (Noonan, Gaumer Erickson, & Morningstar, 2013; Noonan, Morningstar, & Gaumer Erickson, 2008; Repetto, Webb, Garvan, & Washington, 2002). High levels of collaboration across agencies are specific markers of well-established and successful transition services in secondary schools. Transition teams with great involvement of community agencies and local services "are better able to (a) share resources, (b) hold informational fairs, and (c) influence local policies and procedures" (Noonan et al., 2013, p. 97). Interagency collaboration is essential for transition planning for all students with disabilities and clearly evident in high-performing districts. In their study of 29 high-performing districts and state-level transition coordinators across five states in the United States, Noonan et al. (2008) identified 11 strategies essential for effective interagency collaboration (see Table 2). Engaging in interagency collaboration has the potential for streamlining inclusive services and supports for children and youth with disabilities and their families (Ysseldyke & Algozzine, 2006).

Fiesta Educativa is an example of a community agency support provider working to build greater relationships with schools and districts. Fiesta Educativa works specifically with state regional centers, schools, and districts to provide assistance with much needed parent training. The organization coordinates annual conferences bringing together speakers with

Table 2.   Essential Strategies for Effective Interagency Collaboration.

Strategies	Description
Flexible scheduling and staffing	Transition coordinator given flexible schedule to collaborate with multiple agencies and families. Services are provided in flexible settings.
Follow-up after transition	Transition coordinators continue assisting families and students even after students exit secondary schooling.
Administrative support for transition	Administrator transition support to allow for flexible schedules, compensation time, paid summer training, and paying substitutes.
Using a variety of funding sources	Schools and districts share funds and resources with agencies.
State-supported technical assistance	States provide technical assistance to schools and districts.
Ability to build relationships	Schools and districts regularly work with high numbers of adult agencies and form relationships with staff.
Agency meetings with students and families	Transition coordinators meet with students, families, and agency representatives ongoing, and beyond the annual IEP.
Training students and families	Schools and districts provide ongoing training for students and families regarding employment opportunities, postsecondary education, and adult agency services.
Joint training of staff	Schools and districts provide joint training opportunities including school staff, family, and agency representatives. Trainings provide opportunities for ongoing relationship building.
Meetings with agency staff and transition councils	Meetings between schools with agency staff are scheduled regularly.
Dissemination of information to a broad audience	Schools provide information to families and students about agency services.

experience in a variety of areas to inform families about services, supports, research, and educational planning. When working directly with schools and districts, Fiesta Educativa provides the necessary curriculum and trainers while schools in turn provide on-site facilities and outreach to families.

Fiesta Educativa's Autism Parent Education Program (APEP) and Fiesta Familiar Program provide parent training on topics including autism, sexuality in adolescents, the difference between diagnosis and eligibility, maintaining records, and mental health and regional center services. Again, regardless of placement, access to on-site school trainings for these programs builds a level of convenience often preferred by families who often juggle between home, employment, therapies, and other various activities for their families. Participating schools in these programs often prefer for training to be conducted exclusively by agency trainers although involving school personnel is recommended in planning for and delivering training (Aceves & Higareda, 2014). Although trainings target families who have children with disabilities, the agency finds many attendees whose children do not qualify for or receive special education services (Aceves & Higareda, 2014; I. Martinez, personal communication, February 10, 2016).

During the 2011–2012 academic year, Fiesta Educativa collaborated with a large urban school district to implement a series of trainings within six school sites. The program involved two elementary schools, one middle school, two high schools, and one special education center. The organization conducted 36 training sessions for 190 parents during the course of the year. In an evaluation of Fiesta Educativa's parent training program, Aceves and Higareda (2014) made several recommendations to maximize community agency-school collaboration (see Table 3). These recommendations could enhance program implementation and better prepare schools to continue more hands-on support of and collaboration with families. Overall, the program allowed for parents to have access to much needed information regarding special education service delivery, methods to support their child at home, access community resources, and communicate with their child's school (Aceves, 2014). Families were incredibly grateful for the information and support the program offered, and the connection with other parent mentors, and the ready access to information in their preferred language.

Table 3. Strategies for Maximizing
Community Agency-School Collaboration.

Strategies	Description
Early planning and preparation	Conduct early joint planning sessions between organization and school site to individualize training topics according to school and family needs.
Content needs-assessment	Administer initial needs assessment with school site staff to identify relevant training topics and determine families' needs.
Co-facilitated training sessions	Design co-facilitated sessions between agency and school to show site representation and expertise and support ongoing parent education.
School site representation	Involve administrative and/or teaching staff during trainings in order to show support and be able to answer site-specific questions for families.

Much of Fiesta Educativa's work depends heavily on parent-to-parent support and mentoring. Parent-to-parent support has demonstrated success with facilitating successful parent outcomes (Shilling et al., 2013). Fiesta Familiar is an example of a parent-driven program conducted in a variety of settings including homes, churches, libraries, civic centers as well as schools within the community, covering topics suggested by parent partici- pants. The trainings are individualized to parents' needs and with the instruction and materials provided in their primary language. Through Fiesta Educativa's school-based training programs, parents learn from other mentor parents' experiences, expertise, challenges, and successes within the schools. The program also allows parents to connect with other parents who have children with similar needs.

A parent mentor who had worked with Fiesta Educativa for numerous years and had gone through their trainings explained how this support had helped her feel more empowered to advocate for her child who was fully included in general education. During a recent IEP meeting she described not being fearful of sharing her perspective or asking the team questions. The IEP was an annual meeting for her 15-year-old son with autism with plans of attending college.

> During the meeting I discussed my son's difficulty with organizing his work, turning in assignments, and having sufficient time to transition between his classes. He is failing three of his classes. My son and I explained to the team his need for additional help with prompting, organization, and transitioning between classes. In the end the team told me that they could not provide him with that level of assistance. In response, I asked the team to document in his IEP what they had just told me. Instead of using our time to talk through some solutions, someone from the team called the district office to check if they could include my comments and their response into my son's IEP document. (Fiesta Educativa, Parent Mentor)

Community parent-to-parent support and training provided this parent with the skills and knowledge necessary to communicate with the team regarding her son's needs. She understood her right to document decisions made by the school and questions asked by herself and her son during the IEP meeting. She also knew that her son had a right to specific services and accommodations to assist him with being successful in his general education classes given his IEP. The parent also knew the school had a responsibility to develop a solution to address her child's specific needs. This example clearly shows the benefits of seeking community training and support for this parent and her child with a disability. The scenario however, also shows the incred- ible effort parents must make in order to request expected services for inclusive placements to appropriately support students with disabilities.

More research is needed to determine how community organizations can create mutually beneficial relationships for school personnel as well as families in an effort to improve inclusive programming for students with disabilities.

CONCLUSION

The present chapter provided an overview regarding the benefits of community-based instruction for students with disabilities educated within inclusive K-12 settings and the importance of community organizations in assisting parents to obtain appropriate inclusive programming for their child with special needs. To further enhance learning opportunities for students with disabilities in inclusive settings, educational programs that include community-based experiences expose students early on to the expectations, benefits, and challenges of living as a member of a community (Andrews et al., 2015; Kim & Dymond, 2010). Special education programs and services can afford students with disabilities meaningful opportunities to acquire the knowledge and skills necessary to help them achieve successful community participation and satisfying postsecondary life experiences. Unfortunately, many families must actively advocate for such programming to truly realize the goal of inclusion and genuine community participation for their child with special needs. The chapter also emphasized the important role community organizations play in supporting families' efforts when advocating for inclusive placements for their child. Community organizations have the ability to provide assistance not always available within schools and districts to advocate for and ensure the quality of such placements.

Overall, it is clear that the collaborative work of schools, community organizations, and families and the resources and policies that support these efforts are essential to realize international and US goals for the full inclusion of individuals with disabilities in our communities. The United Nation's *Convention of the Rights of Persons with Disabilities* (2006) clearly articulated the importance of involving individuals with disabilities in all aspects of community living. Purposeful efforts must be made to ensure there are carefully planned and supported opportunities for this goal to be realized.

REFERENCES

About us. (2016, March 10). Retrieved from http://fiestaeducativa.org/about-us/
Aceves, T. C. (2014). Supporting Latino families in special education through community agency-school partnerships. *Multicultural Education, 21*(3), 45–50.

Aceves, T. C., & Chavez-Valdivia, S. (2016). *Learning rights law center: Beginning TIGER training evaluation*. Unpublished report.

Aceves, T. C., & Higareda, I. (2014). Community organizations supporting special education advocacy with diverse families. In L. Lo & D. Hiatt-Michael (Eds.), *Promising practices to empower culturally and linguistically diverse families of children with disabilities* (pp. 95–112). Scottsdale, AZ: Information Age, Inc.

Andrews, J., Falkmer, M., & Girdler, S. (2015). Community participation interventions for children and adolescents with a neurodevelopmental intellectual disability: A systematic review. *Disability & Rehabilitation, 37*(10), 825–833.

Becker, E., & Dusing, S. (2010). Participation is possible: A case report of integration into a community performing arts program. *Physiotherapy Theory and Practice, 26*(4), 275–280.

Burke, M. M. (2015). Parent advocacy for inclusive education in the United States. In R. G. Craven, A. J. S. Morin, D. Tracey, P. D. Parker, & H. F. Zhong (Eds.), *Inclusive education for students with intellectual disabilities* (pp. 231–248). Charlotte, NC: Information Age Publishing, Inc.

Carter, C., Meckes, L., Pritchard, L., Swensen, S., Wittman, P. P., & Velde, B. (2004). The friendship club: An after-school program for children with Asperger syndrome. *Family Community Health, 27*(2), 143–150.

Cosier, M., Causton-Theoharis, J., & Theoharis, G. (2013). Does access matter? Time in general education and achievement for students with disabilities. *Remedial and Special Education, 34*(6), 323–332.

Fennick, E., & Royle, J. (2003). Community inclusion for children and youth with developmental disabilities. *Focus Autism Other Developmental Disability, 18*, 20–27.

Gaumer, A. S., Morningstar, M. E., & Clark, G. M. (2004). Status of community-based transition programs: A national database. *Career Development for Exceptional Individual, 27*(2), 7–24.

Haring, T. G., & Breen, C. G. (1992). A peer-mediated social network intervention to enhance the social integration of persons with moderate and severe disabilities. *Journal of Applied Behavioral Analysis, 25*, 319–333.

Harry, B., & Klingner, J. (2014). *Why are there so many minority students in special education?* New York, NY: Teachers College Press.

Individuals with Disabilities Education Improvement Act of 2004. 20 U.S.C. §1400 et seq. (2004).

Kalyanpur, M., Harry, B., & Skrtic, T. (2000). Equity and advocacy expectations of culturally diverse families' participation in special education. *International Journal of Disability, Development and Education, 47*, 119–136.

Kasari, C., Rotheram-Fuller, E., & Locke, J. (2012). Making the connection: Randomized controlled trial of social skills at school for children with autism spectrum disorders. *Journal of Child Psychology and Psychiatry, 53*, 431–439.

Kim, R., & Dymond, S. K. (2010). Special education teachers' perceptions of benefits, barriers, and components of community-based vocational instruction. *Intellectual and Developmental Disabilities, 48*(5), 313–329.

Magaña, S., Lopez, K., Aguinaga, A., & Morton, H. (2013). Access to diagnosis and treatment services among Latino children with autism spectrum disorders. *Intellectual and Developmental Disabilities, 51*(3), 141–153.

Mission statement. (2016, March 10). Retrieved from http://www.learningrights.org/#!mission/c1pbe

Morningstar, M. E., Frey, B. B., Noonan, P. M., Ng, J., Clavenna-Deane, B., Graves, P., ... Williams-Diehm, K. (2010). A preliminary investigation of the relationship of transition preparation and self-determination for students with disabilities in postsecondary educational settings. *Career Development for Exceptional Individuals, 33*(2), 80–94.

Noonan, P. M., Gaumer Erickson, A., & Morningstar, M. E. (2013). Effects of community transition teams on interagency collaboration for school and adult agency staff. *Career Development and Transition for Exceptional Individuals, 36*(2), 96–104.

Noonan, P. M., Morningstar, M. E., & Gaumer Erickson, A. (2008). Improving interagency collaboration: Effective strategies used by high-performing local districts and communities. *Career Development for Exceptional Individuals, 31*, 132–143.

Repetto, J. B., Webb, K. W., Garvan, C. W., & Washington, T. (2002). Connecting student outcomes with transition practices in Florida. *Career Development for Exceptional Individuals, 25*, 123–139.

Reynolds, M. C., Gotto, G. S., Arnold, C., Boehm, T. L., Magaña, S., Dinora, P., ... Shaffert, R. (2015). National goals for supporting families across the life course. *Inclusion, 3*(4), 260–266.

Rojewski, J. W., Lee, H., & Gregg, N. (2013). Causal effects of inclusion on postsecondary education and work outcomes of individuals with high incidence disabilities. *Journal of Disability Policy Studies, 25*(4), 210–219. doi:10.1177/1044207313505648

Schleien, S. J., Krotee, M. L., Mustonen, T., Kelterborn, B., & Schermer, A. (1987). The effect of integrating children with autism into a physical activity and recreation setting. *Therapeutic Recreation Journal, 21*(4), 52–62.

Shilling, V., Morris, C., Thompson-Coon, J., Ukoumunne, O., Rogers, M., & Logan, S. (2013). Peer support for parents of children with chronic disabling conditions: A systematic review of quantitative and qualitative studies. *Developmental Medicine and Child Neurology, 55*(7), 602–609.

Shogren, K. A., Wehmeyer, M. L., Palmer, S. B., Rifenbark, G., & Little, T. D. (2015). Relationships between self-determination and postschool outcomes for youth with disabilities. *The Journal of Special Education, 48*(4), 256–267.

Siperstein, G. N., Glick, G. C., & Parker, R. C. (2009). Social inclusion of children with intellectual disabilities in a recreational setting. *American Association of Intellectual and Developmental Disabilities, 47*, 97–107.

The United Nations. (2006). *Final report of the ad hoc committee on a comprehensive and integral international convention on the protection and promotion of the rights and dignity of persons with disabilities.* Retrieved from http://www.un.org/esa/socdev/enable/rights/ahcfinalrepe.htm

Thoma, C. A., Cain, I., & Walther-Thomas, C. (2015). National goals for the education of children and youth with intellectual and developmental disabilities: Honoring the past while moving forward. *Inclusion, 3*(4), 219–226.

Turnbull, A. P., Turnbull, H. R., Erwin, E. J., Soodak, L. C., & Shogren, K. A. (2015). *Families, professionals, and exceptionality: Positive outcomes through partnerships and trust* (7th ed.). Upper Saddle River, NJ: Merrill/Prentice Hall.

Turnbull, A. P., Turnbull, H. R., & Kyzar, K. (2009). Family-professional partnerships as catalysts for successful inclusion: A United States of America perspective. Retrieved from http://www.revistaeducation.mec.es/re349/re349_04ing.pdf

Walker, A. R., Uphold, N. M., Richter, S., & Test, D. W. (2010). Review of the literature on community-based instruction across grade levels. *Education and Training in Autism and Developmental Disabilities, 45*(2), 242–267.

Ysseldyke, J. E., & Algozzine, B. (2006). *Working with families and community agencies to support students with special needs.* Thousand Oaks, CA: Corwin Press.

MEETING STUDENT NEEDS IN AN INCLUSIVE ENVIRONMENT: WAITING FOR THE CHANGE

Bob Algozzine, Kelly Anderson
and Cynthia Baughan

ABSTRACT

Educating students with disabilities in the same classrooms and instructional environments as their natural neighbors and peers (i.e., inclusion) is a promise of significant substance and value for many special educators. When federal legislation mandated that students with disabilities receive a free and appropriate education in least restrictive environments, at least in principle, the schoolhouse doors were opened for all *students. In this chapter, we provide a brief historical review of efforts to educate students with disabilities in inclusive environments and provide direction for what we believe are important practices for creating high-quality inclusive learning environments.*

Keywords: Inclusion; full inclusion; inclusive practices; effective instruction; general education

General and Special Education Inclusion in an Age of Change: Roles of Professionals Involved
Advances in Special Education, Volume 32, 119–136
ISSN: 0270-4013/doi:10.1108/S0270-401320160000032008

A BRIEF HISTORY OF EFFORTS AND FAILURE TO MEET STUDENT NEEDS IN INCLUSIVE ENVIRONMENTS

The inclusion of students with disabilities in general education classrooms with their typically developing peers would seem a relatively straightforward thing to do. The reality however, is that educating all children together in natural environments is and has historically been both a complex and contentious issue for decades. Undeniably, the Education of All Handicapped Children Act (P.L. 94-142) in 1975 and subsequent special education reform and legislation (now the Individuals with Disabilities Education Act, IDEA), opened the door to students with disabilities in terms of providing access to K-12 school environments. As a result of P.L. 94-142, special education evolved and quickly became a separate education system with specialized teacher preparation and credentials, evaluation teams, eligibility determination, categorical labeling, and placements (Connor & Ferri, 2007; Farrell, 2000; Fuchs & Fuchs, 1994; Wang, Reynolds, & Walberg, 1988).

Among the most highly debated provisions of P.L. 94-142 (IDEA) is the long-standing requirement mandating that education of students with disabilities occur in the least restrictive learning environment (LRE) (IDEA, 2004). The LRE provision has evoked extensive discourse in efforts to clarify its meaning for students with disabilities. Some professionals within the field of special education still contend that the division over the inclusion of students with disabilities remains strong today (Friend, 2005). On one side of the debate, professionals question the legitimacy of segregated placements of students with disabilities; doubting the necessity of a completely separate system to meet the academic and social needs of students with disabilities (Fuchs & Fuchs, 1994; Stainback & Stainback, 1984). From this perspective, inclusion of students with special needs is more concerned with the degree to which students with disabilities are actually being included and actively engaged in effective instruction as valued members of their classroom and school communities. Inclusion is not viewed solely as a place or physical placement of students with disabilities in general education settings for a limited portion of the school day primarily on the premise of social benefits. Instead, this perspective directs that students with disabilities are actively engaged in effective instruction with supports and services provided to them within their natural learning environments (Dunn, 1968; Lipsky & Gartner, 1997; Stainback & Stainback, 1984). Conversely, a more traditional special education perspective views the concept of inclusion as a dismantling of services and programs for students with disabilities, ultimately unraveling the spirit and intent behind the enactment of P.L. 94-142 (Connor & Ferri, 2007; Kauffman & Hallahan, 1995). This perception focuses on sustaining the "specialization" of special education arguing that LRE typically necessitates differential placements of students with disabilities for at least a portion of their school day (continuum of specialized settings such as resource and self-contained classrooms).

Since the groundbreaking P.L. 94-142 legislation over 40 years ago, most special educators generally agree that progress has indeed been made in eradicating historically detrimental perceptions related to the "limitations" of children with disabilities in terms of their abilities to learn in general education settings (Petch-Hogan, & Haggard, 1999). The essence of special education is the guarantee that students with disabilities have access to specialized services and individualized education. The paradox of special education as a delivery system of supports and services to students with disabilities however, exists when attempting to align the highly specialized supports and services while also honoring the mandate of access to the LRE (Connor & Ferri, 2007). This contradiction of requiring specialized and individualized education in the least restrictive environment (presumably the general education classroom) has led to varying interpretations and extreme differences in the implementation of inclusive practices for decades in the United States. In many ways, the disparity among these two perspectives continues to hinder further clarification and implementation of inclusive practices today by forcing "a choice" among high-quality and effective instruction and quality interaction and participation with peers in the general education environment (McLeskey, Waldron, Spooner, & Algozzine, 2014).

The basis for the majority of resistance among special education professionals toward the inclusion of students with special needs lies in an overall discontent and lack of trust with general education. An apparent absence of willingness and/or ability to accommodate students with disabilities by general education teachers and administrators has long been used as a rationale for the need for differential special education placements (Fuchs & Fuchs, 1994). For decades, research supported the notion that general education teachers lacked preparedness in teaching and responding to the needs of diverse students, particularly students with disabilities and cultural and linguistic differences (Ladson-Billings, 2000; NCES, 1999; Rushton, 2001). Even with reform efforts such as the Regular Education Initiative (REI) in the 1980s, the two education systems (general and special education) continued to run parallel, functioning primarily independent of one another (Fuchs & Fuchs, 1994). Pugach and Sapon-Shevin (1987) noted that despite efforts on the part of proponents of REI, general education took little notice of special education concerns at the time and the distinctly separate systems continued.

Within the last decade however, two powerful influences have dramatically altered the implementation of inclusive practices for all students (including students with disabilities) in K-12 schools across the United States. With the dramatic shift of diversity among K-12 students across the United States (e.g., socioeconomic status, ethnicity, and cultural and linguistic diversity) during the late 1990s early 2000s, general education began to develop increasing interest and *disability* became one of a multitude of "learner differences" in American classrooms. Today, English Language Learners (ELL) represent the largest and most rapidly growing K-12 student population in U.S. schools, with an increase of 57% from 1995 and 2005 as compared to a 2.6% increase in the general student population (Rueda & Stillman, 2012). In recent years, "[m]ore than 60 percent of students ages 6 through 21 served under IDEA, Part B, (62.1 percent) were educated inside the regular class 80% or more of the day" (U. S. Department of Education, 2015, p. 46). These numbers and conditions have resulted in the need for teachers to be highly knowledgeable and skilled in working with a vast range of students' cognitive and performance abilities, social and emotional needs, and cultural and linguistic differences (Brock, Case, & Taylor, 2013; DeLuca, 2012; O'Hara & Pritchard, 2008). The current wave of change prompting increased inclusive practices in schools was grounded in the reauthorizations of the No Child Left Behind Act (NCLB, 2002), the Individuals with Disabilities Education Act (IDEA, 2004), and the Every Student Succeeds Act (ESSA, 2015) having powerful influence on the way schools and teachers instruct and assess all students (including students with disabilities). The implications of amplified diversity of student populations in American schools and legislation mandating accountability of academic achievement of all students has resulted in significant increase of students with disabilities spending the majority of their school day in general education resulting in shared educational responsibility of general and special education teachers. Today, inclusive classroom configurations and practices are being implemented as a means of responding to added intense accountability and responsibility on teachers to produce clear evidence of the impact of their instruction on the academic progress of *all* K-12 students, including students with disabilities.

For purposes of our discussion on meeting the needs of students in inclusive learning environments, we have chosen to view the inclusiveness of the learning environment as congruent with the effectiveness of daily instruction. Implementation of inclusive classroom practices means students with disabilities are valued and engaged members of a universal community of learners, participating in the same academic, social, and extracurricular activities as their natural neighbors and peers. Three main assumptions underscore our discussion on meeting the needs of all learners through effective instructional practices: inclusive classroom practices benefit all students, not just those students with identified disabilities; educating all students is a collaborative responsibility among general and special education; and effective, responsive instruction coupled with personalized supports is critical toward achieving academic proficiency for all students, including students with disabilities (McLeskey et al., 2014). This is a global view that we believe underlies beliefs and efforts to provide and support free, appropriate education for all, not just some of the people who go to school.

A BRIEF PROPOSAL FOR HOW TO BETTER MEET STUDENT NEEDS IN INCLUSIVE ENVIRONMENTS

McLeskey, Rosenberg, and Westing (2010) describe inclusion not as a placement within the continuum of special education service delivery options, but as the idea that students with disabilities are valued members and active participants in the education community (as cited in McLeskey & Waldron, 2011). This philosophy of inclusion is echoed in the Division for Early Childhood/National Association for the Education of Young Children (DEC/NAEYC, 2009) and the U.S. Department of Health and Human Services/U.S. Department of Education (DHHS/DOE, 2015) joint position statements on early childhood inclusion as they describe the principles of access, participation, and support. The National Professional Development Center on Inclusion (National Professional Development Center on Inclusion [NPDCI], 2011) describes *access* as the removal of physical barriers, provision of a variety of learning opportunities and experiences, and making individualized adaptations as needed to promote learning; *participation* as using a variety of approaches that promote engagement and a sense of belonging; and *supports* as systems-level changes that ensure quality inclusion. These principles suggest that the intent of inclusion is to create environments that foster a sense of community by promoting meaningful and relevant participation and learning for *all* students. Key principles of access and participation and working together frame approaches for creating high-quality inclusive learning environments that support meeting all students' needs.

Access and Participation

The ecological perspective of inclusion focuses on the match between the needs of the student and the learning environment; a perspective that requires classroom and school personnel to be thoughtful, strategic, and reflective as they focus on how to intentionally prepare the environment to create an effective match for each student (Thompson, 2013). This process should begin by designing a learning environment that allows meaningful access to and participation in the general curriculum for all students, including students with disabilities.

Meaningful Access
To meet the true intent of inclusion, access to inclusive settings and the general curriculum must be meaningful and move beyond simply being present to being a part of everything that goes on in the general education setting. Two strategies identified by the National Professional Development Center on Inclusion (NPDCI, 2011) that can be used to promote meaningful access are Universal Design for Learning (UDL) and incorporating Assistive Technology (AT).

Universal Design for Learning. UDL is a framework to promote access to the learning environment for all students by removing physical and structural barriers and providing multiple means of participation (Jimenez, Graf, & Rose, 2007; National Center on Universal Design for Learning, 2011). UDL is a proactive approach intended to be part of the initial design of the environment and instructional lessons (Browder, Hudson, & Wood, 2014), and should provide all learners with opportunities for multiple and flexible means of representation, expression, and engagement (Rose & Meyer, 2002). UDL is "about the pedagogy ... used with students with and without disabilities," and may or may not include the use of technology (King-Sears, 2009, p. 199). Although UDL has received much attention in the discussion of meeting diverse student needs in the general education environment, as asserted by Edyburn (2010), and based on the literature review of Rao, Ok, and Bryant (2014), there is not a substantial amount of evidence that clearly links improved outcomes for students with disabilities and principles of UDL at this time. These authors provide guidance and suggestions for researchers to continue to build this research base.

Intentional efforts to incorporate UDL, such as those described in the Three-Block Model of UDL (Katz & Brownlie, 2010), however, appear to have the potential to not only increase academic engagement, but also social engagement, peer interactions, student autonomy, and inclusion in both elementary and secondary settings (Katz, 2013; Katz & Brownlie, 2010). King-Sears et al. (2015) also provide some evidence that secondary students with high-incidence disabilities performed better on a chemistry task when taught using principles of UDL than students with high-incidence disabilities who received traditional instruction on the task; interestingly, the same effects were not noted for students without disabilities. Additionally, Kortering, McClannon, and Braziel (2008) indicate secondary students with and without disabilities in content area classes view participation in instructional activities that incorporate principles of UDL favorably.

Recommendations in the literature also support incorporating principles of UDL with students with language and reading disabilities to remove curricular barriers and reduce limitations for them accessing and progressing in more complex content area subject matter (e.g., Meo, 2012; Messinger-Willman & Marino, 2010; Thomas, Van Garderen, Scheuermann, & Lee, 2015). Research on UDL has also emphasized the design of "customized scaffolded learning experiences" that incorporate technology with effective instructional practices and curricula (Coyne, Pisha, Dalton, Zeph, & Smith, 2012, p. 164); and, findings suggest that using technology within the UDL framework has been effective for diverse learners (Meyer & Rose, 2005; Rose & Meyer, 2002; Rose, Meyer, & Hitchcock, 2005), such as improving literacy in K-2 learners with significant intellectual disabilities (Coyne et al., 2012). These findings support the assertion of Hitchcock and Stahl (2003) that there is no single solution to providing necessary supports that ensure meaningful access for our diverse student population, and that UDL and AT will likely need to coexist within the classroom.

Assistive Technology. AT is "… any item, piece of equipment, or product system, whether acquired commercially or off the shelf, modified, or customized, that is used to increase, maintain, or improve functional capabilities of individuals with disabilities" (IDEA as cited in Hitchcock & Stahl, 2003, p. 47). Not only is AT clearly recommended in the literature, but it is also mandated in IDEA; IEP teams must consider AT for every student when developing individualized education programs (IEPs). Hitchcock and Stahl (2003) describe AT as "tools ... that enhance personal effectiveness" (p. 48). These tools can be simple (e.g., highlighters) or complex (e.g., voice output device), and should be chosen based on individual student strengths and needs to support students in overcoming limitations that may prevent access and participation in the general curriculum (Messinger-Willman & Marino, 2010), as well as to promote student success (Marino, Marino, & Shaw, 2006). Identifying and implementing individually appropriate AT supports requires knowledgeable and reflective IEP team members. Specifically, successful AT programs have been described as those that include preassessment and collaborative problem-solving (Marino et al., 2006), a process for integrating the AT into the learning context (Edyburn, 2000) and effective implementation (Marino et al.), and systematic evaluation (Marino et al.). Although technology has become a prominent feature in K-12 classrooms, it is unlikely that students with disabilities are benefitting from this technology to the fullest extent possible (Edyburn & Howery, 2014). Furthermore, there is a distinct need to advance the research base related to the effectiveness of technology (Edyburn, 2013) to support students with disabilities in inclusive settings.

Meaningful Participation and Engagement
Promoting participation and a sense of engagement in inclusive environments suggests the experiences of students with disabilities in inclusive settings should be meaningful and relevant, including students with moderate to severe disabilities. Hunt, McDonnell, and Crockett (2012) describe "personally relevant" access to the general curriculum under an ecological curricular framework in which quality of life learning goals are linked to the core curriculum. Trela and Jimenez (2013) further discuss "personally relevant access" as an approach that includes access to age-appropriate general curriculum as well as needed individual supports that creates a curriculum that is "differentiated not different" for students with severe disabilities (p. 117).

Routines-Based Instructional Planning. One model described in the literature for differentiating and planning meaningful participation in the general education curriculum is the Beyond Access Model that was initially used through the years 2002–2008 in 14 federally funded model demonstration schools in New Hampshire (Jorgensen & Lambert, 2012; Jorgensen, McSheehan, & Sonnenmeier, 2010). This approach incorporated a routines-based instructional planning process that includes three key elements: having high expectations for all students, planning for participation in typical instructional routines, and grounding the process in what students without disabilities are doing (Jorgensen & Lambert, 2012). Five questions are used to guide the planning process:

1. What is the general education instructional routine?
2. What are students without disabilities doing to participate in the instructional routine?
3. Can the student with the disability participate in the same way in all components of the instructional routine or does the student need an alternate way to participate?
4. What supports does the student need to participate using alternate means?
5. Who will prepare the supports? (Jorgensen & Lambert, 2012, p. 24).

Research regarding the impact of the Beyond Access Model is limited; however, reported benefits have included improvements in participation and outcomes for students with disabilities, improvements in efficiency and effectiveness of team members, and improvements in school—family partnerships (Jorgensen & Lambert, 2012; Sonnenmeier, McSheehan, & Jorgensen, 2005).

Multitiered System of Support. Another approach to designing effective instructional environments that promotes meaningful participation is the use of a multitiered system of support (MTSS). MTSS has been used to define differing levels of support to promote academic and behavioral progress (e.g., Response to Intervention: Hughes & Dexter, 2011), social-emotional development in young children (e.g., Teaching Pyramid Model: Fox, Dunlap, Hemmeter, Joseph, & Strain, 2003), and appropriate behaviors (e.g., Positive Behavior Support: Carr et al., 2002) for all students. MTSS is typically implemented to identify struggling students early and to provide the intensity of support needed to ensure student progress. Although there are multiple representations of MTSS, these supports are generally based on a multitiered continuum that provides varying levels of support, beginning with universal strategies used with all students and moving toward more intensive individualized interventions as needed. The foundation of MTSS is the broad base, or Tier One (Primary Intervention) that should include high-quality instruction and curricula, and incorporate the principles of UDL. This level of support should be designed to be effective with the majority of students, and provide meaningful access to the general education curriculum for all students. Student progress is regularly monitored and this information is used to determine what level of supports each student needs. MTSS is a promising approach to promote meaningful access and engagement while providing the least intrusive level of individualized support necessary to ensure progress in the general curriculum. For more extensive discussions of the use of MTSS in inclusive settings, see Batsche (2014), Cusumano, Algozzine, and Algozzine (2014), and Johnson and Mellard (2014).

Classroom-Based Interventions. Within MTSS models, classroom-based interventions are used with students who require more intensive targeted group supports (Tier Two, Secondary Intervention) or intensive individualized interventions (Tier Three, Tertiary Intervention) to access and make progress in the general curriculum. Identifying appropriate classroom-based interventions typically requires the efforts of collaborative teams. (See discussion on Problem-Solving Teams below.) Collaborative teams can be used to identify appropriate supports and to assist general education teachers in effectively implementing supports in the inclusive setting (Bahr & Kovaleski, 2006; Bahr et al., 2006; McLeskey & Waldron, 2006; McLeskey et al., 2014; Waldron, McLeskey, & Redd, 2011; Williamson & McLeskey, 2011). There are a wide variety of classroom-based strategies and interventions that have been found to be effective in supporting students with disabilities in inclusive settings. For an in-depth review of evidence-based intensive and individualized interventions that can support meaningful participation and progress in inclusive environments for students with disabilities, see other chapters in *General and Special Education Inclusion in an Age of Change*.

Working Together

Creating an appropriate learning environment that matches each student and supports meaningful access to and participation in the general curriculum often requires the work of collaborative teams. One type of collaborative teaming that has been used to support the development of effective inclusive environments is problem-solving teams (Bahr & Kovaleski, 2006; Bahr et al., 2006; McLeskey & Waldron, 2006; Waldron et al., 2011; Williamson & McLeskey, 2011). Problem-solving teams can be an effective source of support for general education teachers addressing student academic and behavioral challenges.

Problem-Solving Teams
Problem-solving teams work together to analyze and define a problem, identify and support the implementation of appropriate interventions to

address the problem, and monitor the effectiveness of the intervention and student progress (Bahr & Kovaleski, 2006). Participating in problem-solving teams has resulted in general education teachers feeling supported, learning new strategies, and increasing in reflective and improved practice (Williamson & McLeskey, 2011), potentially building the capacity of general education teachers to address the individual needs of students with disabilities within inclusive settings. Improved academic and behavioral student outcomes have also been linked to the team problem-solving process (e.g., Ruble, Dalrymple, & McGrew, 2010; Thompson, 2013; Todd et al., 2011, 2012; Williamson & McLeskey, 2011).

Team-Initiated Problem-Solving
Team-Initiated Problem-Solving (TIPS; Newton et al., 2014) is a model that has been developed to increase the efficiency and effectiveness of Positive Behavior Intervention and Support (PBIS) Teams (Newton et al., 2014). TIPS specifically focuses on the appropriate use of data to guide decision making during the problem-solving process. Newton et al. (2014) describe the components of the TIPS model as:

- *Identify problem with precision, and with a defined goal;*
- *Discuss and select solution (actions) to achieve the goal;*
- *Develop and implement action plan; and*
- *Evaluate progress and status of problem and revise action plan as necessary* (p. 282).

Team members receive training in the TIPS model, as well as technical assistance and environmental supports. (More specific descriptions of these features can be found in Newton et al., 2014.) Research findings indicate that, following TIPS training and supports, PBIS teams can become more effective and exercise fidelity in data-based problem-solving (Newton, Algozzine, Algozzine, Horner, & Todd, 2011; Newton, Horner, Algozzine, Todd, & Algozzine, 2012; Todd et al., 2011, 2012).

Collaborative Consultation
Another approach to team problem-solving is collaborative consultation (Ruble et al., 2010; Thompson, 2013). Collaborative consultation can involve the support of special educators (e.g., Thompson, 2013) or other trained specialists (e.g., Ruble et al., 2010) who work directly with the general education classroom teacher to develop effective inclusive environments. Zins and Erchul (2002) describe the goal of collaborative consultation as one of building capacity; specifically, addressing problems through teaching, role

sharing, and empowerment so that general education teachers are prepared to effectively address similar challenges in the future. Collaborative consultation should lead to more reflective practitioners who are able to evaluate the classroom environment and practices and make adjustment as needed to promote positive student outcomes (Thompson, 2013).

Collaborative consultation can also include a coaching component to support general education teachers who are implementing interventions with student with disabilities. For example, the Collaborative Model for Promoting Competence and Success (COMPASS) was designed to use consultation to develop program plans to address individual student needs for environmental supports and interventions, and then coaching to support teachers in the implementation of the interventions and supports (Ruble et al., 2010).

Research findings indicate that teachers have generally reported satisfaction and acceptance of the support and guidance they received through collaborative consultation (Ruble et al., 2010; Thompson, 2013). Additionally, teachers reported that the changes made to the learning environment and in-class supports resulted in maintaining the inclusive environment for the target child, as well as resulting in additional benefits for the whole class (Thompson, 2013).

Make it Happen

Effective inclusion begins with the assumption that *all* students are valued members of the education community; an assumption that should naturally lead to practices that ensure meaningful access to, participation in, and progress in the general curriculum for *all* students. Moving this philosophical assumption to a reality for our students with disabilities, however, requires a commitment to creating the optimal match between the needs of each student and the supports provided in the learning environment. Creating this match must be an intentional process; a process that involves knowledgeable, thoughtful, strategic, and reflective personnel and teams at the classroom, school, and systems levels.

A BRIEF STATEMENT OF HOPE

We believe there really is no reason to separate people to provide a free, appropriate education to them. Good teaching is good teaching and there are no boundaries on where it will occur or who will profit from it. Instruction that is good for any person should be provided to all people.

We also believe it is wrong to separate people to provide care for them. We accept that there were times when society said there was no other way. We accept that there are people today who disagree with us. Accepting that the past is the past and what made sense to many then may only make sense to a few now. Accepting the views and promises consistently put forward in federal legislation, we believe that focusing on access and participation that is intentional and meaningful and on effective problem-solving to drive instruction that is meaningful and intentional, may be all that it takes to bring about the change of all children learning in any educational environment.

Federal law mandates that students with disabilities have access to and make progress in the general curriculum (Individuals with Disabilities Education Improvement Act; IDEA, 2004). To some, the increasing number of students with disabilities being served in the general education classroom (cf. U. S. Department of Education, 1995, 2005, 2011, 2014, 2015) suggests there is an increase in inclusion; however, simply providing a full- or part-time placement in the general education classroom does not guarantee that students with disabilities are accessing, participating, or making progress in the general curriculum. In fact, research indicates the education setting, in and of itself, does not ensure the use of effective instructional practices that can result in improved outcomes for students with disabilities (McLeskey & Waldron, 2011), or, as required under IDEA, guarantee progress in the general curriculum (Cook, 2002; McCart, Sailor, Bezdek, & Satter, 2014; McLeskey et al., 2010, 2014; Sailor & McCart, 2014; Sailor & Roger, 2005; Shogren, McCart, Lyon, & Sailor, 2015).

Any children failing to profit from the educational menu of experiences provided in schools is wrong. Education should be special for everyone and schools should serve all who go there. Doing less is wrong. Inclusion or providing educational opportunities for all students alongside their natural neighbors and peers remains a highly valued goal for us. Ensuring that effective education practices available and provided to any students are available and provided to all students and that no cultural, ethnic, or other groups are disproportionately placed in ineffective education settings remains an equally important quest. Waiting for the change: Our long and often disappointing search for inclusion continues undaunted by the challenge it has become or the context in which it is unfolding.

REFERENCES

Bahr, M. W., & Kovaleski, J. F. (2006). The need for problem-solving teams: Introduction to the special issue. *Remedial and Special Education, 27*, 2–5.

Bahr, M. W., Walker, K., Hampton, E. M., Buddle, B. S., Freeman, T., Ruschman, N., … Littlejohn, W. (2006). Creative problem solving for general education intervention teams: A two-year evaluation study. *Remedial and Special Education, 27*, 27–41.

Batsche, G. (2014). Multi-tiered system of supports for inclusive schools. In J. McLeskey, N. L. Waldron, F. Spooner, & B. Algozzine (Eds.), *Handbook of effective inclusive schools: Research and practice* (pp. 183–196). New York, NY: Routledge.

Brock, C. H., Case, R., & Taylor, S. S. (2013). Dilemmas in guiding pre-service teachers to explore literacy instruction and diversity. *Teacher Education Quarterly, 40*(1), 81–100.

Browder, D. M., Hudson, M. E., & Wood, L. (2014). Using principles of high quality instruction in the general education classroom to provide access to the general education curriculum. In J. McLeskey, N. L. Waldron, F. Spooner, & B. Algozzine (Eds.), *Handbook of effective inclusive schools: Research and practice* (pp. 339–351). New York, NY: Routledge.

Carr, E. G., Dunlap, G., Horner, R. H., Koegel, R. L., Turnbull, A. P., Sailor, W., Anderson, J. L., … Fox, L. (2002). Positive behavior support: Evolution of an applied science. *Journal of Positive Behavior Interventions, 4*, 4–20.

Connor, D. J., & Ferri, B. A. (2007). The conflict within: Resistance to inclusion and other paradoxes in special education. *Disability & Society, 22*, 63–77.

Cook, M. A. (2002). Outcomes: Where are we now? The efficacy of differential placement and the effectiveness of current practices. *Preventing School Failure, 46*(2), 54–56.

Coyne, P., Pisha, B., Dalton, B., Zeph, L. A., & Smith, N. C. (2012). Literacy by design: A universal design for learning approach for students with significant intellectual disabilities. *Remedial and Special Education, 33*, 162–172.

Cusumano, D. L., Algozzine, K., & Algozzine, B. (2014). Multi-tiered system of supports for effective inclusion in elementary schools. In J. McLeskey, N. L. Waldron, F. Spooner, & B. Algozzine (Eds.), *Handbook of effective inclusive schools: Research and practice* (pp. 197–209). New York, NY: Routledge.

DEC/NAEYC. (2009). *Early childhood inclusion: A joint position statement of the Division for Early Childhood (DEC) and the National Association for the education of young children (NAEYC)*. Chapel Hill, NC: The University of North Carolina, FPG Child Development Institute.

DeLuca, C. (2012). Selecting inclusive teacher candidates: Validity and reliability issues in admission policy and practice. *Teacher Education Quarterly, 39*(4), 7–31.

Dunn, L. M. (1968). Special education for the mildly retarded – Is much of it justifiable? *Exceptional Children, 23*, 5–22.

Education of All Handicapped Children Act. (P.L. 94-142), U.S.C. § 20 Sec. 1400(d) (1975).

Edyburn, D. (2010). Would you recognize universal design for learning if you saw it? Ten propositions for new directions for the second decade of UDL. *Learning Disabilities Quarterly, 33*, 33–41.

Edyburn, D. (2013). Critical issues in advancing the special education technology evidence base. *Exceptional Children, 80*, 7–24.

Edyburn, D., & Howery, K. (2014). How is technology used to support instruction in inclusive schools? In J. McLeskey, N. L. Waldron, F. Spooner, & B. Algozzine (Eds.), *Handbook* of effective inclusive schools: Research and practice (pp. 167–180). New York, NY: Routledge.

Edyburn, D. L. (2000). Assistive technology and students with mild disabilities. *Focus on Exceptional Children, 32,* 1–23.

Every Student Succeeds Act of 2015. (2015, December 10). Retrieved from http://www.ed.gov/ESSA

Farrell, P. (2000). The impact of research on developments in inclusive education. *International Journal of Inclusive Education, 4,* 153–162. doi:10.1080/136031100284867

Fox, L., Dunlap, G., Hemmeter, M. L., Joseph, G., & Strain, P. (2003). The teaching pyramid: A model for supporting social competence and preventing challenging behavior in young children. *Young Children, 58*(4), 48–53.

Friend, M. (2005). *Special education: Contemporary perspectives for school professionals.* Boston, MA: Allyn & Bacon.

Fuchs, D., & Fuchs, L. S. (1994). Inclusive schools movement and the radicalization of special education reform. *Exceptional Children, 60,* 294–309.

Hitchcock, C., & Stahl, S. (2003). Assistive technology, universal design, universal design for learning: Improved learning outcomes. *Journal of Special Education Technology, 18,* 45–54.

Hughes, C. A., & Dexter, D. D. (2011). Response to intervention: A research-based summary. *Theory into Practice, 50,* 4–11.

Hunt, P., McDonnell, J., & Crockett, M. A. (2012). Reconciling an ecological curricular framework focusing on quality of life outcomes with the development and instruction of standards-based academic goals. *Research & Practice for Persons with Severe Disabilities, 37,* 139–152.

Individuals with Disabilities Education Improvement Act of 2004 (IDEA). Pub.L.No.108-446, 118 Stat. 2647 (2004). [Amending 20 U.S.C. § § 1400 et seq.].

Jimenez, T. C., Graf, V. L., & Rose, E. (2007). Gaining access to general education: The promise of universal design for learning. *Issues in Teacher Education, 16,* 41–54.

Johnson, E. S., & Mellard, D. F. (2014). Multi-tiered system of supports for effective inclusion in secondary schools. In J. McLeskey, N. L. Waldron, F. Spooner, & B. Algozzine (Eds.), *Handbook of effective inclusive schools: Research and practice* (pp. 210–228). New York, NY: Routledge.

Jorgensen, C. M., & Lambert, L. (2012). Inclusion means more than just being "in:" Planning full participation of students with intellectual and other developmental disabilities in the general education classroom. *International Journal of Whole Schooling, 8*(2), 21–36.

Jorgensen, C. M., McSheehan, M., & Sonnenmeier, R. M. (2010). *The beyond access model: Promoting membership participation, and learning for students with disabilities in the general education classroom.* Baltimore, MD: Paul H. Brookes Publishing Co.

Katz, J. (2013). The three-block model of universal design for learning (UDL): Engaging students in inclusive education. *Canadian Journal of Education, 36,* 153–194.

Katz, J., & Brownlie, F. (2010). *Teaching to diversity: The three-block model of universal design for learning.* Winnipeg: Portage and Main Press.

Kauffman, J. M., & Hallahan, D. P. (1995). *The illusion of full inclusion.* Austin, TX: Pro-Ed.

King-Sears, M. (2009). Universal design for learning: Technology and pedagogy. *Learning Disabilities Quarterly, 32,* 199–201.

King-Sears, M. E., Johnson, T. M., Berkeley, S., Weiss, M. P., Peters-Burton, E. E., Evmenova, ... Hursh, J. C. (2015). An exploratory study of universal design for teaching chemistry to students with and without disabilities. *Learning Disability Quarterly, 38*, 84–96.

Kortering, L. J., McClannon, T. W., & Braziel, P. M. (2008). Universal design for learning: A look at what algebra and biology students with and without high incidence conditions are saying. *Remedial and Special Education, 29*, 352–363.

Ladson-Billings, G. (2000). Fighting for our lives: Preparing teachers to teach African American students. *Journal of Teacher Education, 51*, 206–214.

Lipsky, D. K., & Gartner, A. (1997). *Inclusion and school reform: Transforming America's classrooms*. Baltimore, MD: Brooks Publishing.

Marino, M. T., Marino, E. C., & Shaw, S. F. (2006). Technology decisions for students with high incidence disabilities. *Teaching Exceptional Children, 36*, 18–25.

McCart, A., Sailor, W., Bezdek, J., & Satter, A. (2014). A framework for inclusive educational delivery systems. *Inclusion, 2*, 252–264. doi:10.1352/2326-6988-2.4.252

McLeskey, J., Rosenberg, M., & Westing, D. (2010). *Inclusion: Effective practices for all students*. Upper Saddle River, NJ: Prentice Hall.

McLeskey, J., & Waldron, N. (2006). Comprehensive school reform and inclusive schools. *Theory & Practice, 45*, 269–278. doi 10.1207/s15430421tip4503_9

McLeskey, J., & Waldron, N. (2011). Education programs for elementary students with learning disabilities: Can they be both effective and inclusive? *Learning Disabilities Research & Practice, 26*, 48–57.

McLeskey, J., Waldron, N. L., Spooner, F., & Algozzine, B. (2014). *Handbook of research and practice for inclusive schools*. New York, NY: Routledge.

Meo, G. (2012). Curriculum planning for all learners: Applying universal design for learning (UDL) to a high school reading comprehension program. *Preventing School Failure, 52*(2), 21–30.

Messinger-Willman, J., & Marino, M. T. (2010). Universal design for learning and assistive technology: Leadership considerations for promoting inclusive education in today's secondary schools. *NASSP Bulletin, 94*, 5–16.

Meyer, A., & Rose, D. H. (2005). The future is in the margins: The role of technology and disability in education reform. In D. H. Rose, A. Meyer, & C. Hitchcock (Eds.), *The universally designed classroom: Accessible curriculum and digital technologies* (pp. 13–35). Cambridge, MA: Harvard Education Press.

National Center for Education Statistics [NCES] (1999). *The condition of education, 1999*. Washington, DC: Institute of Education Sciences. Retrieved from http://nces.ed.gov/pubsearch/pubsinfo.asp?pubid = 1999022

National Center on Universal Design for Learning. (2011). *UDL guidelines – Version 2.0: Research evidence*. Retrieved from http://www.udlcenter.org/research/researchevidence

National Professional Development Center on Inclusion (2011). *Research synthesis points on practices that support inclusion*. Chapel Hill, NC: The University of North Carolina, FPG Child Development Institute, Author. Retrieved from http://npdci.fpg.unc.edu

Newton, J. S., Algozzine, B., Algozzine, K., Horner, R. H., & Todd, A. W. (2011). Building local capacity for training and coaching data-based problem solving with positive behavior intervention and support teams. *Journal of Applied School Psychology, 27*, 228–245.

Newton, J. S., Horner, R. H., Algozzine, B., Todd, A. W., & Algozzine, K. (2012). A randomized wait-list controlled analysis of the implementation integrity of team-initiated problem solving process. *Journal of School Psychology, 50*, 421–441.

Newton, J. S., Todd, A. W., Algozzine, B., Algozzine, K., Horner, R. H., & Cusumano, D. L. (2014). Supporting team problem solving in inclusive schools. In J. McLeskey, N. L. Waldron, F. Spooner, & B. Algozzine (Eds.), *Handbook of effective inclusive schools: Research and practice* (pp. 275–289). New York, NY: Routledge.

No Child Left Behind Act of 2001. 22 U.S.C. § 9101 (2002).

O'Hara, S., & Pritchard, R. H. (2008). Meeting the challenge of diversity: Professional development for teacher educators. *Teacher Education Quarterly, 35*(1), 43–61.

Petch-Hogan, B., & Haggard, D. (1999). The inclusion debate continues. *Kappa Delta Pi Record, 35,* 128–131.

Pugach, M., & Sapon-Shevin, M. (1987). New agendas for special education policy: What the national reports haven't said. *Exceptional Children, 53,* 295–299.

Rao, K., Ok, M. W., & Bryant, B. R. (2014). A review of research on universal design educational models. *Remedial and Special Education, 35,* 153–166.

Rose, D., & Meyer, A. (2002). *Teaching every student in the digital age: Universal design for learning.* Alexandria, VA: ASCD.

Rose, D., Meyer, A., & Hitchcock, C. (2005). *The universally designed classroom: Accessible curriculum and digital technologies.* Cambridge, MA: Harvard Education Press.

Ruble, L. A., Dalrymple, N. J., & McGrew, J. H. (2010). The effects of consultation on individualized education program outcomes for young children with autism: The collaborative model for promoting competence and success. *Journal of Early Intervention, 32,* 286–301.

Rueda, R., & Stillman, J. (2012). The 21st century teacher: A cultural perspective. *Journal of Teacher Education, 63,* 245–253.

Rushton, S. (2001). Applying brain research to create developmentally appropriate learning environments. *Young Children, 56*(5), 76–82.

Sailor, W., & McCart, A. (2014). Stars in alignment. *Research and Practice for Persons with Severe Disabilities, 39*(1), 55–64.

Sailor, W., & Roger, B. (2005). Rethinking inclusion: Schoolwide applications. *Phi Delta Kappan, 86,* 503–509.

Shogren, K. A., McCart, A. B., Lyon, K. J., & Sailor, W. S. (2015). All means all: Building knowledge for inclusive schoolwide transformation. *Research and Practice for Persons with Severe Disabilities, 40,* 173–191. doi:10.1177/1540796915586191

Sonnenmeier, R. M., McSheehan, M., & Jorgensen, C. M. (2005). A case study of team supports for a student with autism's communication and engagement within the general education curriculum: Preliminary report of the beyond access model. *Augmentative and Alternative Communication, 21,* 101–115.

Stainback, W., & Stainback, S. (1984). A rationale for the merger of special and regular education. *Exceptional Children, 51,* 102–111.

Thomas, C. N., Van Garderen, D., Scheuermann, A., & Lee, E. J. (2015). Applying a universal design for learning framework to mediate the language demands of mathematics. *Reading and Writing Quarterly, 31,* 207–234.

Thompson, C. (2013). Collaborative consultation to promote inclusion: Voices from the classroom. *International Journal of Inclusive Education, 17,* 882–894. doi 10.1080/13603116.2011.602535

Todd, A. W., Horner, R. H., Berry, D., Sanders, C., Bugni, M., Currier, A., ... Algozzine, K. (2012). A case study of team-initiated problem solving addressing student behavior in one elementary school. *Journal of Special Education Leadership, 25,* 81–89.

Todd, A. W., Horner, R. H., Newton, J. S., Algozzine, R. F., Algozzine, K. M., & Frank, J. L. (2011). Effects of team-initiated problem solving on decision making by school-wide behavior support teams. *Journal of Applied School Psychology*, *27*, 42–59.

Trela, K., & Jimenez, B. A. (2013). From different to differentiated: Using "ecological framework" to support personally relevant access to general curriculum for students with significant intellectual disabilities. *Research and Practice for Persons with Severe Disabilities*, *38*, 117–119.

U.S. Department of Education. (1995). *Seventeenth annual report to congress on the implementation of the individuals with disabilities education act*. Washington, DC: Author. Retrieved from http://www2.ed.gov/pubs/OSEP95AnlRpt/index.html

U.S. Department of Education. (2005). *Twenty-seventh annual report to congress on the implementation of the individuals with disabilities education act*. Washington, DC: Author. Retrieved from http://www2.ed.gov/about/reports/annual/osep/2005/parts-b-c/index.html

U.S. Department of Education. (2011). *30th annual report to congress on the implementation of the individual with disabilities education act, 2008*. Washington, DC: Office of Special Education and Rehabilitation Services, Office of Special Education Programs. Retrieved from http://www2.ed.gov/about/reports/annual/osep/2008/parts-b-c/30th-idea-arc.pdf

U.S. Department of Education. (2014). *Thirty-sixth annual report to congress on the implementation of the individuals with disabilities education act*. Washington, DC: Author. Retrieved from http://www2.ed.gov/about/reports/annual/osep/2014/parts-b-c/index.html

U.S. Department of Education. (2015). *Thirty-seventh annual report to congress on the implementation of the individuals with disabilities education act*. Washington, DC: Author. Retrieved from http://www2.ed.gov/about/reports/annual/osep/2015/parts-b-c/37th-arc-for-idea.pdf

U.S. Department of Health and Human Services & U.S. Department of Education. (2015). *Policy statement on inclusion of children with disabilities in early childhood programs*. Retrieved from http://www2.ed.gov/policy/speced/guid/earlylearning/joint-statement-full-text.pdf

Waldron, N. L., McLeskey, J., & Redd, L. (2011). Setting the direction: The role of the principal in developing an effective inclusive school. *Journal of Special Education Leadership*, *24*, 51–60.

Wang, M. C., Reynolds, M. C., & Walberg, H. J. (1988). Integrating the children of the second system. *Phi Delta Kappan*, *70*, 248–251.

Williamson, P., & McLeskey, J. (2011). An investigation into the nature of inclusion problem-solving teams. *The Teacher Educator*, *46*, 316–334.

Zins, J. E., & Erchul, W. P. (2002). Best practices in school consultation. In A. Thomas & J. Grimes (Eds.), *Best practices in school psychology* (4th ed., pp. 625–643). Bethesda, MD: The National Association of School Psychologists.

ACADEMICS AND THE CURRICULUM IN INCLUSIVE CLASSROOMS: AN EXAMPLE OF HISTORICAL THINKING

Margaret P. Weiss and Anthony Pellegrino

ABSTRACT

Both broad and discipline-specific curriculum standards have shifted from a focus on learning discrete content material to a broader understanding of the processes used by disciplinary experts. Using the example of historical thinking in history/social studies, we discuss how this shift may impact students with disabilities and their participation in the general education curriculum and classroom. Specific examples of what close reading and sourcing look like in the classroom and how researchers in special education have addressed them are provided. We conclude with how this shift in thinking about process over the regurgitation of facts may be both advantageous and overwhelming to students with disabilities and their teachers.

Keywords: Historical reasoning; disciplinary literacy; students with disabilities

General and Special Education Inclusion in an Age of Change: Roles of Professionals Involved
Advances in Special Education, Volume 32, 137–152
Copyright © 2016 by Emerald Group Publishing Limited
ISSN: 0270-4013/doi:10.1108/S0270-4013201600000320009

Changes in legislation in the last 10−15 years have placed more and more students with disabilities in the general education curriculum and in the general education classroom. In 1988−1989, for example, approximately 30% of students with disabilities spent more than 80% of their time in general education classrooms and, by 2013, 61% did (American Youth Policy Forum, 2002; U. S. Department of Education, 2013). This increase in participation comes at a time when there has been a broad shift in focus of the curriculum from accumulation of knowledge, as in memorizing facts and procedures, to the integration of knowledge with the application and use of skills necessary for higher order thinking. In history, for example, these changes are evident in the ways teachers challenge students to think historically by employing skills to analyze and interpret historical evidence rather than recall names and dates of the past as a measure of learning. Given the characteristics of students with disabilities who have difficulty with these skills, particularly those with learning disabilities (LD), changes in instruction and learning expectations to develop them may have an impact on how, when, and if they can successfully participate in general education classrooms (Bulgren, Graner, & Deshler, 2013). It is critical that special educators understand these changes so that they can effectively integrate their expertise in evidence-based practices, task analysis, and student characteristics into the instruction their students receive. In that context, the purpose of this chapter is to describe these broad curricular changes and what they mean for students with disabilities, using the example of social studies and learning opportunities created through evidence-based practices associated with historical thinking.

CONCEPTUAL CHANGE IN CURRICULUM

The conceptual shift in curriculum can be seen both in broad curriculum standards and within individual disciplines. For example, though much controversy surrounds them, the Common Core State Standards have been adopted by 42 states across the country (Common Core State Standards Initiative, 2016). Developers state that the key shifts for English Language Arts standards include using complex texts, academic language, evidence from texts, and content-rich nonfiction (Common Core State Standards Initiative, 2016, Key Shifts in English Language Arts). These are mirrored in shifts in Common Core mathematics standards, described as developing conceptual understanding, procedural skills, and the ability to apply both.

The Common Core Standards focus on developing the critical-thinking, problem-solving, and analytical skills students will need to be successful (Common Core State Standards Initiative, 2016, Key Shifts in Mathematics).

In addition to the broad standards included in the Common Core, several discipline-specific groups have also shifted their focus. For example, the Next Generation Science standards tout a focus on a deep understanding of content and the application of that content (Next Generation Science Standards, 2012). The National Council for the Social Studies states, "civic competence ... requires that citizens have the ability to use their knowledge about their community, nation, and world; to apply inquiry processes; and to employ skills of data collection and analysis, collaboration, decision-making, and problem-solving" (National Council for the Social Studies, n.d., para 1). Advocates emphasize that this focus on integration and application is necessary for today's changing world and that instruction to achieve these standards will prepare students to be college and career ready (U.S. Department of Education, n.d.). Though each state defines college and career ready in a slightly different way, most include academic knowledge; critical thinking and/or problem solving; and social emotional learning, collaboration, and/or communication (American Institutes for Research, 2014). Citing discouraging results from the NAEP and comparisons on international standardized tests, leaders insist these revised standards and focus will lead to desired instructional reform (U.S. Department of Education, 2009).

WHAT DOES THIS MEAN FOR THE CLASSROOM?

The emphasis on building broader conceptual knowledge within a discipline requires the development and refinement of the reading and writing skills used by experts. Social studies educator and researcher Monte-Sano (2010) asserted that "ways of thinking and reasoning associated with a particular discipline are embedded in subject-specific texts and tasks and must be attended to if we as educators are to help ...." (p. 540). This discipline literacy begins with representation or understanding of a task, such as developing an argument, and extends to the appropriate use of sources, language, and format in communicating ideas. It is the task of developing naïve learners into individuals who independently use some form of the same skills and processes that experts do. To get students there, instruction must be reoriented from the traditional paradigm where teachers give students information and students parrot it back in similar form.

The use of a cognitive apprenticeship model is one way instruction might be different in a classroom organized to develop disciplinary literacy. Several researchers (e.g., Brown, Collins, & Duguid, 1989; Englert, Berry, & Dunsmore, 2001; Tisdale, 2001) have written about the concept of cognitive apprenticeship in which knowledgeable individuals (teachers) scaffold novices (students) through learning experiences that help them acquire the tools necessary for use in the discipline. In a cognitive apprenticeship in any discipline, teachers provide students with instruction and then model completion of tasks so that students understand their expectations. Then, students practice those skills and processes on increasingly challenging but authentic tasks with robust feedback and further practice opportunities. To be successful, cognitive apprenticeships "require access to the discourse or language of the discipline, mediational tools of the discipline, and a supported context that included appropriate scaffolding" (Bouck, Okolo, Englert, & Heutsche, 2008, p. 22). Current practices in the social studies provide an example of the development of discipline literacy through a cognitive apprenticeship model.

History Education Practices

Evidence-based practices in history/social studies education have evolved beyond asking students to merely memorize names and dates of the past. Along with attention to experiences of less included individuals, groups, and events, the way we approach teaching history has transformed to include disciplinary strategies that emphasize skills which enable students to acquire the means to interpret historical evidence and determine historical significance based on analysis of resources.

Perhaps the most significant part of the changes in history pedagogy originated decades ago from those who investigated how cognitive psychology might provide explanations of how students develop conceptual understanding, generalizations, and mental models in history (e.g., Wineburg, 2001; Zaccaria, 1978). Historical content, which includes the study of abstract concepts, remote cultures, and a time far different from our own, requires students to learn and develop ways of knowing regarding values, beliefs, perspectives, and experiences. These ways of knowing rely on application of skills to: (a) source documents, (b) look for corroborative and contradictory evidence, and (c) assess accuracy and reliability of that evidence (Wineburg, 1997). To that end, scholars have advocated for history teachers to teach skills-based practices that facilitate students' ability to think historically (Barton, 2011; Wineburg, 1997). Developing these skills allows students to analyze sources, consider the context of the topic under study, and ultimately make historical claims (teachinghistory.org, 2013). Incorporating both the learning and thinking skills associated with the ways in which historians study the past has become the essence of historical thinking. Efforts to get students to think historically are facilitated through practice opportunities structured with a combination of resources and questions that challenge students to grapple with historical evidence. The level of structure embedded in lessons to foster historical thinking allows students of varying abilities to achieve a deeper understanding of history, beyond only names and dates, to find relevance in the ways people have lived, the choices they have made and how those impact our lives today.

To harness the close coupling of knowledge and skills critical to meaningful learning in history, practice opportunities in certain skills are valuable. Skills to think historically, for example, begin with those elemental to understanding text. And texts used in classrooms where students are taught to think historically are not often a traditional textbook. Instead, teachers find more value in challenging students to work with primary sources including original texts, images, and other artifacts. Beginning with original sources allows students to learn analysis and interpretation skills that bring them closer to the past as it happened, but requires specific skills including close reading and sourcing that lead to a deeper sense of the significance of learning about the past.

READING AS FOUNDATIONAL FOR
HISTORICAL THINKING

In the act of thinking historically, applying reasoning strategies while reading to determine explicit and implicit meaning and evaluating bias and perspective are fundamental and come from practice opportunities using historical resources. Barksdale (2013) explained how we can "zoom in" and zoom out" (p. 233) when reading, thereby using text to learn more than just comprehending the words on a page. By this, he noted that there are times when understanding from text requires readers to see a picture beyond what is in the text specifically. Including a wider understanding of context, for example, assists readers in understanding why an author used specific references to develop his message. Other times, it is beneficial to zoom into a text to dissect details from the author's words. Here, we might find language references from the text that offer insights into the author's intended message. Interpreting text and finding meaning in these ways are part of what is referred to as close reading. Neumann (2010) asserted that such reading "can yield an accurate though tentative reconstruction of the past" (p. 492).

In classrooms, students who are taught to close read text gain far more knowledge from text and learn to identify components of text that support deeper learning (Fisher & Frey, 2014). Brown and Kappes (2012) defined close reading as involving

> an investigation of a short piece of text with multiple readings done over multiple instructional lessons. Through text-based questions and discussion, students are guided to deeply analyze and appreciate various aspects of the text, such as key vocabulary and how its meaning is shaped by context; attention to form, tone, imagery, and/or rhetorical devices; the significance of word choice and syntax, and the discovery of different levels of meaning as passages are read multiple times. (p. 2)

History educators often use close reading practices described by Brown and Kappes as a means to support their students' understanding of text. As such, they ask readers to engage in practices including identifying an author's claims from the text and using the text as evidence to support a larger historical question or topic. Fang and Pace (2013) noted that

> Simply reading a text multiple times and asking more questions do little to help students who are already struggling with challenging texts. Students need tools for independently unpacking the often dense and abstract language of disciplinary texts. We suggest that teachers examine texts with students by considering how language choices construct knowledge and value in disciplinary contexts. Such an explicit, functional focus on language is critical because it facilitates access to meaning, promotes the use of text evidence to support interpretation, scaffolds writing, supports subject area learning, and builds capacity for independence. (p. 106)

From this perspective, teachers might ask students, for example, "What evidence does the author use to make the claim?" and "What language does the author use that offers some examples or evidence of his/her perspective?" From questions like these, close reading challenges learners to focus on the information in a text in ways that emphasizes the importance of the deeper meaning of text. Through this approach, close reading fundamentally compels students to see text as ripe for interpretation; active rather than static; and relevant to a deeper understanding. It involves asking text-dependent questions in concert with offering readers the ability to think beyond the text (Fisher & Frey, 2014). Also, close readers imagine the implications of the text for other readers by discerning contextual and sub-textual references. Contending with sources by close reading then leads learners to ask "What is the text doing?" in concert with "What does the text say?" Together, these help students see the ideas in the text, the author's perspective, and incorporate the context necessary to situate the text in a broader understanding of the topic and its significance. These are connected skills needed to support student learning in history, and the teacher's role is to provide scaffolds for students trying to make sense of complex content.

DIVING DEEPER THROUGH EXAMPLES

The practice of close reading as an instrument to engage students in historical thinking typically comes with coordination of several texts that may support or challenge each other or a larger narrative (Boyles, 2013). Using a series of texts related to Abraham Lincoln, for example, a teacher may complicate the notion of Lincoln as the "Great Emancipator" by including text of a speech Lincoln gave during his 1858 campaign for U.S. Senate where he stated that "I have no purpose, directly or indirectly, to interfere with the institution of slavery" and "I … am in favor of the race to which I belong having the superior position" (Teaching American History, n.d., para. 28). These statements force readers to confront the traditional narrative of Lincoln and beg for clarity of his positions on race and slavery. Including this speech along with letters to his friends and colleagues where he openly sympathizes with the goals of abolitionists helps paint a picture of a man of his time − a politician − struggling to confront race. Students cannot simply read these texts and take each at face value. They must dig deeper and confront reasons why Lincoln may have made these statements. They must ask, "Who is Lincoln addressing in this speech?" "How might that environment have influenced his words?" It further compels students to consider the broader situation of the Civil War period and try to empathize with people of that time. In these instances, students are actively interacting with text rather than absorbing it passively.

In concert with close reading, when confronted with historical resources, students should learn to "source" documents and other artifacts. By this, we mean that even before reading a text, students determine who wrote or created the text and when and where the text was written or created. These clues help the reader situate the text in the larger historical context and consider how that contextual knowledge helps inform the message from the text. Knowing that Lincoln's speech, for example, came while running for the U.S. Senate in 1858 gives readers a sense that the words were written in a political context. Further, knowing that his audience at the time was composed largely of proslavery constituents from southern Illinois is important information when interpreting the language on race and slavery. Sourcing the speech with those pieces of information provides far deeper insights into the time period and Lincoln as a politician and an individual of his time. And it becomes clear that students need more information, additional perspectives, and more resources to understand the sixteenth president.

It is also important to note that close reading can (and should) involve reading sources other than traditional text. Students can, for example, close read a painting, looking for meaning and considering the artist's purpose (Zwirn & Libresco, 2010). The 1872 painting by John Gast titled *American Progress*, for example, offers several powerful, yet relatively simple symbolic images of Manifest Destiny (U.S. Library of Congress, n.d.). As such, it can be used for those beginning to consider close reading of a variety of sources. Like close reading of art, music is also ripe for this type of activity. Listening to Bob Dylan's 1963 song *Masters of War* offers listeners straightforward lyrics to interpret as well as an emotive tone to the music that harmonizes (to the extent possible with Dylan) with the lyrical messages (Sherwin, 2014). Combining this with the famous farewell address from President Dwight Eisenhower in early 1961, in which he warns Americans of a looming "military-industrial complex" offers readers a powerful depiction of Cold War fears Americans faced during a time further complicated by the nascent movement toward attention to social justice issues (U.S. National Archives, Our Documents, n.d.).

More subtly, famous Russian composer, Dmitri Shostakovich, wrote a homage to his hometown of Leningrad in his 7th Symphony. It was composed during the years-long siege by the Nazis during World War II. Its music offers insights into the unconscionable suffering of the people of Leningrad and reflects their plight through music that emotes the dual terror of Stalin and Hitler. These are merely a few examples from a fast-growing body of historical resources available digitally for teachers endeavoring to engage their students in historical thinking.

Teachers seeking to engage students in close reading should select texts and excerpt them as necessary to be manageable for their student population. When excerpting text, teachers are wise to begin by considering lesson objectives. They may ask, for example, "What will students be expected to learn from these texts, and how does this close reading activity help achieve objectives?" Relatedly, teachers must develop appropriate supports for readers to effectively respond to these questions. This may include vocabulary aquisition strategies such as preteaching definitions of specific vocabulary words found in the text, asking students to identify unfamiliar words, and highlighting certain words or phrases that help readers identify tone, or perspective.

Further, teachers may identify concepts that require additional development. Ideas such as democracy and justice are worth exploring conceptually to allow the larger text to better resonate. Finally, teachers must develop questions that challenge readers to consider context and subtext, leading to their consideration of author's purpose, claims, and the evidence gleaned to make those determinations (Werz & Saine, 2014).

Historical Thinking and Students with Disabilities

This description of historical thinking using the skills of close reading and sourcing provides an example of the expectations for students within a curriculum that centers on developing discipline literacy. In this example, students are expected to use information from multiple primary and secondary sources to develop an understanding in order to answer broad historical questions. This extension to interpreting and evaluating the evidence requires, at a minimum, the skills of understanding the task; reading, comprehending, and interpreting the sources; and implementing a strategy to follow to task completion. With such complexity, it would be far easier to resign to the notion that students with learning disabilities are incapable of thinking historically. After all, students with LD, who are in general education classrooms at a higher rate than any other disability category except speech-language impairments (U.S. Department of Education, 2013), often struggle with all of these skills (Bulgren et al., 2013). Inherent in the definition of a learning disability is difficulty with language that may affect listening, thinking, speaking, reading, writing, spelling, and math. In school, these difficulties manifest in levels different from their peers in reading fluency, reading comprehension, and vocabulary acquisition (Hallahan, Lloyd, Kauffman, Weiss, & Martinez, 2005; Vaughn & Wanzek, 2014). In addition, students with LD often have difficulties with memory, strategic thinking, and executive function, including their ability to interpret directions, break down and complete a task, self-regulate, and generalize these skills across tasks and content areas (Bulgren, Deshler, & Lenz, 2007; Hallahan et al., 2005). Difficulties in any of these areas will have an impact on the development of the skills of historical thinking. However, the integration of evidence-based practices in special education into instruction in strategies such as close reading and sourcing shows promise.

In a line of research directed at teaching discipline literacy in history, Susan de La Paz and several colleagues have integrated and examined Self-Regulated Strategy Development (SRSD), a close reading/sourcing systematic strategy, and a writing strategy to help students with learning disabilities and others become successful historical thinkers. Overall, this line of research has offered insights into the ways learners can engage in historical thinking. As such, it has been an important part of understanding how best to support diverse learners in new curricular paradigms designed to get students to problem solve and think critically rather than memorize and respond to convergent questions. Specifically, SRSD "incorporates a process by which students gradually take ownership of learning" (De La Paz, Morales, & Winston, 2007). They move from teacher describing and modeling a SRSD strategy to supported practice with feedback to independent implementation. The close reading/sourcing strategy, itself, is specific enough to provide individual steps to accomplish the task but general enough that it can be applied to each similar task. For example, in Stage 1 where a student must source a document, the questions include, "Who said or wrote this document? What was the author's purpose? Do the reasons make sense? Do you find evidence of bias – specific word choice? Or only giving one point of view?" (De La Paz et al., 2007, p. 136). The strategy is taught and practiced in the general education classroom but, often, additional practice is provided in a subsequent skills or support class. In addition, the close reading/sourcing strategy is often coupled with a strategy for developing an argument in writing.

In a 2005 study of these strategies, de La Paz included 70 eighth-grade students of varying abilities in an experimental condition that received instruction in both the close reading/sourcing strategy and a persuasive writing strategy and a control condition that received "business as usual" instruction. Teachers in the experimental condition began with an anchoring activity that developed interest in the first topic. The teachers then proceeded through the stages of SRSD to teach both strategies in a 12-day unit. The students who mastered the strategy in the experimental condition wrote longer essays that were more persuasive, included a greater number of arguments, and were more historically accurate than those in the control group (De La Paz, 2005). These students were thinking historically by drawing on their analysis of evidence to make reasoned interpretations and evaluations. When looking across groups within the experimental condition, the students identified as talented writers and those of higher ability outperformed those with LD on most measures; however, by the end of the intervention, the essays of students with LD had improved to the pretest levels of the more skilled writers. Though challenges remained with developing historical understanding at all levels, students better understood and felt more confident in using historical reasoning skills after a brief unit of instruction (De La Paz, 2005).

In 2010, de La Paz and Felton took this idea further and compared the persuasive essays of two groups of students in eleventh-grade history classes. Students were of varying abilities but none had disabilities. Both groups used the same materials in instruction but one group received instruction in the close reading/sourcing strategy described earlier and the other group did not. At pretest, the control group wrote longer essays with more claims, better claim development, and higher overall quality. At posttest, students in the experimental group wrote longer essays with a greater probability of being identified as high quality than those in the control group. In addition, the groups were comparable on the number of claims and those in the experimental group were more likely to include citation or reference to the documents used than those in the control group (De La Paz & Felton, 2010). In this case, even students without disabilities improved their strategy use and writing, leading the researchers to assert that the explicit teaching of a strategy does not just benefit students with disabilities.

In addition to teaching a strategy, Monte-Sano and de La Paz (2012) found that the relation of the task to the strategy was critical to student outcomes. In this study, the authors varied the writing task students were asked to complete after participating in strategy instruction. Students were asked to either: (a) imagine themselves as a historical agent, (b) consider an author's motivations or purposes in documents, (c) compare/contrast two documents, or (d) answer a cause question (e.g., Why did Churchill and Truman speak out against the Soviet Union and Communism in 1946 and 1947?). They found that "31% of the variance in the historical quality of students' writing can be explained by the writing task, in combination with other background factors" (Monte-Sano & de La Paz, 2012, p. 289). Why is this important? Because, at times, tasks are adapted for students with disabilities with the idea that personalizing it will increase engagement and outcomes. In this result, we find that that change may not fit the objective of integrating a close reading/sourcing strategy into a document analysis.

Finally, in De La Paz and Wissinger (2015), researchers examined the effects of genre and content knowledge on eleventh-grade students' historical thinking. In this study, participants had varying levels of reading and writing abilities as well as varying levels of content knowledge. Students with disabilities were included in the study and given a read aloud accommodation for the historical documents. Participants were given a package of materials related to the Gulf of Tonkin incident. They were given 20 minutes to read the documents and 40 minutes to create either a summary or an argument. Findings indicated that students with adequate levels of content knowledge "performed better on a disciplinary reading measure when composing arguments and students with limited content knowledge demonstrated greater comprehension when composing summaries" (p. 110). Scores for students with disabilities were not different from their peers on the historical thinking measure, writing quality, or number of words in the essay when given the reading accommodation (De La Paz & Wissinger, 2015).

The critical features of these examples are important to identify. The curricular objective was twofold: (a) develop content knowledge and (b) develop discipline literacy. To address difficulties in the area of developing content knowledge for students with disabilities, instructional activities included anchoring activities such as a mock trial of native Americans accused of massacring American citizens, accommodations such as read alouds or text to speech of the included documents, and supplemental textbook material. To address the development of discipline literacy, teachers taught a systematic strategy using the instructional steps of SRSD and this instruction was often reinforced in a separate special education classroom. There was flexibility within both the instruction and the material to differentiate for student need while still working to achieve the curricular objectives. Within these examples, students with disabilities made progress in both curricular objectives.

Concluding Thoughts

What can the example of historical thinking teach special educators about content knowledge, disciplinary literacy, and adapting to changing learning expectations brought on by new standards and our deepening understanding of how students learn? This increased focus on process may actually be advantageous for students with disabilities for several reasons. First, the complexity involved with thinking like a historian seems daunting for teachers of students with disabilities. Breaking the process down to steps and specific engagement strategies, however, offers a manageable entre to historical thinking. As such, it allows teachers to recognize that breaking down learning strategies into appropriate and manageable steps supports student learning, regardless of disability. Asking students to identify the author of a text, or record what they see in a historical image is a first step in historical thinking. Second, if done correctly, teachers are not standing at the front of the room, lecturing for long periods of time. Instead, students may watch the modeling of a strategy by a teacher and then they are working in small groups or individually at tasks that can be designed to fit individual needs. For example, strong readers may provide support in reading while other students may have a higher level of background knowledge due to their individual interests in a topic. Third, the objective of developing historical thinking skills is not the same as the objective of memorizing a series of facts, dates, and names that can become an endless string of disconnected items to a struggling student. The repeated use of a close reading/sourcing strategy provides an organizing schema that may help them plug facts into a larger concept. Fourth, using primary and secondary sources may generate more interest in historical topics than the standard textbook. In addition, these sources can be chosen to meet varying reading levels, unlike standards texts (Hughes & Parker-Katz, 2013). Finally, through this example of historical thinking, we endeavor to highlight the ways special education teachers can actively participate as the learning specialist, critical to students processing and applying historical thinking skills. We hypothesize that these ideas, teaching and practicing the skills of disciplinary literacy in a systematic and explicit way, apply to all disciplines and not just history/social studies.

CHALLENGES REMAIN

Though these examples provide a promising level of evidence that students with disabilities can meet the curricular objective of learning critical skills of discipline literacy, many challenges remain. First, a challenge within the discipline of history education and many other content areas, is to insure both novice and expert teachers have the ability to draw upon various ideas of teaching beyond that which they have come to experience as students themselves, which, more often than not, continues the practice of memorizing facts, not analysis and discovery. Although much qualitative research has demonstrated positive effects of utilizing practices consistent with historical thinking in the history/social studies literature and using explicit instruction in teaching strategies is well demonstrated in the special education literature, the resiliency of the traditional pedagogy such as didactic learning from a single source, the textbook, with support from a lecture mimicking the contents thereof, remains. In this classroom, both the student with disabilities and the special education teacher often feel overwhelmed by content and vocabulary that is disconnected and hard to learn (Swanson & Deshler, 2003).

Second, there is always the challenge of instructional time and clearly articulated objectives that can be appropriately matched to instructional activities. In our experience, content teachers often say they do not have time to teach strategies when there is so much content to cover. Not only does this impact the strategies necessary for disciplinary literacy but also the requisite skills of vocabulary acquisition, self-regulation, and reading and writing basics that are often weak in students with disabilities. Teaching all of these skills within the context of content area courses alone while also continuing to add content knowledge may be too large a task. Additional instruction outside of the content area course may be necessary. Finally, there is an urgent need to match the changing curricular focus on process and application to the way in which student progress is measured. How can we expect teachers to commit to the instructional change required to meet these curricular standards when they are evaluated on student performance on measures of knowledge of discrete facts and not process? Though we purposefully avoided discussion of testing and evaluation in this chapter, it is imperative that the evolution of curriculum standards such as the Common Core State Standards to a more process-oriented approach must be aligned to the assessment of student outcomes within this curriculum. Otherwise, the push to develop students as disciplinary thinkers who can use systematic processes learned through scaffolded, explicit instruction to gain content knowledge will not be successful.

REFERENCES

American Institutes for Research. (2014). *Overview: State definitions of college and career readiness.* Retrieved from http://www.ccrscenter.org/sites/default/files/CCRS%20Defintions%20Brief_REV_1.pdf

American Youth Policy Forum. (2002). *Twenty-five years of educating children with disabilities: The good news and work ahead.* Washington, DC: Author.

Barksdale, S. T. (2013). Good readers make good historians: "Can we just settle it on 'a lot of people died'"? *History Teacher, 46*, 231–252.

Barton, K. C. (2011). History: From learning narratives to thinking historically. In W. B. Russell (Ed.), *Contemporary social studies: An essential reader* (pp. 109–139). Charlotte, NC: Information Age Publishing.

Bouck, E. C., Okolo, C. M., Englert, C. S., & Heutsche, A. (2008). Cognitive apprenticeship into the discipline: Helping students with disabilities think and act like historians. *Learning Disabilities: A Contemporary Journal, 6*(2), 21–40.

Boyles, N. (2013). Closing in on close reading. *Educational Leadership, 70*(4), 36–41.

Brown, J. S., Collins, A., & Duguid, P. (1989). Situated cognition and the culture of learning. *Educational Researcher, 1*, 32–42.

Brown, S., & Kappes, L. (2012). *Implementing the common core state standards: A primer on "close reading of text"*. Washington, DC: Aspen Institute.

Bulgren, J. A., Deshler, D. C., & Lenz, B. K. (2007). Engaging adolescents with LD in higher order thinking about history concepts using integrated content enhancement routines. *Journal of Learning Disabilities, 40*, 121–133.

Bulgren, J. A., Graner, P. S., & Deshler, D. D. (2013). Literacy challenges and opportunities for students with learning disabilities in social studies and history. *Learning Disabilities Research & Practice, 28*, 17–27.

Common Core State Standards Initiative. (2016). *Preparing America's students for success*. Retrieved from http://www.corestandards.org

De La Paz, S. (2005). Effects of historical reasoning instruction and writing strategy mastery in culturally and academically diverse middle school classrooms. *Journal of Educational Psychology, 97*, 139–156.

De La Paz, S., & Felton, M. K. (2010). Reading and writing from multiple source documents in history: Effects of strategy instruction with low to average high school writers. *Contemporary Educational Psychology, 35*, 174–192.

De La Paz, S., Morales, P., & Winston, P. M. (2007). Source interpretation: Teaching students with and without LD to read and write historically. *Journal of Learning Disabilities, 40*, 134–144.

De La Paz, S., & Wissinger, D. R. (2015). Effects of genre and content knowledge on historical thinking with academically diverse high school students. *The Journal of Experimental Education, 83*, 110–129.

Englert, C. S., Berry, R., & Dunsmore, D. (2001). A case study of the apprenticeship process: Another perspective on the apprentice and the scaffolding metaphor. *Journal of Learning Disabilities, 34*, 152–171.

Fang, Z., & Pace, B. (2013). Teaching with challenging texts in the disciplines: Text complexity and close reading. *Journal of Adolescent Literacy, 57*(2), 104–108.

Fisher, D., & Frey, N. (2014). *Close reading and writing from sources*. Newark, DE: International Reading Association.

Hallahan, D. P., Lloyd, J. W., Kauffman, J. M., Weiss, M. P., & Martinez, E. A. (2005). *Learning disabilities: Foundations, characteristics and effective teaching* (3rd ed.). Boston, MA: Pearson.

Hughes, M. T., & Parker-Katz, M. (2013). Integrating comprehension strategies into social studies instruction. *The Social Studies, 104*, 93–104.

Monte-Sano, C. (2010). Disciplinary literacy in history: An exploration of the historical natural of adolescents' writing. *Journal of Learning Sciences, 19*, 539–568.

Monte-Sano, C., & de La Paz, S. (2012). Using writing tasks to elicit adolescents' historical reasoning. *Journal of Literacy Research, 44*, 273–299.

National Council for the Social Studies. (n.d.). *National curriculum standards for social studies: Executive summary.* Retrieved from http://www.socialstudies.org/standards/execsummary

Neumann, D. J. (2010). "What is the text doing?" Preparing pre-service teachers to teach primary sources effectively. *The History Teacher, 43*, 489–511.

Next Generation Science Standards. (2012). *Conceptual shifts in the next generation science standards.* Retrieved from http://www.nextgenscience.org/sites/default/files/Conceptual %20Shifts%20in%20the%20Next%20Generation%20Science%20Standards%20POST %20PUBLIC%20May%20Draft.pdf

Sherwin, A. [AllySherwin] (2014, March 17). *Bob Dylan, masters of war* [Video file]. Retrieved from https://www.youtube.com/watch?v=exm7FN-t3PY

Swanson, H. L., & Deshler, D. (2003). Instructing adolescents with learning disabilities: Converting a meta-analysis to practice. *Journal of Learning Disabilities, 36*, 124–135.

Teaching American History. (n.d.). *The Lincoln–Douglas debates 1st debate: Abraham Lincoln, Stephen A. Douglas, Ottawa, Illinois.* Retrieved from http://teachingamericanhistory. org/library/document/the-lincoln-douglas-debates-1st-debate/. Accessed on August 21, 1858.

Teaching History. (2013). *What is historical thinking?* Teachinghistory.org%20blog. Retrieved from http://teachinghistory.org/historical-thinking-intro

Tisdale, K. (2001). Dissention and distress in a cognitive apprenticeship of reading. *Reading Research and Instruction, 41*, 51–82.

U.S. Department of Education. (2009). *U.S. performance across international assessments of student achievement: Special supplement to the condition of education.* Retrieved from http:// www.air.org/sites/default/files/downloads/report/ConditionofEdSpecial2009_0.pdf

U.S. Department of Education. (2013). *Digest of education statistics.* Washington, DC: Author.

U.S. Department of Education. (n.d.). *College and career ready standards and assessments.* Retrieved from https://www2.ed.gov/policy/elsec/leg/blueprint/faq/college-career.pdf

U.S. Library of Congress Prints and Photographs Division. (n.d.). *John Gast's American progress.* Washington, DC: Author. Retrieved from http://www.loc.gov/pictures/item/97507547/

U.S. National Archives. Our Documents. (n.d.). *Farewell address by President Dwight D. Eisenhower, January 17, 1961. Final TV Talk.* Speech Series, Papers of Dwight D. Eisenhower, 1953–1961. Washington, DC, Eisenhower Library, National Archives and Records Administration.

Vaughn, S., & Wanzek, J. (2014). Intensive interventions in reading for students with reading disabilities: Meaningful impacts. *Learning Disabilities Research and Practice, 29*, 46–53.

Werz, J., & Saine, P. (2014). Using digital technology to complement close reading of complex texts. *New England Reading Association Journal, 50*(1), 78–82.

Wineburg, S. (1997). Beyond "breadth and depth": Subject matter knowledge and assessment. *Theory into Practice, 36*(4), 255–261.

Wineburg, S. (2001). *Historical thinking and other unnatural acts: Charting the future of teaching the past.* Philadelphia, PA: Temple University Press.

Zaccaria, M. A. (1978). The development of historical thinking: Implications for the teaching of history. *History Teacher, 11*, 323–340.

Zwirn, S., & Libresco, A. (2010). Art in social studies assessments. An untapped resource for social justice. *Art Education, 63*(5), 30–35.

INCLUSIVE EDUCATION MOVING FORWARD

James M. Kauffman, Dimitris Anastasiou,
Jeanmarie Badar, Jason C. Travers
and Andrew L. Wiley

ABSTRACT

Change is not synonymous with improvement. Improvement of special education requires better instruction of individuals with disabilities. Although LRE and inclusion are important issues, they are not the primary legal or practical issues in improving special education. Federal law (IDEA) requires a continuum of alternative placements, not placement in general education in all cases. To make actual progress in education of students with disabilities, a single and strict principle of equality or/and antidiscriminatory legal instruments, such as the CRPD, is not enough. Social justice as a multifaceted principle can serve the education of the whole spectrum of special educational needs in national and international contexts. Responsible inclusion demands attention to the individual instructional needs of individuals with disabilities and consideration of the practical realities involved in teaching. If inclusive education is to move forward, it must involve placing students with disabilities in general

General and Special Education Inclusion in an Age of Change: Roles of Professionals Involved
Advances in Special Education, Volume 32, 153–178
Copyright © 2016 by Emerald Group Publishing Limited
All rights of reproduction in any form reserved
ISSN: 0270-4013/doi:10.1108/S0270-401320160000032010

education only if that is the environment in which they seem most likely to learn the skills that will be most important for their futures.

Keywords: Instruction; realities; law; attitudes; individualization; international context

HISTORY AND MEANINGS

General and special education are changing, as the title of this book suggests. But change does not necessarily mean progress, the field is improving, or our knowledge about educating students with disabilities has advanced. Change itself is not synonymous with improvement. Change can also mean regression, depending on the measure of movement. In this chapter, we try to focus on forward movement or substantive progress related to inclusion — what we see as improvements in the lives and prospects for individuals with disabilities, not merely change or difference in their education. We necessarily mention nonexamples and failures to clarify change without progress, differences that can be observed without movement toward the goal of substantive improvement of the education of and social justice for individuals with disabilities.

Perhaps Warnock (2005) most clearly distinguished between meaningful inclusion and inclusion that does not represent substantive progress. She argued for including students with disabilities in meaningful and appropriate education *wherever that was best provided*, not meaning necessarily "under the same roof" or in the same building or class as those without disabilities. This definition makes effective education the priority, not location. Although the term "full inclusion" has typically referred to educating all students in general education at all times, its priority of placement rather than effective instruction is neither appropriate nor consistent with reality (Anastasiou, Kauffman, & Di Nuovo, 2015; Hornby, 2014; Kauffman & Badar, 2014b; Kauffman, Ward, & Badar, 2016). On the contrary, we believe effective instruction of the learner with a disability, not placement, is the most important objective of special education. Despite decades of research and advocacy for full inclusion, we are aware of no convincing evidence demonstrating its efficacy in reaching desired educational outcomes for learners with disabilities.

We are aware of opinions that it is never appropriate to place a student in a specialized classroom or school and that education is only appropriate when it occurs in general education classrooms. That viewpoint ignores important realities, discounts and dismisses the meaning of disability, is inconsistent with U.S. law and regulations governing special education (Bateman, 2017; Bea, 2016), and will not help the nations of the world effectively educate students with disabilities. Rather, we see inclusion as the most appropriate setting where effective instruction in meaningful tasks that are relevant to the student's future can be assured (Ayres, Lowrey, Douglas, & Sievers, 2011; Hornby, 2014). Research clearly supports this model of inclusion – placement in general education when that is the most appropriate place for the student because he/she can be taught there most effectively. However, no research supports the inclusion of *all* students in general education (Hornby, 2014). Thus, judgment is required about where each individual student should be placed, given *his/her* instructional and social needs. Special education is fundamentally about *individuals*, and it precludes the uniform educational placement of students comprising any group in a particular educational environment (Kauffman, 2015b).

Judgment about where education should occur is one of special education's perpetual issues. Decisions about placement must be made for individuals, not groups (Bateman, 1994; 2017). Individuals with disabilities comprise an extremely diverse group, and judgment of the best place to educate a person must be made *after* assessment of an individual's educational needs. Moreover, such judgment must be based on logical consideration of the best scientific evidence available. Empirical evidence and logic do not support *full* inclusion, but they do support placement in the LRE (least restrictive environment) – the inclusion in general education of those who learn best there. A critical point here is that inclusion is not an intervention. That is, it is not an instructional strategy or method, but a belief about where instruction is most effectively delivered. Inappropriate inclusion in general education does more harm than good, and inclusion in specialized schools and classes can be highly effective. We need more research about the types of schools and classes in which students with particular learning needs are taught most effectively (Hornby, 2014; Kauffman, 2015a; Warnock, 2005). The fact that inclusion results in the same or better outcomes for *some* or *most* students is not convincing evidence that it will do so for *all*. And therein lies the rub for proponents of full inclusion. The failure of any individual(s) to benefit from the general education setting belies the full inclusion mantra, "*all means all.*"

An important objective of special education is advancing social justice in the education of all children. Belief in full inclusion without reliable evidence supporting it is not a path to social justice, and dogmatic adherence to its ideology does not make it true. Scientific evidence and sound logic are our best guides to finding truth and can provide tools to achieve social justice. Although proponents of full inclusion believe inclusion in general education is *always best* and make claims that research supports their view, the belief is dogmatic, inherently irrational, and without convincing evidence (see Bateman, in press; Hornby, 2014; Kauffman et al., 2016; Zigmond & Kloo, in press). However, full inclusion is inimical to achieving social justice for all students. Social justice depends on access to effective instruction which, in turn, requires recognition of the differences between disabilities and other diversities (Anastasiou, Kauffman, & Michail, 2016; Kauffman & Landrum, 2009; Zigmond & Kloo, 2017).

The history of special education is rife with stories of students with disabilities who were unserved or very poorly served (see Gerber, 2017; Kauffman, 1981). The shoddy treatment of individuals with disabilities has included needless separation from general education in many cases. We agree that more students than in the past can and should be included in social and academic life in general education, but only when such involvement confers benefits equal or superior to those obtained in specialized settings. This means opportunities for appropriate inclusion must always be sought, but cannot come at the expense of appropriate and effective instruction. Effective instruction ought to be the primary concern of special educators, who must not allow other issues (e.g., societal attitudes or lofty ideals), important as they may be, to usurp effective instruction. Otherwise, many students with disabilities again will be treated shoddily, albeit with a different rationale than in the past. In our view, sacrificing the individual's instructional improvement for the sake of advancing the societal value of inclusion does not indicate progress. On the contrary, we believe advancing toward a more socially just and inclusive society is contingent on effectively educating students with disabilities to realize their desired outcomes, which means placing them in general education only when that is where they will best learn the skills most important to their futures. This requires preserving the full continuum of placement options for practical, philosophical, legal, and contextual reasons.

PRACTICAL REALITIES AND DOING WHAT IS BEST FOR STUDENTS

Part of effective instruction is considering the practical details of what a practice or policy requires. As is true of most proposals for change, "the devil is in the details." Inclusion of students with disabilities is no exception. We call attention to a few of the organizational, practical, and logistical details a policy of full inclusion requires. These realities too often are not considered. Our discussion here includes questions about the practicality or feasibility of inclusion that must be answered. They are questions that become more difficult to answer satisfactorily as inclusion approaches "full." We also want to make clear that not all of these questions or their answers depend entirely on the severity of a student's disability. That is, some of these questions and their answers may be more difficult for students with what are usually considered "mild" disabilities than for those with severe or obvious disabilities.

Whose Interests Are Being Served?

Many schools view "nonacademic" times such as P.E., Art, Music, Library, Lunch, Recess, Assemblies, and Field Trips as the best and most obvious times for students with disabilities to be included with same-age peers. Often these students are not able to complete the tasks required in these settings, but they are said to benefit "socially" from interactions with typically developing students.

- In a P.E. class, the teacher is supposed to be addressing the *physical* needs of students. A student with significant physical and/or cognitive disabilities can often be years behind his/her peers in the development of physical skills. Therefore, these students tend to participate only marginally in a class with same-age peers (e.g., students using wheelchairs may sit on the sidelines throughout P.E. and yet be said to be "participating"), and their very different physical goals are never addressed. Is it appropriate to sacrifice a child's physical needs (in a P.E. class) for some supposed *social* benefit? The same logic might be applied to Music, Art, Library, Assemblies, and Field Trips. Is it acceptable to expect a student to sit through lessons and activities that are far beyond his/her developmental capabilities, just to "rub shoulders" with general education students? Wouldn't this student's time be better spent doing activities that further his/her development (not to mention that he/she might actually enjoy as opposed to being marginalized or bored)?
- When it comes to lunch and recess, a similar line of thinking leads to some of the same questions: Whose interests are being served when a student with disabilities who is bothered by loud noises is expected to eat lunch in a noisy cafeteria? Is it better for that student to spend lunch with his hands over his ears than be offered a quiet eating place with a few peers, where he/she might actually learn to engage in a conversation?

When does "participation" in a curriculum become pretense, an attempted justification for the student's being placed in a general education class that subjects him/her to humiliation or pity because his/her expected level of performance is so far from that of the average in the group and failure to provide more effective instruction?

Instructional Environment

A student has an individual education program (IEP) *because* he/she has not progressed as expected in general education and requires specialized instruction and programming to achieve expected academic and/or social progress (Bateman, 2017). Students with IEPs require instruction that is fundamentally different from that being provided to most other students in the general education classroom. This includes but is not limited to below-grade-level reading or math instruction or an environment with reduced distractions and interruptions.

- Does it make sense for a special education teacher to try to provide instruction that is *fundamentally different* to an individual or small group within the context of a larger classroom with 10–20 other students and numerous distractions? Does it not make more sense for this instruction to be delivered in a quiet classroom with reduced external stimuli and distractions?
- Good teachers fill their walls with relevant information that may provide students with visual cues or learned strategies to help them with learning tasks. If a student is working significantly below grade level (e.g., a 2nd grader or older student who is still learning letter sounds), how will these types of academic supports be available in the general education setting?
- Proponents of inclusion often claim damage is done to students' self-esteem when they are "segregated" for instruction. How is it less damaging to a student's self-esteem to engage in below grade-level instruction in full view of his/her peers?

Scheduling

Most Special Education teachers are responsible for implementing IEPs for students at more than one grade level. Most grade levels follow different schedules, and this is sometimes true of different teachers of the same grade. Important questions include:

- How can a special educator provide instructional or behavioral support for students who need it when there are schedule conflicts (i.e., when he/ she is needed in more than one place at a time)?
- Is placing an instructional aide with a student (or in a classroom) an adequate substitute for having a special educator provide the needed specialized support?
- How can a special educator participate in coplanning and coteaching when he/she is managing student's from various grade levels (in most schools, teachers share planning time with others at their grade level)? Is it reasonable to expect a special educator to plan appropriate, individualized, targeted instructional support for several students at the same time (assuming the instruction will be implemented by someone else)?
- Unless a special educator is fully involved in coplanning with general education teachers, does "coteaching" really mean the general education teacher teaches, and the special education teacher acts as an overqualified aide in the classroom?
- When a school tries to maintain a continuum of services and provides a self-contained class but expects students from that class to be included at certain times (usually lunch and "specials"), how can a special educator provide effective instruction when students from various grade levels are coming and going throughout the day?
- When a school has a special educator assigned to each grade level (which is far from typical), unless all the students with IEPs are placed in the same classroom, the same problem exists: No teacher can be in more than one place at a time.

We have raised only a few questions about practical realities and doing what best serves the student's interests. At times, it is very difficult to separate our own interests and commitments from those of the student. Commitment to an idea or ideology can lead us to develop attitudes, beliefs, or philosophical perspectives that are misleading and ultimately destructive of students' best interests. Open-mindedness helps us evaluate the practical realities involved in movement toward better inclusion because we appreciate the nitty-gritty issues raised by any philosophical perspective or "theoretical" proposal. Full consideration of practical realities also helps us avoid short-changing students' and teachers' ability to function effectively, sacrificing more satisfactory options to maintain philosophical purity, or making hollow promises of support.

ATTITUDES AND PHILOSOPHICAL PERSPECTIVES

Positive change in the educational experiences of students with disabilities is achievable, but not without examining attitudes and philosophical perspectives. Philosophical perspectives on inclusive education are important because they both enable and constrain – sometimes powerfully – thinking and acting in relation to educating students with disabilities. This is especially true for philosophical perspectives that allow no or very few exceptions to the expectation that all students, regardless of their individual learning needs, will be taught in the same setting or the same program (Wiley, 2015). The primary concern of advocates of full inclusion ("all means all") is unifying education such that there are no or very few lines of demarcation between students, teachers, instruction, programs, and settings (Burrello, Sailor, & Kleinhammer-Tramill, 2012; explore also the Schoolwide Integrated Framework for Transformation [SWIFT], 2015). The core and sacred value of the full inclusion movement appears to be *equal treatment* for all students. From this perspective, anything that involves different treatment (e.g., labeling, specialized settings, individualized learning expectations [unless differentiated for *all* students], and special education delivered outside the general education classroom) is harmful and unjust, while all efforts to abolish different treatment (or abandon "silos") are assumed to be beneficial and a sure path to social justice for students with disabilities.

Moral values that are resistant or impervious to tradeoffs are known as protected values. Extreme, "no exceptions" perspectives based entirely or almost entirely on one protected value (e.g., equal treatment) inhibit the ability to be open-minded and think critically about limitations and downsides related to that value (Ditto & Liu, 2011). The belief that inclusion is right in every case is a form of moral absolutism, and moral absolutism significantly increases and intensifies well-known errors in reasoning like confirmation bias. Confirmation bias entails the selective attention to evidence for an already accepted conclusion and/or biased evaluation of contradictory evidence and arguments (Nickerson, 1998; Sinatra, Kienhues, & Hofer, 2015). These biases make it extremely difficult to think open-mindedly about protected values and may lead to distorted perceptions of the actual (versus preferred) harms and benefits associated with that value.

Although protected values come in all political stripes, we offer one example typically associated with conservatism – economic freedom. When economic freedom, based on the ideals of free market capitalism, is elevated to the status of a sacred or protected value, the ability to think open-mindedly about potential downsides or negative consequences associated with unregulated economic freedom is compromised. The denial of scientific evidence for global climate change is perhaps the most familiar manifestation of this phenomenon, although there are many others (Gawande, 2016). Similarly, elevating economic freedom above all other sources of moral value can bias someone to believe that publicly funded programs (e.g., public education, "food stamps," Medicare, Social Security, what has been called "Obamacare") are harmful and ineffective in all cases. Again, such cognitive biases operate across the political spectrum and are associated with strong beliefs about any divisive moral issue (e.g., gun control, the death penalty, contraception, abortion, and same-sex marriage).

Full inclusion is a prime example of how this moral approach to empirical issues can mislead individuals to accept (and disseminate) the idea. Full inclusion proponents may conclude that all children should be educated in general education environments based on beliefs that separating children for specialized treatment violates equal treatment (i.e., cherished value). It's important to point out that full inclusion is the cherished belief, not the educational outcomes of individuals with disabilities. Believers embrace full inclusion as *principally right* and therefore morally superior (i.e., moral judgment) to every possible alternative. This moral position is beyond the empirical sphere and therefore impervious to arguments based on scientific evidence. However, full inclusion advocates may buttress their argument via appeals to consequences. In order to justify their belief, full inclusion proponents may present evidence that an individual (or some individuals) appears to benefit from inclusion (biased reasoning). This fallacious argument fails to demonstrate that all children (i.e., "all means all") benefit from full inclusion, but also fails to account for the type of benefit (i.e., academic, social, behavioral) and whether it confers some long-term advantage in ways superior to benefits of a specialized setting. It is worth noting the argument that *some* students benefit from full inclusion is not a valid reason to accept the belief that *all* students benefit from full inclusion (i.e., hasty generalization, a type of *nonsequitur* fallacy).

People are entitled to their philosophical perspectives, including those that are extreme. The danger is that ideologically constrained thinking, weakly tied to facts and logic, contributes to injustice via misguided action or inaction. In the case of inclusive education, cognitive biases are evident when advocates of full inclusion incorrectly claim that "research shows" inclusion in general education is beneficial for all students, or that separate placements are always inappropriate or ineffective. The truth is that research on the relationship between placement and student outcomes is inconclusive, in part because — as we have argued in this chapter — quality of instruction is the critical variable, not location of instruction (Zigmond & Kloo, 2011).

Advocates of full inclusion might deny that their beliefs are based on moral absolutism, to which we would say, good. Rejecting moral absolutism frees us to pursue a richer vision of social justice for students with disabilities, one that is built on multiple sources of moral value.

Effectively educating students with disabilities requires focused, sustained action based firmly on clear thinking, scientific evidence, and compassion. Divisive and circular debates about full inclusion have surely impeded, or at least distracted from, the collaborative and thoughtful work needed to make real (vs. illusory) progress in educating students with disabilities. We acknowledge the emotional appeal of arguments for blurring or erasing all distinctions between students, instruction, and settings. However, an open-minded evaluation of these arguments, based on logic, historical evidence, and observations of educational systems that do not make these distinctions, suggests that failing to draw lines, make distinctions, or speak clearly about differences will cause far more harm to students with disabilities than good.

To make progress in inclusion, we must recognize and avoid philosophical perspectives on inclusive education that do not lead to the better outcomes for students with disabilities. Improving instruction and services is a moral imperative because of the life-long benefits that accrue from maximizing students' learning and independence. We do not believe this perspective precludes us from addressing other important concerns in fully inclusive education, such as concerns related to belonging, acceptance, and dignity. We see these concerns as integral to the appropriateness and effectiveness of instruction and services, regardless of where these services are provided. Like efforts to improve instruction, efforts to promote belonging, acceptance, and dignity must also be guided by logic, evidence, and compassion, and they must not be impeded by a philosophical perspective that arbitrarily or unjustly limits our ability to respond fully to the individual needs and unique circumstances of all students with disabilities.

LEGAL MANDATES AND CATEGORICAL PERSPECTIVES

The Education of All Handicapped Children Act of 1975 (i.e., Public Law 94—142) and its subsequent reauthorizations (IDEA, in 2004 titled the

Individuals with Disabilities Education Improvement Act) was a monumental achievement for the civil and social rights of children with disabilities and their families (Martin, 2013). This law not only provides legal protections to a historically marginalized group, but also ensures access to specific benefits (i.e., entitlements). Other laws complement the legal protections and entitlements afforded under IDEA, including the Americans with Disabilities Act of 1990 (ADA) (e.g., right to access and reasonable accommodations). We regard these laws as representations of a progressive society that values educating citizens with disabilities for participation in a secular democracy.

IDEA and ADA can be perceived as blunt instruments for assuring the civil rights of students with disabilities. Bluntness is a necessary characteristic of law because it must allow the consideration of unique circumstances when making decisions about educating individuals, but law also must be sufficiently specific to ensure enforceability (Howe & Miramontes, 1992). Although debate about various aspects of these laws abounds, the bulk of controversy surrounding inclusive education stems primarily from interpretations of two fundamental principles of IDEA, namely the right to a "free and appropriate public education" (FAPE) and the delivery of services in the "LRE." Much emphasis (e.g., case law, scholarly work) has been placed on the effects of disability eligibility categories, what constitutes an "appropriate" education, and what is meant by "least restrictive."

Special Education Eligibility Categories

Although refinement of the law is necessary from time to time, revisions can be either beneficial or harmful. The eligibility categories of the IDEA are intended to identify individuals who are entitled to legal benefits and protection from the majority. Despite this, some have advocated that the eligibility categories be removed from the law (e.g., Harry & Klingner, 2014). Although stereotypes about people with disabilities can (and do) result in prejudice, oppression, and marginalization, we are unconvinced that eliminating eligibility (i.e., disability) categories will translate to better outcomes for individuals with disabilities. One is inclined to ask whether abstaining from identifying a child as having a disability (i.e., labeling) results in the disability ceasing to exist; does refusing to establish the presence of a disability mean the person does not have the disability?

Although seemingly bizarre, full inclusion advocates have a history of pretending children do not actually have intellectual (and other) disabilities by arguing that disabilities are entirely social constructions (Danforth & Rhodes, 1997; Hall, 2005; Kliewer, Biklen, & Petersen, 2015). Such ideas are accompanied by stories of alleged liberation, acceptance, and inclusion of people who use methods like facilitated communication, a thoroughly debunked communication tactic (Mostert, 2001, 2010, 2014; Travers, Tincani, & Lang, 2014) that has become increasingly tolerated and promoted by full inclusion proponents (Ashby, 2011; Ashby & Causton-Theoharis, 2009, 2012; Kasa-Hendrickson, Broderick, & Hanson, 2009; Stubblefield, 2011). Such beliefs and behavior demonstrate a complete failure to recognize the importance of hard-won federal protection under the law for students with disabilities and their families, but also discounts or entirely ignores a mountain of evidence about the complex interplay of genetic, neurological, developmental, and environmental factors that give rise to disabling conditions.

Furthermore, no evidence indicates that changing labels from typical language (e.g., autistic child; learning disabled child) to person-first language (e.g., child with autism; child with learning disability) or to nondisability terms (i.e., child with tier 3 needs in mathematics; child who gets tier 2 interventions in reading) will have any meaningful effect on improving educational outcomes of a child with a disability. The attempt to discard useful (and well-established) disability categories in favor of less precise terms is potentially harmful to education outcomes because disability and its manifestations in child functioning are disregarded rather than recognized. This will undoubtedly have the effect of making individualization exceedingly difficult, thereby undermining access to effective instruction and obstructing progress toward desired outcomes.

Elimination of specific labels only creates new space for different terms. Over time, new terms acquire the stigma that motivated the previous change in terminology. This cycle likely can only be disrupted by effectively educating learners with disabilities to become adults who, through living their life and participating in a pluralistic society, erode stereotypes and stigma. In other words, elimination of eligibility categories is a futile attempt to reduce stigma in the absence of effective, individualized education. Stigma associated with disability originates from various sources, but the terms used to articulate the stigma are merely artifacts of that phenomenon; stigma is not caused by the term itself. We contend that recognizing disability as a manifestation of the diversity of human life and educating individuals to achieve their desired outcomes represent a truly progressive position that directly addresses stigma associated with disability. Attention to superficial issues like the rapid evolution of politically correct language only serves to distract from that effort (Kauffman & Badar, 2013, 2014a; Kauffman, 2013).

To agree with full inclusion proponents that disability categories ought to be removed from federal and state special education law, one must (a) discount the relevance of federal protections and guarantees; (b) reject and/ or deny an extensive body of literature about disability etiologies and manifestations; (c) convince one's self that, for example, severe autism in a four-year-old child is a social construction; (d) subscribe to a set of beliefs and engage in a repertoire of behavior associated with disproven, unproven, and pseudoscientific nonsense; and (e) fail to recognize that stigma is not caused by labels themselves. Abandonment of eligibility categories is antithetical to equity of opportunity for individuals with disabilities, a path toward further marginalization, and a degradation of individuals by rejecting the reality of their disabilities. For these reasons, we view the suggestion that disability categories be jettisoned to be profoundly regressive, a belief that ultimately dismantles the rights and protections afforded under United States laws to children with disabilities and their families.

Appropriate Education and the Least Restrictive Environment

The IDEA clearly outlines a continuum of placements, including the location where services will be provided, contingent on stakeholders' consideration of the needs of individuals with disabilities. The least restrictive environment (LRE) is the place where instructional benefit is best received, depending on the learner. This feature not only protects children with disabilities and their families from unilateral decisions of the majority (e.g., changes in service delivery based on policy changes of school administrators), but also ensures that students with disabilities have *access to* and *participate in* meaningful instruction. These concepts are fundamental to the IDEA and the ADA (see Bea, 2016). The primary purpose of these laws is to prevent discrimination on the basis of disability by requiring individualized decisions about instruction and guaranteeing access and participation in education. Importantly, these laws do not state that children must be educated in any particular environment, but do suggest access and participation in general education *as appropriate*. Exposure to a curriculum certainly does not mean the student has meaningful access (Fuchs et al., 2015). We therefore contend that it is sometimes inappropriate and harmful to withhold from students with disabilities access to specialized education environments.

Some students, such as those with autism and other developmental disabilities, engage in a range of severe behaviors that impede their learning and the learning of others. Although rare, some individuals' behavior may result in permanent self-injury or death (e.g., eye gouging; head banging). Some individuals also may engage in severe aggression, causing temporary or permanent injury to peers. Such individuals benefit from highly specialized environments with well-trained behavior specialists who are equipped to predict, understand, and replace such behaviors. We contend that providing such services in, for example, a 10th grade physics classroom or 4th grade general education classroom (see Ayres et al., 2011; Fuchs et al., 2015) is more restrictive for a student with the self-injurious or aggressive behavior because it limits the type and extent of behavioral interventions and supports that can be provided. Furthermore, such service delivery is detrimental to his/her relationships with others and overall quality of life, not to mention failure to learn the general education or any meaningful curriculum. There is no benefit a physics class or other general education environment can offer a student with such behavior that would supersede the benefit of improving his or her behavioral functioning. Yet this sort of argument is used to deride the right to make decisions based on individual needs guaranteed by law in favor of "all means all" fully inclusive education.

The notion that all children should be educated in the general education classroom replaces progressive values regarding the rights of the individual (a fundamental element of the IDEA) with a collectivist, utopian vision. Not all inclusive education proponents adopt this absolutist ideology (see Hornby, 2014). Some students with disabilities excel in general education with supplementary supports and services. However, the primary assumption of full inclusion is that general education is an *inherently superior environment compared to a specialized one* for all students. In other words, a typical educational environment will result in an education for the student with a disability that will be on par with, if not superior to, an education that is tailored to her/his unique needs. It's worth noting the bizarre belief that students with disabilities will be expected to perform in a manner consistent with peers via exposure to general (i.e., nonspecialized) environments and differentiation made therein (Fuchs et al., 2015). Not only does this seem to discount the very meaning of having a disability, but it also advances an idea that doing less will result in performance that exceeds what might be expected in a specialized environment. Such notions go beyond rational arguments about how special education ought to be improved and trespasses into avenues of wishful thinking.

Fallacious reasoning of full inclusion is perhaps more clear when applied to other contexts. For example, if applied to the medical field, generalized chemotherapy and radiation treatment of cancer would be regarded as inherently superior to specialized/targeted treatment protocols based on the cancer type, tumor size, growth rate, location, and so on (i.e., the individual's particular treatment needs). Perhaps we ought to move patients from intensive care units to general hospital wards to ensure that everyone has the same type and level of care. Or, perhaps, we should abandon the idea of operating rooms and instead require surgeons to operate in regular hospital rooms so that everyone can be together in the same environment. As bizarre as these ideas are, they reflect precisely the mentality of so-called progressive reformers of special education. Somehow, many special (and general) educators have become convinced that providing less specialized reading instruction or trying to do it in the context of general education is better than providing more specialized instruction in a specialized place. This peculiar thinking illustrates how ideology distorts perception and gives rise to harmful practices in the name of progressive education.

The no-holds-barred approach to advancing fully inclusive education ("all means all") also is antithetical to progressive values. Progressivism values intellectual honesty, rigorous debate, and objective evidence as fundamental to making decisions, yet self-proclaimed progressive reformers have suggested these foundations of reason themselves are ideologies (Brantlinger, 1997). A progressive education platform, at least in the liberal tradition, would be comprised of open dialog, consideration of the evidence, and logically consistent debate. However, an array of dishonest tactics have been used to convince educators to adopt inclusive education ideology and to discard the reliance on individualized decisions about how to best educate children. False equivalencies are offered to generate fear and recruit professionals to join the full inclusion crusade. For example, the use of the term "segregation" to refer to specialized classrooms is used to instill fear of being maligned as a bigot for not joining in the inclusion movement. "Segregation" falsely insinuates that highly specialized instructional environments are in all ways inferior to general education. False dichotomy is proffered to wide-eyed future educators who are told they must either be for full inclusion or against it when, as we espouse, some students may be best served in the general education environment while others are best educated in separate/specialized settings.

Understanding and meeting the particular needs of learners with disabilities depends on understanding what their disability is, how it affects their lives (and the prospective life an individual and other stakeholders envision), and how to best support students in attaining desired outcomes. Disabilities are authentic conditions that put individuals at risk for marginalization. The IDEA and ADA are as or more important than ever before for ensuring protections for individuals with disabilities, given increasingly limited resources. Such protections include the right to effective instruction in the LRE (i.e., the location and types of services that confer the most educational benefit for the individual). Full inclusion is regressive in that it regards such protections and rights as harmful and fails to account for students who require highly specialized types of instruction and environments that cannot (and should not) be afforded in, for example, a 12th grade English literature course or 2nd grade general education classroom.

INTERNATIONAL CONTEXTS AND THE CRPD

Movement toward inclusion is international, as exemplified by the United Nations' Convention on the Rights of Persons with Disabilities (CRPD; see United Nations, 2006). In December, 2006, the Plenary of the General Assembly of the UN adopted the CRPD, which went into effect on May 3, 2008. Article 24 of the CRPD recognizes the right of the persons with disabilities (PWD) to education, spelling out obligations of States Parties (nations) to adopt measures that "ensure an inclusive education system at all levels and life-long learning." As of October, 2015, 159 countries had ratified the Convention (thus became "State Parties").

The United Kingdom and Mauritius expressed specific reservations or/and declarations concerning Article 24, particularly Clauses 2(a) and 2(b). For example:

> The United Kingdom Government is committed to continuing to develop an inclusive system where parents of disabled children have increasing access to mainstream schools and staff, which have the capacity to meet the needs of disabled children. The General Education System in the United Kingdom includes mainstream, and special schools, which the UK Government understands is allowed under the Convention.

> The United Kingdom reserves the right for disabled children to be educated outside their local community where more appropriate education provision is available elsewhere. Nevertheless, parents of disabled children have the same opportunity as other parents to state a preference for the school at which they wish their child to be educated.

Similarly, Mauritius responded to Article 24.2 (Article 24.1 is not cited in the reply of the Republic of Mauritius, hence there is no #1 in the quotation):

With regard to Article 24.2(b), the Republic of Mauritius has a policy of inclusive education which is being implemented incrementally alongside special education.

Thus, the following subparagraphs of the CRPD are not universally accepted even among State Parties:

2. In realizing this right, States Parties shall ensure that:

   a. Persons with disabilities are not excluded from the general education system on the basis of disability, and that children with disabilities are not excluded from free and compulsory primary education, or from secondary education, on the basis of disability;
   b. Persons with disabilities can access an inclusive, quality and free primary education and secondary education on an equal basis with others in the communities in which they live; (CRPD, 2006)

Further clarifications about the interpretation of the aforementioned controversial subparagraphs are needed. The nonexclusion language, used in subparagraph 2(a), aimed to affirm the right to receive education. However, in legal terms across several international contexts with long tradition in special education (e.g., the United States, the United Kingdom, and Finland), students with disabilities are not pulled out of the general classroom on the basis of disabilities per se, but on the basis of their individual and special educational needs that should be met in the most appropriate way in order to achieve educational progress (Anastasiou & Keller, 2017; Anastasiou, Gardner, & Michail, 2011). Undoubtedly, placement in special education settings a priori on the basis of disability would be prejudicial and discriminatory. The IDEA (section 614(d)), requires an IEP for every student who is eligible for special education services, not for every person with a disability. Orthopedic impairments or chronic health problems not relevant to learning can be addressed by accommodations through the allocation of space or other arrangements and are not considered specialized instruction (Hallahan, Kauffman, & Pullen, 2015). In addition, the wording in subparagraph 2(b) of the CRPD may exclude remote special schools that are far from homes but not every type of special education unit (class or school) on the condition that they are accessible in a given community.

The above countries' declarations and reservations are related to the infamous and ambiguous phrase "full inclusion" in subparagraph 2(e) of the CRPD, which states:

   c. effective individualized support measures are provided in environments that maximize academic and social development, consistent with the goal of full inclusion. (CRPD, 2006)

"Full inclusion" was subjected to considerable debate during the travaux préparatoires (preparatory works) of the CRPD, despite the shameful fact that the special education community did not participate in the preparation of Article 24. The absence of input from special education experts might have made a significant difference in the final wording of Article 24, although experts often have differences of opinion with regard to special education philosophy and practice. But neither have Non-Governmental Organizations (NGOs) always spoken with one voice. For example, the UK-based *Centre for Studies on Inclusive Education* (CSIE) lobbied for emphasis on full inclusion and was disproportionately more influential in drafting the CRPD compared to its influence in the United Kingdom. The selective criteria for participants from the NGOs were not clear. Finally, the European Union was the agent insisting on "full inclusion" in the eighth and final session of discussion of the wording of the CRPD. Nevertheless, the wording of Article 24 was a matter of serious disagreement among national delegates and disability movement agents in the critical last three discussions (6th, 7th, and 8th sessions).

Subparagraph 2(e) of Article 24 of the CRPD is remarkably self-contradictory. The subparagraph included the clauses "effective individualized support" in "environments that maximize academic and social development," both of which fall into a special educational needs paradigm. Therefore, the clauses seemed to recognize special instruction that met the specific needs of the individual student with a disability. In addition, many agents involved in the travaux préparatoires used the key word "environments" to clearly denote environments beyond the general or "regular" education classroom. However, if the meaning of the phrase "goal of full inclusion" as stated in 2(e) is interpreted in the sense of inclusion debate in the United States and United Kingdom, then this seems a direct contradiction to the emphasis on individualization and specialized environments; the two propositions are mutually exclusive. Subparagraph 2(e) can be coherent and meaningful if "full inclusion" has the meaning of "*full participation in the community*," or "a fully inclusive society." But such an interpretation is not relevant to the full inclusion debate in the special education literature. Despite the fact that subparagraph 2(e) was introduced by the European Union and had the support of UNESCO, very important disability organizations such as the *World Federation of the Deaf, The World Blind Union*, and *The World Federation of the Deaf-Blind* strongly opposed the terminology "full inclusion." Upon passage of the CRPD, these groups reinterpreted "full inclusion" as "totally supportive environments." For example, the *World Federation of the Deaf* (WFD) not only advocated for such a meaning for students who are deaf, but also argued for an inclusive education as the *LRE*: Many policy-makers today strongly support full inclusion in education, which they interpret to mean full-scale mainstreaming of all disabled students with all students in regular schools near their homes.

Although such a goal may be generally appropriate for many disabled learners who can hear and interact with their peers and teachers, WFD has serious differences regarding implementation of this concept for Deaf learners:

> WFD holds that *the least restrictive environment* for a Deaf learner is whatever is the most enabling environment for that learner. *Full inclusion for a Deaf learner means a totally supportive, signing and student-centred environment.* This permits the learner to develop to his/her full educational, social and emotional potential. This is stated also in the Convention on the Rights of Persons with Disabilities. (World Federation of the Deaf, n.d.; [emphasis added])

Consequently, the following two statements, a and b, are *false*: (a) the CRPD is a UN treaty in which the *people of interest* through their organizations shaped the final document, and (b) the CRPD has strong support from the *entire* disability community. The meaning of "full inclusion" in the CRPD is seriously misleading. Logically, "full inclusion" in the full context of Article 24 and its travaux préparatoires must mean fully supportive environments, not always placement in general education.

Without surrounding context, including discussions before adoption of the CRPD, "full inclusion" cannot be interpreted accurately. The CRPD Committee's Concluding Observations (COs) sent to China, Argentina, and Paraguay were openly critical of specialized education schools (Argentina) and systems (China, Paraguay) for not relying entirely on fully inclusive (i.e., general education) settings for all students. Moreover, in the cases of China and Argentina, the CRPD Committee's COs clearly suggested the reallocation of resources from the special education system to inclusive education in "mainstream schools."

However, as of 2008–2009 (the most recent data available) only 0.2% of the school population in China, 0.3% in Paraguay, and about 1% in Argentina received special education services across a continuum of placements (Anastasiou & Keller, 2014). It is disturbing and tragic that the CRPD Committee focused exclusively on condemning the minimal services available rather than advocating the rights of children with disabilities to an appropriate education.

Different interpretations of Article 24 of the CRPD have created serious dilemmas for some States Parties and perhaps for the members of the Committee itself. Despite the best intensions of the creators of the CRPD, interpretation of "full inclusion" has led to confusion in the disability rights movement, dissenting voices in special education, and inconsistency in the scientific community. The best interests of people with disabilities will not be served by ignoring problems in the wording and presumed meaning of statements, imagining the benefits of placement of students with disabilities in general education, or transferring resources from special education to general education. Sensitivity to the educational interests of children with disabilities requires the best *specialized* instruction for those who are excluded from education altogether or are underserved in many nations of the world. In many nations of the world, there are deep-rooted and structural inequalities going far beyond the superficial antidiscriminatory spirit of Article 24 (Anastasiou & Kauffman, in preparation; Anastasiou & Keller, 2017). For example, whereas Italy represents the single national example of implementation of a nearly fully inclusive education system, the available data show that "the everyday reality in Italian classrooms is more complex and not as encouraging as one might hope" (Anastasiou et al., 2015, p. 439). Similarly, in Ghana, general education is improving, but special and inclusive education remain stagnant, mainly due to unclear or dogmatic approaches to inclusion (Ametepee & Anastasiou, 2015).

Unfortunately, "clarification" of the CRPD Committee recently interpreted the terms "inclusion" and "inclusionary" as referring to full inclusion, meaning no options for placement other than general education, defunding alternative placements, and eliminating parental choice regarding placement of the child. Paragraph 10 of the CRPD Committee's interpretation released in September, 2016, includes, "Notably, education is the right of the individual learner, and not, in the case of children, the right of a parent or caregiver. Parental responsibilities in this regard are subordinate to the rights of the child" (CRPD Committee GC-4, 2016, p. 3). However, paragraph 45 begins, "Article 7 asserts that, in all actions, the best interests of the child shall be a primary consideration" (CRPD Committee GC-4, 2016, p. 16). Thus, the implicit assumption is that the 18 Committee members monitoring the CRPD, not parents or educators, will determine what is in the best interests of the child – full inclusion.

SUMMARY AND CONCLUSIONS

Inclusion should mean placing a student with disabilities in general education only when stakeholders are convinced it is where the student will best learn the skills most important to their futures. The judgment about where a student is most likely to learn necessary skills should involve choice from a full continuum of placement options. Such judgment requires careful attention to the practical matters involving instruction so that neither students nor teachers are short-changed in their ability to function effectively, sacrificed for the sake of philosophical purity, or left with hollow promises of support. Choice from a continuum of placement options requires open-mindedness about advantages and disadvantages of various placements. Efforts to promote belonging, acceptance, and dignity, as well as learning, must also be guided by logic, evidence, and compassion. Such efforts must not be impeded by a philosophical perspective that arbitrarily or unjustly limits the ability to respond fully to individual students' needs and circumstances. Inclusionary practices must also be guided by the letter and spirit of a nation's laws and regulations. In the United States, federal law in 2016 required a full continuum of alternative placements, disallowing arbitrary placement of all children with disabilities in general education and requiring consideration of the needs of individuals, not groups, in all aspects of special education (Bateman, 2017; Bea, 2016). "Inclusion" has various meanings, and in some nations "inclusion" refers to including students in public education, even if this means serving some students some in environments not intended to meet the needs of more typical individuals.

If change in education is to be progressive, not regressive, it must be guided by clear thinking about the nature of disabilities in the context of education. We do not understand why, given the nature of disabilities, any of the following three quotations should be seen as rational.

Not only are very few students with disabilities meeting proficiency on NAEP — better known as the Nation's Report Card — but large achievement gaps between students with and without disabilities remain. (Council for Exceptional Children, Policy Insider, 2015, emphasis in original)

But the lack of movement on scores means that students with disabilities gained no ground on closing the wide achievement gap between themselves and students who do not have disabilities ... Most students covered under these federal laws are not cognitively impaired. (Samuels, 2015)

Thirty years of research shows us that when all students are learning together (including those with the most extensive needs) AND are given the appropriate instruction and

supports, ALL students can participate, learn, and excel within grade-level general education curriculum, build meaningful social relationships, achieve positive behavioral
outcomes, and graduate from high school, college and beyond. (SWIFT, 2015)

Are special education experts naïve when they believe the achievement gap
between students with and without disabilities might be closed (i.e., gaps
between average scores can be entirely eliminated and the central tendency
phenomenon can be circumvented) by offering less specialized instruction?
If not, why make such statements as those by the Council for Exceptional
Children and Samuels? Are we really to believe that all students, bar none
(the SWIFT website includes the mantra "all means all" repeated by many
adults and children), will graduate from high school ready for college or
employment? If not, why the emphasis on *all*? Should the grace of acceptance allow some individuals *not* to be included in some classes? Might
a 15-year-old who needs extensive supports to perform daily tasks be an
exception? Or do such cases simply not exist? If they do, is it only because
they have not been given appropriate instruction and supports? We do
ourselves no favors by exaggerating claims, expressing faux horror when
confronted with unpleasant realities, or requiring that all students attain
the same educational (i.e. academic, social, behavioral) outcomes.

The threat to special education posed by the ideology of full inclusion, meaning all children with disabilities are placed in general education, is real (see The Special Edge, 2016; detailing a state plan for
California that is clearly contrary to a federal appeals court opinion
regarding the requirements of IDEA — Bea, 2016). Moreover, we caution that this threat is not necessarily related to severity of the disability.
In some cases, it may be easier to "include" a student in general education and claim that he or she is best taught there when the disability is
severe than when the disability is considered "mild." Martin (2013)
has cautioned:

Experts in learning disability today report real fears that educators might make the case
that special treatment programs, e.g., special education and special teachers of children
with learning disabilities, should be ended and the children "included" in the regular
classroom. This fear is, and I share it, that we will return to the time before PL 94–142,
when large numbers of children in regular education received no real instruction.
Eventually they lost interest and dropped out. (p. 227)

Much of the controversy about inclusion has to do with how students are
best grouped for instruction, and we believe that a diversity of knowledge
and skills requires a diversity of relatively homogeneous groups (i.e., relatively high homogeneity in the skills being taught) for the most effective

instruction possible (Kauffman, Landrum, Mock, Sayeski, & Sayeski, 2005). Inclusion could be made better by focusing on including students with disabilities in groups for effective instruction in needed skills, not on placing students in heterogeneous groups of students incorporating those without disabilities. The way forward for inclusion, if it is to represent real progress, requires remembering the history of the struggle to achieve appropriate education of all children with disabilities (Martin, 2013), improving instruction in special education, maintaining the full continuum of placement options, and including students in general education only as appropriate.

REFERENCES

Ametepee, L. K., & Anastasiou, D. (2015). Special and inclusive education in Ghana: Status and progress, challenges and implications. *International Journal of Educational Development, 41*, 143–152. doi:10.1016/j.ijedudev.2015.02.007

Anastasiou, D., Gardner, R., & Michail, D. (2011). Ethnicity and exceptionality. In J. M. Kauffman & D. P. Hallahan (Eds.), *Handbook of special education* (pp. 745–758). New York, NY: Routledge.

Anastasiou, D., & Kauffman, J. M. (in preparation). Commentary on article 24 of the CRPD: The right to education. In I. Bantekas, D. Anastasiou, & M. Stein (Eds.), *Commentary on the UN convention on the rights of persons with disabilities*. New York: Oxford University Press.

Anastasiou, D., Kauffman, J. M., & Di Nuovo, S. (2015). Inclusive education in Italy: Description and reflections on full inclusion. *European Journal of Special Needs Education, 30*, 429–443. doi:10.1080/08856257.2015.1060075

Anastasiou, D., Kauffman, J. M., & Michail, D. (2016). Disability in multicultural theory: Conceptual and social justice issues. *Journal of Disability Policy Studies, 27*, 3–12. doi:10.1177/1044207314558595

Anastasiou, D., & Keller, C. (2017). Cross-national differences in special education: A typological approach. In J. M. Kauffman, D. P. Hallahan, & P. C. Pullen (Eds.), *Handbook of special education* (175, 2nd ed.). New York, NY: Routledge.

Anastasiou, D., & Keller, C. (2014). Cross-National differences in special education coverage: An empirical analysis. *Exceptional Children 16, 80*, 353–367. doi:10.1177/0014402914522421

Ashby, C. E. (2011). Whose "voice" is it anyway?: Giving voice and qualitative research involving individuals that type to communicate. *Disability Studies Quarterly, 31*(4). Retrieved from http://dsq-sds.org/article/view/1723. Accessed on June 20, 2016.

Ashby, C. E., & Causton-Theoharis, J. (2012). "Moving quietly through the door of opportunity": Perspectives of college students who type to communicate. *Equity & Excellence in Education, 45*(2), 261–282.

Ashby, C. E., & Causton-Theoharis, J. N. (2009). Disqualified in the human race: A close reading of the autobiographies of individuals identified as autistic. *International Journal of Inclusive Education, 13*(5), 501–516.

Ayres, K. M., Lowrey, K. A., Douglas, K. H., & Sievers, C. (2011). I can identify Saturn but I can't brush my teeth: What happens when the curricular focus for students with severe disabilities shifts. *Education and Training in Autism and Developmental Disabilities, 46*, 11–21.

Bateman, B. D. (1994). Who, how, and where: Special education's issues in perpetuity. *Journal of Special Education, 27*, 509–520.

Bateman, B. D. (2017). Individual education programs for children with disabilities. In J. M. Kauffman, D. P. Hallahan, & P. C. Pullen (Eds.), *Handbook of special education* (2nd ed.). New York, NY: Taylor & Francis.

Bea, C. T. (2016). Opinion. *Ninth circuit court of appeals, May 20*. Pasadena, CA.

Brantlinger, E. (1997). Using ideology: Cases of nonrecognition of the politics of research and practice in special education. *Review of Educational Research, 67*, 425–459.

Burrello, L. C., Sailor, W., & Kleinhammer-Tramill, J. (Eds.). (2012). *Unifying educational systems: Leadership and policy perspectives*. New York, NY: Routledge.

Convention on the Rights of Persons With Disabilities. (2006). *United nations*. Retrieved from http://www.un.org/disabilities/convention/convention.shtml. Accessed on September 19, 2016

Convention on the Rights of Persons with Disabilities, Committee. (CRPD-G). (2016, September 2). *General comment No. 4 on article 24: Right to inclusive education*. New York, NY: United Nations.

Council for Exceptional Children, Policy Insider. (2015). *NAEP results show wide achievement gaps between students with, without disabilities*. Retrieved from http://www.policy-insider.org/2013/11/naep-results-show-wide-achievement-gaps-between-students-with-without-disabilities.html. Accessed on November 29.

Danforth, S., & Rhodes, W. C. (1997). Deconstructing disability: A philosophy for inclusion. *Remedial and Special Education, 18*(6), 357–366.

Ditto, P. H., & Liu, B. (2011). Deontological dissonance and the consequentialist crutch. In P. Shaver & M. Mikulincer (Eds.), *The social psychology of morality: Exploring the causes of good and evil* (pp. 51–70). New York, NY: APA Books.

Fuchs, L. S., Fuchs, D., Compton, D. L., Wehby, J., Schumacher, R. F., Gersten, R., & Jordan, N. C. (2015). Inclusion versus specialized intervention for very-low-performing students: What does access mean in an era of academic challenge? *Exceptional Children, 81*, 134–157. doi:10.1177/0014402914551743

Gawande, A. (2016, June 10). *The mistrust of science*. Retrieved from http://www.newyorker.com/news/news-desk/the-mistrust-of-science. Accessed on June 13, 2016.

Gerber, M. M. (2017). A history of special education. In J. M. Kauffman, D. P. Hallahan, & P. C. Pullen (Eds.), *Handbook of special education* (2nd ed.). New York, NY: Taylor & Francis.

Hall, E. (2005). The entangled geographies of social exclusion/inclusion for people with learning disabilities. *Health & Place, 11*(2), 107–115.

Hallahan, D. P., Kauffman, J. M., & Pullen, P. C. (2015). *Exceptional learners: An introduction to special education* (13th ed.). Upper Saddle River, NJ: Pearson.

Harry, B., & Klingner, J. (2014). *Why are so many minority students in special education?* (2nd ed.). New York, NY: Teachers College Press.

Hornby, G. (2014). *Inclusive special education: Evidence-based practices for children with special needs and disabilities*. New York, NY: Springer.

Howe, K. R., & Miramontes, O. B. (1992). *The ethics of special education*. New York, NY: Teachers College Press.

Kasa-Hendrickson, C., Broderick, A., & Hanson, D. (2009). Sorting out speech: Understanding multiple methods of communication for persons with autism and other developmental disabilities. *Journal of Developmental Processes, 4*, 116–133.

Kauffman, J. M. (1981). Introduction: Historical trends and contemporary issues in special education in the United States. In J. M. Kauffman & D. P. Hallahan (Eds.), *Handbook of special education* (pp. 3–23). Englewood Cliffs, NJ: Prentice Hall.

Kauffman, J. M. (2013). Labeling and categorizing children and youth with emotional and behavioral disorders in the USA: Current practices and conceptual problems. In T. Cole, H. Daniels, & J. Visser (Eds.), *The Routledge international companion to emotional and behavioural difficulties* (pp. 15–21). London: Routledge.

Kauffman, J. M. (2015a). Opinion on recent developments and the future of special education. *Remedial and Special Education, 36*, 9–13.

Kauffman, J. M. (2015b). Why exceptionality is more important for special education than exceptional children. *Exceptionality, 25*, 225–236. doi:10.1080/09362835.2014.986609

Kauffman, J. M., & Badar, J. (2013). How we might make special education for students with emotional or behavioral disorders less stigmatizing. *Behavioral Disorders, 39*, 16–27.

Kauffman, J. M., & Badar, J. (2014a). Better thinking and clearer communication will help special education. *Exceptionality, 22*, 17–32. doi:10.1080/09362835.2014.865953

Kauffman, J. M., & Badar, J. (2014b). Instruction, not inclusion, should be the central issue in special education: An alternative view from the USA. *Journal of International Special Needs Education, 17*, 13–20.

Kauffman, J. M., & Landrum, T. J. (2009). Politics, civil rights, and disproportional identification of students with emotional and behavioral disorders. *Exceptionality, 17*, 177–188.

Kauffman, J. M., Landrum, T. J., Mock, D. R., Sayeski, B., & Sayeski, K. L. (2005). Diverse knowledge and skills require a diversity of instructional groups: A position statement. *Remedial and Special Education, 26*, 2–6. doi:10.1177/07419325050260010101

Kauffman, J. M., Ward, D. M., & Badar, J. (2016). The delusion of full inclusion. In R. M. Foxx & J. A. Mulick (Eds.), *Controversial therapies for autism and intellectual disabilities* (2nd ed., pp. 71–86). New York, NY: Taylor & Francis.

Kliewer, C., Biklen, D., & Petersen, A. (2015). At the end of intellectual disability. *Harvard Educational Review, 85*(1), 1–28.

Martin, E. W. (2013). *Breakthrough: Federal special education legislation* (pp. 1965–1981). Sarasota, FL: Bardolf. doi: 10.17763/haer.5.1.j260u3gv2402v576

Mostert, M. P. (2001). Facilitated communication since 1995: A review of published studies. *Journal of Autism and Developmental Disorders, 31*, 287–313.

Mostert, M. P. (2010). Facilitated communication and its legitimacy – Twenty-first century developments. *Exceptionality, 18*, 1–11.

Mostert, M. P. (2014). An activist approach to debunking FC. *Research and Practice for Persons with Severe Disabilities, 39*, 203–210.

Nickerson, R. S. (1998). Confirmation bias: A ubiquitous phenomenon in many guises. *Review of General Psychology, 2*, 175–220.

Samuels, C. (2015, October). *NAEP scores for students with disabilities show wide achievement gap.* Retrieved from http://blogs.edweek.org/edweek/speced/2015/10/naep_scores_for_students_with.html. Accessed on November 29, 2015.

Schoolwide Integrated Framework for Transformation [SWIFT]. (2015, November). Retrieved from http://www.swiftschools.org. Accessed on November 29, 2015.

Sinatra, G. M., Kienhues, D., & Hofer, B. K. (2015). Addressing challenges to public under-standing of science: Epistemic cognition, motivated reasoning, and conceptual change. *Educational Psychologist, 49*, 123–138.

Stubblefield, A. (2011). Sound and fury: When opposition to facilitated communication func-tions as hate speech. *Disability Studies Quarterly, 31*(4). Retrieved from http://dsq-sds.org/article/view/1729/1777. Accessed on November 17, 2015.

The Special Edge. (2016, spring). Rohnert Part, CA: Napa County Office of Education.

Travers, J. C., Tincani, M., & Lang, R. (2014). Facilitated communication denies people with dis-abilities their voice. *Research and Practice for Persons with Severe Disabilities, 39*, 195–202.

United Nations. (2006). *Convention on the rights of persons with disabilities.* Retrieved from http://www.un.org/disabilities/convention/conventionfull.shtml. Accessed on October 13, 2015.

Warnock, M. (2005). *Special educational needs: A new look.* Impact No. 11. London: Philosophy of Education Society of Great Britain.

Wiley, A. L. (2015). Place values: What moral psychology can tell us about the full inclusion debate in special education. In B. Bateman, J. W. Lloyd, & M. Tankersley (Eds.), *Enduring issues in special education: Personal perspectives* (pp. 232–250). New York, NY: Routledge.

World Federation of the Deaf. (n.d.). Education *rights for deaf children: A policy statement of the world federation of the deaf.* Author. Retrieved from http://wfdeaf.org/databank/policies/education-rights-for-deaf-children. Accessed on October 13, 2015.

Zigmond, N., & Kloo (2017). General and special education are (and should be) different. In J. M. Kauffman, D. P. Hallahan, & P. C. Pullen (Eds.), *Handbook of special education* (2nd ed.). New York, NY: Taylor & Francis.

INCLUSION IN GENERAL AND SPECIAL EDUCATION IN AN AGE OF CHANGE: CONCLUDING THOUGHTS

Jeffrey P. Bakken and Festus E. Obiakor

ABSTRACT

Our world is changing and also getting smaller. We now know what is happening outside our narrow confines — this means that we must all be involved in solving educational, societal, community, and global problems in inclusive fashions. For example, in education, we must be collaborative, consultative, and cooperative in solving school problems and in advancing school programs. To a large measure, inclusion in general and special education has become imperative in today's educational programming. Though it is seen by some as complex and appears to attract conflicting perspectives, it enhances different professional viewpoints and practices that help general and special education learners to maximize their fullest potential. Some schools end up doing inclusion well and others continue to work on it; however, many believe it has made education more efficient and effective. Inclusion strives to include all students with and without disabilities within the general education classroom and

General and Special Education Inclusion in an Age of Change: Roles of Professionals Involved
Advances in Special Education, Volume 32, 179–185
ISSN: 0270-4013/doi:10.1108/S0270-401320160000032011

curriculum. This chapter discusses our conclusive thoughts on inclusion and where we think it is headed in the future.

Keywords: Inclusion; least restrictive environment; general education; special education; training; resources

WHY WE MUST BE INCLUSIVE

Today, we live in a complex multicultural world; and technology has endeavored to make it simpler. But, one can argue that the same technology is making our multicultural world more difficult (Obi, Obiakor, Gala, & Magee, 2013). One can go to the internet today and see all kinds of divisive activities that do not advance our society and our world. We believe in progressive futuristic ideas that creatively challenge us to move toward inclusion. In other words, we believe in encouraging meaningful changes that advance our society and our world. From our perspective, "many of us have stopped seeing, talking, hearing, and thinking. We have stopped seeing the beauties in all of us; we have stopped talking — we now text all the time; we have blocked our ears from hearing anything positive about our fellow humans, society, and world; and we have stopped thinking about productive futuristic solutions" (Obiakor, 2014, p. 1). Sadly, if you listen to talk radio today, the more divisive you are, the more we hear your voice. "Meaningful 'seeing, talking, hearing, and thinking' are slowly losing their ways. We are now consumed by the mentality of wanting the instant gratification — 'I want it and I want it now for me, myself, and I' seems to be the modus vivendi (i.e., way of life)" (Obiakor, 2014, p. 1).

As scholars and educators, we understand the pain or risk involved in leaving our comfort zones to go beyond our narrow confines. In fact, we know that it is easy to join the status quo, do what everyone does, learn how everyone learns, teach how everyone teaches, or write about what everyone writes about. In addition, we know the comfort in seeing like everyone, talking like everyone, behaving like everyone, sounding like everyone, or thinking like everyone. In reality, to do what we do and be successful at what we do, we must see differently, create differently, think differently, learn differently, write differently, and value differently. Clearly, it takes hard work and dedication to "see beyond the eyes." In this regard, some critical questions deserve our attention as educators and learners. How can we value our human differences or our multicultural world if we do not include all voices? How can we respect our multidimensional talents if we see our talents narrowly? How can we value our interindividual and intraindividual differences if we see our differences narrowly? How can we be excited about learning new things if we see our learning narrowly? How can we cherish our sacred existence as human-beings if we see our existence narrowly? In more specific terms, how can we solve perennial educational problems confronting our students, teachers, service providers, communities, and governments if we do not see how they matter to us? We argue that if we do not broaden our horizons and get outside our comfort zones, we will be destined to see the narrow picture and fail ourselves as humans in an increasingly complex society. As a perennial problem, exclusion is dangerous, discriminatory, prejudicial, retrogressive, and antihuman. But, we must be inclusive to advance our education, society, and humanity. We do know that inclusion is innovative, creative, painstaking, collaborative, consultative, and cooperative. We also know that without inclusion, we cannot build multicultural bridges in general and special education.

Our challenging question must always be, How do we build inclusive and multicultural bridges that move us beyond our narrow confines to advance general and special education? In our view, life is like a big elephant; you might be able to see one side of it. However, to see all its sides, we must eliminate intentional or unintentional barriers that will prevent us from walking all around it. People tend to make judgments based on one experience. Sadly, even when we acknowledge our limitations, we still generalize based on our biased findings. We must recognize that generalizability problems exist in all that we do. This should force us to be inclusive to see more and do more! In our schools, we have continued to misidentify, misassess, mislabel/miscategorize, misplace, and misinstruct some of our students because they look, talk, and behave differently (see Obiakor, 2001). We have continued to use special education as a "placement" opportunity instead of an "intervention" opportunity (Obiakor & Smith, 2012). And, we have continued to waste so much money to puritanically exclude our students and send our youth to jail instead of investing in their education. To go beyond our narrow confines to build inclusive bridges, we must begin to open our eyes and hearts to acknowledge our human differences, talents, and limitations. By being inclusive, we challenge our traditional assumptions and look for multidimensional ways to solve problems. For example, Sensoy and DiAngelo (2011) challenged us to consistently ask the question, "Is everyone really equal?" In the same dimension, Gorski (2014) challenged us to go beyond "cultural proficiency" to create and sustain an equitable learning environment. We are clearly convinced that failure will be an inevitability unless we challenge to be truly inclusive in our general and special education programming.

INCLUDING STUDENTS WITH DISABILITIES

How students with disabilities have been served in the last 10–15 years has changed over time, especially in regards to the general education classroom and the general education curriculum. For example, in 1988–1989, approximately 30% of students with disabilities spent more than 80% of their time in the general education classroom receiving instruction from teachers on the general education curriculum. In 2013, however, the number of students with disabilities receiving instruction in the general education classroom more than doubled to 61% being served in this environment (U.S. Department of Education, National Center for Education Statistics, 2016).

Including students with disabilities in the least restrictive environment (LRE) has always been at the forefront of special education; but many times in the past, students were pulled out of the general education classroom because the thought was that these students could not be successful in this environment and needed a more individualized instructional setting. The fear was that students with disabilities would fall further and further behind their peers academically. As the data suggests, however, more students with disabilities are now receiving instruction in the general educational environment than ever before. The question that results is: How do we ensure that these students are successful in an inclusive environment? The individualized education program (IEP) team needs to make sure that the inclusive classroom is the LRE for the student with disabilities. This type of environment will not necessarily be conducive to all students with disabilities. The determination of placing a student with disabilities into an inclusive environment should be made on an individual case-by-case basis. The services that are provided within this type of environment will be very important in determining the students' success. For example, differentiation is an incredibly important tool to help those with disabilities to succeed in an inclusive classroom. Differentiation involves providing a range of activities and using a variety of strategies for children with different abilities (from students who have learning disabilities to those that are gifted) to successfully learn in the same classroom.

Teacher training is another aspect that is very important to the success of students with disabilities in an inclusive environment. What knowledge and training does the general education teacher have working with students with disabilities? What knowledge and training does the special education teacher have with the general education curriculum? How might the special education teacher support the general education teacher and the student with disabilities? How might the general education teacher support the general education teacher and students without disabilities? How will communication and collaboration between general and special education teachers be achieved? These questions must be answered to address inclusion when putting a student with disabilities in an inclusive environment. A child receiving special education services may participate fully in the same program as general education children with supports from the special education teacher, or may participate in a limited way, as they are able. In some rare occasions, students may work exclusively on goals in their IEP in a general education classroom alongside typically developing peers. For inclusion to truly succeed, special educators and general educators must work closely together, collaborate, communicate effectively, and compromise. It definitely requires that teachers have training and support to overcome the challenges they must meet together in teaching students with and without disabilities in the general education classroom.

Benefits of inclusion are many and for students with disabilities include "(a) increased social initiations, relationships and networks with student without disabilities; (b) greater opportunities for interactions with other students with disabilities; (c) peers serving as role models for academic, social, and behavior skills; (d) greater access to the general curriculum; (e) realistic expectations; and (f) families feeling more as a part of the school climate and community. In addition, students without disabilities also benefit. These benefits include (a) an increased appreciation and acceptance of students with disabilities, (b) the development of meaningful friendships, (c) learning to respect others that are different than yourselves, and (d) increased understanding and acceptance of diversity" (Bakken, 2017).

FUTURE PERSPECTIVES

It is clear that inclusion is a service delivery model that positively impacts students with and without disabilities and should be a consideration for all students regardless of the type or severity of the disability they possess. In fact, research has shown that there are positive benefits academically and socially for students with and without disabilities. However, the key is for teachers and other related professionals to be prepared (through education and training) and have time to plan (general and special education teacher together). Simply stating that a classroom is inclusive without the proper supports in place would be a fallacy.

There is a lot of work to be done before an inclusive classroom begins; and the work must continue daily and into the future for it to be successful. Supporting inclusion must come from all staff, teachers, and administration to make a positive and lasting impact. Everyone must buy into this inclusion concept to make it successful. The future is very bright for inclusion – it is no more a far-fetched concept. General and special education teachers need sufficient time dedicated within the educational day at school for planning and collaborating. These professionals may also need additional skills training and professional development to be successful. Lastly, it must be mentioned that it could be possible that additional resources may be necessary for implementing inclusive programs. In theory, inclusion is a very good concept, but to implement it many areas need to be addressed to make it successful.

CONCLUSION

In this chapter, we have given our conclusive where thoughts on inclusion. We conclude that it is a concept that explicates we are today as a changing society and world. Our demographics are changing and it behooves us to have educational programs that reflect where and who we are. Inclusion represents our positive response to individual differences, differentiated instruction, multicultural valuing, innovative programming, human interactions, racial appreciation, diversity valuing, and instructional modification. When we exclude students, we fail to value their humanity and ability in our heterogeneous community. This is the situation that students with disabilities find themselves in our educational programs. It is critical that we go beyond theory to practice in inclusive programming at all levels. In the end, we will not advance as a society if we fail to listen to the voices of students, parents, teachers and professionals, community leaders, and government agencies. When we educate students together and work together, we win together individually and collectively.

REFERENCES

Bakken, J. P. (2017). General and special education in an age of change: An introduction. In J. P. Bakken & F. E. Obiakor (Eds.), *General and special education in an age of change*

(Vol. 31, pp. 1–12). Advances in Special Education. Bingley, UK: Emerald Group Publishing Limited.

Gorski, P. C. (2014). *Imagining equity literacy*. Retrieved from http://www.tolerance.org/blog/imagining-equity-literacy

Obi, S. O., Obiakor, F. E., Gala, D. D., & Magee, S. (2013). Diversity, technology, and global interactions: Educational implications. In S. Abebe (Ed.), *Diversity in education: An integrated framework beyond chalk and talk* (pp. 157–181). Ronkonkoma, NY: Linus Learning.

Obiakor, F. E. (2001). *It even happens in "good" schools: Responding to cultural diversity in today's classrooms*. Thousand Oaks, CA: Corwin Press.

Obiakor, F. E. (2014, May). *"Seeing beyond the eyes:" In honor of hard work and dedication*. Keynote Speech delivered at the Academic Honors Dinner, Valdosta, GA: Valdosta State University.

Obiakor, F. E., & Smith, R. (2012). *Special education practices: Personal narratives of African American scholars, educators, and related professionals*. New York, NY: Nova Science Publishers.

Sensoy, O., & DiAngelo, R. (2011). *Is everyone really equal?: An introduction to key concepts of social justice education*. New York, NY: Teachers College Press.

U.S. Department of Education, National Center for Education Statistics. (2016). *Digest of education statistics, 2014* (NCES 2016-006). Retrieved from http://nces.ed.gov/fastfacts/display.asp?id = 59. Accessed on June 22, 2016.